CW00350658

The cross from a distance

Titles in this series:

NEW STUDIES IN BIBLICAL THEOLOGY 18

Series editor: D. A. Carson

The cross from a distance

ATONEMENT IN MARK'S GOSPEL

Peter G. Bolt

APOLLOS

INTERVARSITY PRESS
DOWNERS GROVE, ILLINOIS 60515

™*InterVarsity Press, USA*
P.O. Box 1400, Downers Grove, IL 60515-1426, USA
World Wide Web: www.ivpress.com
Email: email@ivpress.com

APOLLOS (an imprint of Inter-Varsity Press, England)
Norton Street, Nottingham NG7 3HR, England
Website: www.ivpbooks.com
Email: ivp@ivpbooks.com

© *Peter G. Bolt 2004*

InterVarsity Press®, *USA, is the book-publishing division of InterVarsity Christian Fellowship/ USA*®, *a movement of students and faculty active on campus at hundreds of universities, colleges and schools of nursing in the United States of America, and a member movement of the International Fellowship of Evangelical Students. For information about local and regional activities, write Public Relations Dept., InterVarsity Christian Fellowship/USA, 6400 Schroeder Rd., P.O. Box 7895, Madison, WI 53707-7895, or visit the IVCF website at <www.intervarsity. org>.*

Inter-Varsity Press, England, is closely linked with the Universities and Colleges Christian Fellowship, a student movement connecting Christian Unions throughout Great Britain, and a member movement of the International Fellowship of Evangelical Students. Website: www.uccf.org.uk

Scripture quotations marked NRSV *are from the* New Revised Standard Version of the Bible, Anglicized Edition, *copyright 1989 by the Division of Christian Education of the National Council of the Churches of Christ in the USA. Used by permission. All rights reserved.*

Scripture quotations marked ESV *are from* The Holy Bible, English Standard Version, *copyright* © *2001 by Crossway Bibles, a division of Good News Publishers. Used by permission. All rights reserved.*

Unmarked Scripture quotations are in Peter Bolt's own translation.

USA ISBN 978-0-8308-2619-3
UK ISBN 978-1-84474-049-9

Set in Monotype Times New Roman
Typeset in Great Britain by CRB Associates, Reepham, Norfolk

Printed in the United States of America ∞

Library of Congress Cataloging-in-Publication Data
A catalog record for this book is available from the Library of Congress.

British Library Cataloguing in Publication Data
A catalogue record for this book is available from the British Library.

P 25 24 23 22 21 20 19 18 17 16 15 14 13 12 11 10 9 8 7 6 5 4

Y 27 26 25 24 23 22 21 20 19 18 17 16 15 14 13 12 11 10 09

Contents

Series preface

New Studies in Biblical Theology is a series of monographs that
address key issues in the discipline of biblical theology. Contributions
to the series focus on one or more of three areas: 1. the nature and
status of biblical theology, including its relations with other discip-
lines (e.g. historical theology, exegesis, systematic theology, historical
criticism, narrative theology); 2. the articulation and exposition of the
structure of thought of a particular biblical writer or corpus; and
3. the delineation of a biblical theme across all or part of the biblical
corpora.

Above all, these monographs are creative attempts to help thinking
Christians understand their Bibles better. The series aims simultan-
eously to instruct and to edify, to interact with the current literature,
and to point the way ahead. In God's universe, mind and heart
should not be divorced: in this series we will try not to separate what
God has joined together. While the notes interact with the best of the
scholarly literature, the text is uncluttered with untransliterated
Greek and Hebrew, and tries to avoid too much technical jargon.
The volumes are written within the framework of confessional
evangelicalism, but there is always an attempt at thoughtful engage-
ment with the sweep of the relevant literature.

At a time when many theologians are tempted to depreciate the
role of the cross in the canonical Gospels, or at very least to interpret
it in highly restricted ways, the sheer barbarity of the cross can still
capture the public imagination, as the recent film by Mel Gibson
shows – a film that opens by quietly quoting part of Isaiah 53. But the
best use of Mel Gibson's work will take place when, as a result of
watching his film, viewers turn to Scripture to find out for themselves
what the primary sources actually say. And here, in this study of the
Gospel of Mark, Dr Peter Bolt is an enormously engaging and
informed guide. Section after section of the Gospel comes into
sharper focus, as more and more of Mark is read in the light of the
movement and direction of its thought. Interwoven with the exegesis

is a great deal of useful interaction with a wide range of well-chosen literature, and incisive meditation on what this cross-saturated text says to us today. Dr Bolt combines careful reading and profound theological synthesis, all of it shaped to issue a clarion call to eschew idolatry and abandon mere 'religion'. The result is a book that will stimulate and edify any serious Christian reader, and will doubtless become the grist for countless sermons on the Gospel of Mark.

D. A. Carson
Trinity Evangelical Divinity School

Author's preface

The contents of this book were originally delivered as the 2003 Moore College Annual Lectures at Moore Theological College, Sydney. I am grateful to the acting Principal, Mr Michael Hill, for the invitation to deliver these lectures and for the provision of one term's study leave for their preparation, and to Dr John Woodhouse for his encouragement of me in these plans, which were laid out before he arrived as Principal. I also appreciate the fact that my colleagues on the faculty covered for me in various ways during my extraordinary study leave.

The book has profited from interaction with those who originally attended the lectures. I am also grateful for several generations of Moore College fourth-year students in 'The Atonement in Bible and History' course, who engaged with me in discussion of Mark's views of the atonement. It has been my great privilege to share this class with my colleague Robert Doyle, from whom I have learnt much in regard to God's gracious work of atonement. I am immensely grateful to my two research assistants, Matthew Olliffe and Geoffrey Lin, whose willing work on my behalf made my preparation much easier. Thanks must also go to Don Carson for his perceptive suggestions and quiet encouragements in my preparation of the manuscript for publication.

The strange world of the first century continues to fascinate. A world that would crucify any human being is barbaric, let alone one that would crucify the Son of God. Even though these events seem so far away, this is still our world.

The good news of Jesus Christ is even more fascinating. Our destruction of the Son of God should have driven us further away from God. Instead, in that very event, God came close to us! This is our salvation.

I trust that these explorations into Mark's account of that great event will help others to stand in wonder before the God who has come close to us in the cross of Jesus Christ, and to live in hope of the better things to come.

Peter G. Bolt

9

Abbreviations

AG	*Anthologia Graeca*; W. H. Paton, *The Greek Anthology* 5, Cambridge, MA: Harvard University Press; London: Heinemann, 1918, reprinted 1979
AV/KJV	The Authorized (King James) version of the Bible, 1611
BAGD	W. Bauer, W. F. Arndt, F. W. Gingrich & F. W. Danker, *A Greek–English Lexicon of the New Testament and Other Early Christian Literature*, 2nd edn, Chicago, IL: Chicago University Press, 1979
CD	K. Barth, *Church Dogmatics*, 4 vols., Edinburgh: T. & T. Clark, 1956–75
CIL	*Corpus Inscriptionum Latinarum*, 17 vols., Berlin: de Gruyter, 1863–
Danby	H. Danby (ed.), *The Mishnah: Translated from the Hebrew with Introduction and Brief Explanatory Notes*, Oxford: Oxford University Press, 1958
DK	H. Diels & W. Kranz (eds.), *Die Fragmente der Vorsokratiker*. Zurich: Weidmann, 1985
ESV	The English Standard Version of the Bible, 2001
EVV	English versions
fr.	fragment(s)
IG	*Inscriptiones Graecae*, 47 vols., Berlin: de Gruyter, 1815–
LSJ	H. G. Liddell, R. Scott & H. S. Jones, *Greek–English Lexicon*, Oxford: Clarendon, 9th edn, 1968
LXX	The Septuagint (Greek version of the Old Testament)
MM	J. H. Moulton and H. Milligan, *The Vocabulary of the Greek Testament, Illustrated from the Papyri and Other Non-Literary Sources*, London: Hodder & Stoughton, 1930
MSS	manuscripts

MT	Masoretic Text
NASB	The New American Standard Bible, 1960–95
NEB	The New English Bible, 1961–70
NewDocs	New Documents Illustrating Early Church History, ed. G. H. R. Horsley, 9 vols., North Ryde, NSW: Macquarie University, 1981–
NIV	The New International Version of the Bible, 1973–84
NRSV	The New Revised Standard Version of the Bible, 1989–95
PG	Patrologia cursus completus . . . Series graecae, 166 vols., Paris: Petit-Montrouge, 1857–83
PL	Patrologia cursus completus . . . Series prima [latina], 221 vols., Paris: J.-P. Migne, 1844–65
Q	Quelle (German), a presumed 'sayings' source of the synoptic Gospels
RSV	The Revised Standard Version of the Bible, 1952–71
RV	The Revised Version of the Bible, 1881
SVF	H. von Arnim, Stoicorum veterum fragmenta, 3 vols., Leipzig: Teubner, 1903–5
TDNT	Theological Dictionary of the New Testament, ed. G. Kittel and G. Friedrich, 10 vols., Grand Rapids, MI: Eerdmans, 1964–
TLG	Thesaurus Linguae Graecae database, University of California, Irvine; <http://ptolemy.tlg.uci.edu/~tlg>

Introduction

At nine o'clock in the morning on 3 April in the year now known as
AD 33,[1] a Jew, Jesus of Nazareth, was put to death on a Roman cross.
That event changed the world. Why?
There were many who proclaimed Jesus' death to the world. Mark
was one of them. This series of lectures will explore what Mark has to
say about the cross of Jesus Christ.

Why address the topic?

There are several reasons why this is an important topic to address.

The exegetical reason

First, there is simply the exegetical issue. The importance of the cross
of Christ to the Gospels, and especially to Mark's Gospel,[2] has often
been noticed. Because they devote so much narrative space to the
cross, they have been called 'passion narratives with extended
introductions'.[3] This is certainly true of Mark. Of sixteen chapters,
three are dedicated to the passion narrative (18%), but six more deal
with Jesus' journey to the cross (which takes it up to 56%). Even
before we get to that journey, the cross of Christ casts its shadow over
the early stages of Mark's story.[4] If the cross has such prominence in
Mark, it is worth asking *why* it is so important. What is the
significance of Jesus' death to this Gospel that Mark released upon
the world so long ago?

[1] The two most likely dates for Jesus' crucifixion are 7 April AD 30 or 3 April AD 33.
For the arguments for AD 33, see A. D. Doyle 1941; Maier 1968; Hoehner 1977: chs.
4, 5.
[2] E.g. the passion is the climax of the Gospel (E. A. Russell 1985: 207); the Gospel is
the story of Jesus' death (R. E. Brown 1986: 21); it is 'the Gospel of the cross' (Grassi
2000: ix); the crucifixion is its 'central, focal point' (E. A. Russell 1985: 218).
[3] Kähler 1964: 80 n. 11.
[4] Grassi 2000: 9–12, 16; R. E. Brown 1986: 21; Culpepper 1978: 584; J. B. Green &
Baker 2000: 38.

The polemical reason

Secondly, there is the polemical issue. In the past, one of the marks of Protestantism in general, and of evangelical Protestantism in particular, has been a focus on the cross of Christ. In this tradition, Jesus' death has been understood in a forensic context, as the great event in which the Son of God gave his life as a substitute for us, so that he bore the wrath of God, the due penalty for our sin, instead of us. This view of Christ's work on the cross, often described as the penal substitutionary view of the atonement, has long been criticized by those outside the evangelical tradition. More recently, it has also begun to be criticized by some within evangelicalism.[5] Even though I shall not often explicitly address the details of this debate, it should be kept in mind as we examine Mark's teaching on the atonement. What contribution can Mark make to this important discussion? The question should not be: Can we squeeze Mark's view of the atonement into a predetermined theory derived from our dogmatics? but rather: Does the theory find any support from Mark? We also need to be open to the fact that our study of Mark may force us to improve our dogmatic formulations. We may, in the end, agree that penal substitutionary atonement is supported by Mark, and at the same time agree that this dogmatic formulation needs to be constantly enriched with the complexity of the biblical data.[6]

The practical reason

Then there is the practical reason. When we seek to share the good news of Jesus Christ with others, what should we say?

Evangelicalism has had a high commitment to evangelism. In the context of evangelistic ministry, it is easy for ministers of the gospel to develop their own favourite ways of sharing the good news of Jesus Christ. These can tend towards stereotypical phraseology, and the explanation of Jesus' death can be given in a fairly abstract fashion. Some of the images and illustrations that have been developed within evangelicalism have rightly been criticized for their serious inadequacies – if not heresies! – even though they have had a pride of place in gospel presentations for many years. Once gospel ministers have

[5] See e.g. J. B. Green & Baker 2000. For a brief overview of the discussion on the atonement within evangelicalism, see Boyd & Eddy 2002: ch. 8. Although Hickinbotham (1944) defends penal substitutionary atonement in Mark's story, he does so from a fairly 'dogmatic' (rather than exegetical) angle.
[6] This seems also to be N. T. Wright's plea; see 1998: 297.

developed their own favourite way of presenting the good news, these methods can become like a straight-jacket to gospel preaching. As a friend once said to me, 'I find it hard to say what I want to say from the Gospels.' Should it not be the other way around? If the Gospels are our foundational documents, themselves written to proclaim the gospel of Jesus Christ, then we need to hear what they have to say, and to modify our own presentation of the gospel in line with these original sources. Our presentation of the gospel can only be the richer for the experience. How can Mark's teaching on the cross correct and inform our own preaching of the gospel to the contemporary world?

Approach and method

The approach: story, history, theology

It will be my contention in this book that the *details of Mark's story* of the cross should inform our understanding of the meaning of Jesus' death. The Gospel of Mark operates in three arenas, each of which must be taken seriously. It is at one and the same time narrative, history and theology. First, it is a narrative – in fact, a very well-told story, using all the devices of a good storyteller to convey the message of the cross in a holistic, emotion-filled way. But secondly, through that narrative, we gain access to the historical event of Jesus' crucifixion. This most important historical event can be dated: it took place at 9 o'clock in the morning on 3 April in the year now known as AD 33.[7] The Gospel of Mark tells us many of the historical details of that event. And, thirdly, because God reveals himself in this event through this story, I shall be arguing that it is the very historical details, as reported by Mark's narrative, that display the theological significance of Jesus' death,[8] that is, the ongoing significance of Jesus' death for all time.

The method

To understand Mark's view of the atonement, I shall adopt the following method.

The cross in Mark's story. Each chapter will attempt to expose what a particular section of Mark's story says about the cross. We

---

[7] For details see n. 1 above (p. 13).

[8] Cf. R. E. Brown 1986: 18: 'Not biography but theology dominated the choice of events to be narrated, and the OT was the theological source-book of the time.'

shall gradually progress through the Gospel of Mark, enabling us to build up a fairly comprehensive understanding of the death of Jesus.

The informing theology (Old Testament). Because Mark invites readers to understand the story of Jesus in the light of the Old Testament, we shall be paying particular attention to any Old Testament teaching that seems to inform Mark's presentation. Time and again we shall find that the Old Testament provides the theological framework that illuminates and enriches the details of Mark's presentation.

The readers then. Mark's Gospel is a persuasive document. The story of the crucified Christ was evidently written to make an impact upon its readers. As we engage with Mark's message of the cross, we shall therefore, on several occasions, take a brief glance at the first-century Greco-Roman world that Mark sought to persuade.[9] How would Mark's story of the cross have been heard back then?

The readers now. And finally, as we glance at Mark's message to his early readers, we shall find ourselves looking at our own world too. Mark is a narrative of the historical events surrounding Jesus Christ. But, in the end, these are theological events, because they are God's events. Mark's story therefore still communicates to contemporary audiences. As a narrative, Mark draws us into his story of Jesus. As he does so, we are brought into contact with the historical events in which God has made himself known for all time. Mark's narrative will be explained in the belief that this ancient text still speaks to contemporary readers.[10]

---

[9] Scholars have long debated whether the Gospels were designed for a Christian or a non-Christian audience. In my view, the Gospels arose in the context of the early Christian mission in order to support the work of this mission; see Bolt 1998a; cf. Bornkamm's (1960: 17) view that the Gospels 'grow out of the proclamation and are in its service', a view endorsed by D. W. B. Robinson (n.d.). Because of the importance of the message about Jesus, any human being is a potential 'audience' for these documents. The story of Jesus was worth the telling, and the ultimate aim in committing the gospel to written, narrative form was to see the world converted to Christ (i.e. an evangelistic purpose). This would take place, however, through anchoring the churches in the events of the gospel (i.e. a proximate goal: nurturing of the Christians), thus enlisting and encouraging them in Christ's mission.

[10] Cf. Grassi 2000: ix: 'All the actual biblical texts should be read slowly and reflectively since they have a power of their own. The ancient method for reading the Bible is to involve yourself so deeply that you feel yourself as part of the story. This means that *you are actually there*. This is not a piece of pious fiction but based on the way the text was written. It was designed as a living drama in which the audience is there as part of the action.'

The cross at a distance: God up close

At the climax of Mark's Gospel, Jesus hung on the cross, absolutely alone, deserted by God and people. But at that lonely hour, the narrative introduces some characters who have not appeared previously. In Mark 15:40 we read that a group of women were watching the crucifixion 'from a distance' (*apo makrothen*). In a sense, these women can be our point of reference. They are given a stance towards the cross that we ourselves share.

The cross is at a distance. It is an event that occurred long ago, in a world and culture that, in many ways, seem so foreign to our own. But, if we understand this cross correctly, we discover that it is there, in that distant cross, that we see God up close.

Chapter One

The cross and
the abolition of religion

The bridegroom in Mark's story of the cross

The cross enters the story

The first overt reference to the cross in Mark is Jesus' parable about
the bridegroom who will be taken away (2:19–20).[1] For sure, at this
stage in the narrative, this saying may have been rather 'enigmatic' to
Mark's readers (Hagner 1998: 100), but it nevertheless points ahead
to the climax of the Gospel, when Jesus is crucified.[2] So that we can
understand the contribution this parable makes to Mark's story of the
cross, it is important to set it within its narrative context.

Mark's narrative movements

A careful reading of Mark's Gospel reveals that, after a most
important prologue, which sets the stage for the story to follow
(1:1–13), the narrative has five main movements:

---

[1] 'Apart from a possible reference in Mk 2.20, there is no saying of Jesus in the first
half of the Gospel relevant to his death': Grayston 1990: 164. Some have disputed the
identification of this saying as a prophecy of the passion: Lane 1974: 111, with Cremer
1965: 5, 126. For Marshall (1989: 90, cf. 232), the accusation of blasphemy in 2:7
means that 'for the first time in the story the death of Jesus comes faintly into view'.
This may be so, but the death of Jesus is several steps removed from the surface of
the narrative. The death of John (1:14) certainly foreshadows the cross (as pointed
out by many; e.g. R. E. Brown 1986: 21), but this is by type rather than by explicit
reference.

[2] Cf., among others, E. A. Russell 1985: 208–209, 214; and Dewey (1995: 148),
who places this unit at the centre of a series of conflict stories arranged in a concentric
structure around this unit, which she describes as dealing with fasting and crucifixion.
'Thus, Mark employed the controversy stories theologically to place Jesus' life in the
context of his death, and he used them in his narrative construction to show how
Jesus' death historically was to come about.' Dewey 1980 provides a full-length
treatment. (Grayston [1990: 170] charges her with oversimplifying a complicated
discussion.)

In this chapter we shall examine the bridegroom parable, which is part of Mark's first main movement (1:14 – 4:34). We shall also look at Mark's second major movement (4:35 – 8:26), which tells the story of Jesus dealing with the perishing and, as a related theme, portrays the appropriate response to his actions, namely faith. But before turning to the parable, we shall briefly review the story so far.

The story so far

Mark's prologue opens with the arrival of John the Baptist, in fulfilment of Isaiah 40:3, who prepared the way for the long-awaited forgiveness of sins (1:2–5; Isa. 40:1–2).[3] When Jesus is baptized by John (1:9–11), the voice from heaven declares him to be the Christ, the Son of God of Psalm 2:7, and the servant of Isaiah 42:1. Once he is marked out as the suffering servant, according to the prophecy of Isaiah, his path is clear. He is to go to his death in order to bring about the forgiveness of sins and the new deal for Israel, which would flow out even to the nations of the world.[4] The story then focuses upon Jesus' authority, which is eventually revealed to be the authority of the Son of Man to forgive sins in the land (of Israel) (2:10). Because he has this authority to forgive, the second subsection (2:13 – 3:6) shows Jesus calling sinners. This is the immediate context for Jesus' parable about the bridegroom who is present and then taken away.

The bridegroom present and taken away

In the second subsection, Jesus finds himself in conflict with the religious leaders of the land.

The Christ and cosmic conflict

By this stage of the story, he has already engaged in a cosmic conflict

---

[3] For an analysis of forgiveness in Mark, see Bolt 1998b.

[4] It has been a matter of some dispute whether and to what extent Jesus fulfils the servant prophecies. See, for example, the important work by Hooker (1959) and, more recently, the discussion in Bellinger & Farmer 1998. For my own part, see Bolt 1991b.

with Satan and the unclean spirits (1:13; 1:21–28; 1:34, 39). This will continue into the third subsection (3:11–12), but the story has already shown that this demonic conflict also has its human counterpart. Jesus has already been in conflict with the religious authorities (1:22, 27, 44; 2:6–7, 10).

In the third subsection, this conflict will come to a head in the great debate between Jesus and the scribes from Jerusalem (3:22–30). This scene aligns the opposition of the religious leaders with the opposition of Satan. This cosmic conflict forms the backdrop to the conflict between Jesus and the religious authorities that will eventually take him to the cross. The parable of the bridegroom is one of four scenes that contribute to this rising conflict between Jesus and the religious authorities.

Eating with sinners (2:13–17)

In the first scene, Jesus calls Levi, the tax collector (2:13–17), as he had previously called four brothers (1:16–20). This results in a joyful feast with other sinners, who are glad that forgiveness of sins is now available (vv. 15–16). It irks the religious people that Jesus is feasting with sinners (v. 16), but he tells them he is exactly where he ought to be. The doctor is among the sick,[5] for he has 'not come to call the righteous, but sinners' (2:17). The long-awaited forgiveness of sins promised by the prophets (e.g. Isa. 40:1–2; Jer. 31:31–34; Zech. 13:1), and anticipated by John's baptism, has now arrived. Jesus, the Son of Man, is authorized to bring forgiveness to the land. He therefore mingles with the sinners. This brings him into direct conflict with the religious, who think they are already righteous. At this point in the story, Jesus tells the parable of the bridegroom who will be taken away.

The bridegroom taken away (2:18–22)

Introduction: the question about fasting

Mark introduces the parable by anchoring it in a specific event: 'Now John's disciples and the Pharisees were fasting' (v. 18a). This gave rise

---

[5] See e.g. the saying of Pausanias, son of Pleistoanax (Plutarch, *Apophthegmata Laconica* 230F), when asked why he went into exile from Sparta: 'Physicians are wont to spend their time, not among the healthy, but where the sick are'. Dio Chrysostom, *Orationes* 8.5, justified the presence of the wise among the fools with the saying: 'The good physician should go and offer his services where the sick are most numerous.' In the later words of Basil the Great, he is the physician who stoops to our sickness 'breathing its foul breath, that he may heal the sick'; *Letter* 8: *To the Caesareans.*

to a question put to Jesus: 'Why are John's disciples and the disciples of the Pharisees fasting, but your disciples are not?'[6]

At its core, fasting was associated with mourning (1 Sam. 31:13; 2 Sam. 1:12; Esth. 4:3; cf. Judith 8:6; 1 Macc. 1:25–28).[7] If you were bereaved, you grieved, and in your grief you refrained from eating any food. You fasted because of the deep sorrow raised by the death of someone you loved. By extension, fasting was also associated with mourning over sinfulness. A person could be so grieved at their sin that they fasted (e.g. 1 Sam. 7:6; 1 Kgs 21:27; and perhaps 2 Sam. 12:16–23). But it should not be forgotten that behind this fasting associated with the grieving over sin lay the basic meaning of fasting in association with mourning.[8]

Now, it is difficult to say what kind of fast was actually going on in this story.[9] Whatever the reason for the particular fast, what is Jesus'

[6] Despite the generalizing tendency of some translations (e.g. AV/KJV, RSV, NASB, NRSV, ESV: '... do ... do not ...'), the simple present (NEB, NIV: '... are ... are not ...') should be used here, since v. 18a clearly shows that a specific fast is under discussion.

[7] Fasting associated with mourning was a widespread custom in the ancient world. See Guthrie 1962.

[8] Note that Matthew's parallel (9:15) uses *penthein.*

[9] The text itself does not identify the reason for the fast occupying the Pharisees and the disciples of John. (The text implies that both groups were involved in the same fast. This would exclude the suggestion that John's disciples were mourning his death. See Rawlinson 1931: 31; V. Taylor 1966: 209; Cranfield 1977: 108f.) By the first century AD, the Jews were so famous for their fasting practices that Caesar Augustus, who was renowned for being a light eater, once boasted that on a particularly lean day he had fasted even more than a Jew on the Sabbath (Suetonius, 2 [*Divis Augustus*].76.2). Fasting was a particular feature of the piety of certain groups within Judaism, such as the Qumran community and the Pharisees. It was the custom of the Pharisees to fast twice a week (Luke 18:12; cf. *Ta'anit* 12a and *Didache* 8.1). Since they expected Jesus' disciples to be fasting, however, and since John's disciples were already fasting, presumably this was not a Pharisaic fast, but it was a fast in which the ordinary Israelite could also be expected to be engaged. Does that narrow it down any further?

Beginning in the post-exilic period, Judaism had developed set fasts at particular times of the year. Esther refers to the fast associated with Purim (Esth. 9:31; cf. 4:3, 16), and Zechariah mentions four regular fasts (8:19; cf. 7:3, 5). If these fasts were still in operation in the first century, this incident could, of course, be associated with any of them.

But it is also worth noting that fasting was associated with the annual Day of Atonement. It is often claimed that this was the only fast actually *prescribed* by the law (e.g. Lane 1974: 108; Anderson & Culbertson 1986: 314), but, in fact, fasting *per se* was not prescribed at all. Instead, the law required the Day of Atonement to be a 'day of affliction', a term that has a much broader scope than simply fasting (see Milgrom 2000: 20–23). The law urged 'affliction of soul' (Lev. 23:27, 29; cf. Lev. 16) which the LXX takes as being humble of soul (*tapainōsete tas psychas*). This may have included fasting – and in later Jewish practice it almost certainly did – but to be precise, the law did not specifically require fasting. Lane (1974: 109) notes that *t'nyt* occurs only once in the Hebrew Bible (Ezra 9:5; cf. 8:21), 'but had become a technical term for fasting by the time of the codification of the rabbinic material'. Instead, the law required an justification for this perceived breach of piety? Jesus replies in a series of metaphors and parables: the parables of the bridegroom (vv. 19–20), the patch (v. 21) and the new wine (v. 22).

The bridegroom is here! Time for joy

The emotional power of the parable of the bridegroom comes through playing with the opposite emotions associated with weddings and funerals, with joy and with mourning.

The presence of the bridegroom. The call for fasting is a call for mourning, but Jesus wants his hearers to recognize that this is a time for joy.[10] Jesus pictures himself as a bridegroom in the midst of wedding celebrations. This time of great joy exempts his disciples from the present fast.

The image is found in reverse on occasions when a wedding feast was turned to sorrow. 1 Maccabees (9:37–42) describes an actual event in which Jonathan and Simon avenged the murder of John by attacking a wedding: 'the wedding was turned into mourning and the voice of their musicians into a funeral dirge' (v. 41, NRSV).[11] The tragedy of this dramatic contrast was also used metaphorically to describe the Jews' loss of everything in the Babylonian exile. Several times Jeremiah pictured the coming exile in terms of the voice of the bridegroom and bride being heard no more (Jer. 7:34; 16:9; 25:10).[12] The prophet Joel also used this image to speak of the prospect of the coming judgment day (Joel 2:15–16).

---

appropriate recognition of the Israelites' humble station before God. It could be argued that even simply being involved in the Day of Atonement was a humbling experience, for it reminded participants that they had sinned and there was nothing they could do about their sin, except receive God's provision in this day of sacrifice.

So was this a Day of Atonement fast? Perhaps not, if the surrounding stories indicate near contemporaneous events, for the readiness of the grain for harvesting in 2:23–28 would indicate that this was spring (so Lightfoot 1950b: 10), or early summer (France 2002: 144), whereas the Day of Atonement was in autumn. If it was, however, then this makes this unit even more relevant to our discussion of the cross. Presumably it would be a most remarkable thing indeed not to be engaged in the rituals associated with the Day of Atonement. Small wonder that this was questioned! If the law did not specifically require fasting, Jesus was not strictly in breach of the law, but, nevertheless, he had evidently offended some Jewish religious sensibilities and some would have considered him in breach of the tradition, which, for them, amounted to the same thing. Note, too, that the Day of Atonement began the sabbatical year and the year of jubilee.

[10] This is also the import of the Q saying, Matt. 11:16–19 = Luke 7:31–35. For Matthew, see Schnackenburg 2002: 106–107.

[11] The book of Tobit describes a similar event (Tobit 3:5–14).

[12] Cf. Josephus, *Jewish War* 6.301, where Jesus, son of Ananias, cries out against the temple in words reminiscent of Jeremiah: 'A voice against Jerusalem and the sanctuary; a voice against the bridegroom and bride; a voice against all the people.'

Those calling upon Jesus and his friends to fast are moving in the wrong direction, for, in fact, the coming of Jesus is more like a funeral that is turned into a wedding banquet. Jeremiah and Isaiah spoke of the salvation beyond exile in terms of the voice of the bride and bridegroom returning to Israel once again (Jer. 33:11). Isaiah pictured formerly desolate Jerusalem being adorned as a bride (Isa. 61:10 – 62:5). In an earlier portion of his prophecy, Isaiah also looked forward to a great time of feasting at the end of the ages, when God would do away with death and mourning and tears and spread out a banquet for his people (Isa. 25:6–8). This is a picture of future resurrection life (cf. 26:19), for God promised that on this day he would remove the shroud of death that covers the nations and swallow up death for ever.[13] Mourning will be abolished, for resurrection life will have come!

Jesus and his disciples do not participate in the ritual of mourning, for the bridegroom has come. This is not a time for fasting, because the cause of humanity's mourning is about to be removed for ever. It is a time for great joy.

The bridegroom taken away. But a period for mourning will also come. In verse 20, Jesus looks ahead to the time when the bridegroom will be taken away. *Then* his disciples will fast. Jesus is not saying that one day his disciples will practise the ritual of fasting. He is using the rite to speak of the reality with which fasting was associated, namely mourning. There will come a time when the bridegroom is taken away and then his disciples will mourn – not in ritual, but in reality. In this saying, Jesus is alluding to the cross.[14] He has been commissioned as the servant of the Lord. The parable may even contain a subtle allusion to the servant's role, for the word used for 'taken away' occurs twice in the Greek (Septuagint) version of the final

[13] This has long been a disputed point. Scholars are divided over whether these chapters (esp. 25:8; 26:19) speak of individual resurrection, or metaphorically of national resurrection and new beginning. For a discussion of the issues, see e.g. Motyer 1993: 209–210; B. Doyle 2000: 315–320. Prejudice against the view that Isaiah's apocalypse is a reference to individual resurrection has often arisen from the opinion that resurrection belief arose late in Israel's history, under Persian influence. Indeed, even some who find resurrection in Isaiah's apocalypse propose for this reason that it is a late addition to the book. If, however, resurrection belief was *not* due to Persian influence, but was adequately grounded in Israel's own conceptions of God (see Bremmer 2002; Kaiser & Lohse 1981: 91; Petterson 2000: 9–11), then an allusion to resurrection in Isa. 24 – 27 does not seem so foreign after all.

[14] 'This section contains the first hint of the Passion on the lips of Jesus in Mark. What has happened to the forerunner will be repeated in the case of him who comes after him. When that happens, the disciples will have good reason to fast and mourn.' Cranfield 1977: 111.

servant song (Isa. 53:8).[15] Although his presence is now a moment of great joy, at some time in the future the disciples will mourn,[16] as he endures the horrendous death that God has in store for the servant of the Lord.[17]

The arrival of the last days

In his parable of the bridegroom (2:19–20), Jesus' language evokes Old Testament passages about the last days: 'days are coming' (*eleusontai de hēmerai*);[18] 'and then' (*kai tote*); 'in that day' (*en ekeinēi tēi hēmerai*).[19] Jesus had begun his ministry with the announcement, 'The times are fulfilled; the kingdom of God has drawn near' (1:15). One era has drawn to an end; another is about to dawn (cf. 10:30). In the midst of these last days, the bridegroom will be taken away.

Jesus reinforces this expectation with two more parables that make the same point. *The parable of the patch* (v. 21)[20] is a warning not to try to absorb Jesus into Judaism, or even into what John the Baptist was doing. The Old Testament law and John the Baptist pointed towards Jesus in all his newness. To expect him to conform to the practices of first-century Jewish piety is as inappropriate and foolish as sticking a patch of unshrunken cloth on to an old garment. He has not come to patch up this old system. This human religion is simply a part of a fallen world that God is about to roll up like a garment and throw away (cf. Ps. 102:26–28 = Heb. 1:10–12; Hag. 2:6; Heb. 12:26; Jeremias 1963: 118). *The parable of new wine* (v. 22) makes a similar point. The joy of harvest-time was a common prophetic symbol of the

[15] There are marked differences between the Greek and Hebrew versions of Isaiah 53, perhaps especially in vv. 8–11; see Sapp 1998. Both Hebrew and Greek, however, depict the servant as being 'taken away'.

[16] When Matthew's apocalyptic discourse is read in a similar way as I propose for Mark's in ch. 3 below, Zech. 12:10 is applied to the crucifixion; cf. Matt. 24:30. This 'mourning' is also demonstrated in Luke 23:27–31; Acts 2:37.

[17] If the fast was for the Day of Atonement (see n. 9 above, p. 21), then this would suggest that the time of the disciples' future mourning would be their Day of Atonement mourning. This would be a hint that the death of Jesus was a (?the) Day of Atonement.

[18] Instead of the future tense, the LXX uses the present, but it nevertheless refers to the future: 1 Sam. 2:31; 2 Kgs 20:17; Isa. 39:6; Jer. 7:32; 9:24 (EVV 9:25); 16:14; 19:6; 23:5, 7; 37:3 (MT 30:3); 38:27 (MT 31:27); 38:31 (MT 31:31); 31:12 (MT 48:12); 30:18 (MT 49:2); 28:52 (MT 51:52). See also MT Jer. 33:14; 51:47; and Amos 4:2; 8:11; 9:13.

[19] *En ekeinēi tēi hēmerai*: e.g. Dan. 12:1; Zech. 12:8–9; 14:6; *kai tote* evokes the kind of 'eschatological timetable' in Mark 13:26–27.

[20] The rabbis had a similar saying, so it may not have been entirely new for Jesus' hearers: cf. Mishnah, R. Joshua, 'For old cases an old decision, for new cases a new'; *Yadaim* 4.3; see Danby: 73.

new age,[21] and so too was the image of new wine (*oinos neos*).[22] God's salvation beyond judgment was pictured in terms of Israel once again enjoying the fruit of the land, including the blessings of wine (Hos. 2:22). A statement in Amos (9:13–14, ESV)[23] begins with exactly the same words as in Jesus' parable:

> 'Behold, the days are coming,' declares the LORD,
>   'when the plowman shall overtake the reaper
>   and the treader of grapes him who sows the seed;
> the mountains shall drip sweet wine,
>   and all the hills shall flow with it.
> I will restore the fortunes of my people Israel,
>   and they shall rebuild the ruined cities and inhabit them;
> they shall plant vineyards and drink their wine.'

When this new wine begins to drip from the hills as the new age was dawning, it is complete foolishness to expect it to be contained by the old wineskins. Both parables 'bear on the newness of that which has come into the world with Jesus',[24] and point out the folly of trying to

---

[21] Jeremias 1963: 118–119. He notes that harvest also includes the last judgment, with which the new age begins (Joel 3:13). 'New wine' can also be utilized as a judgment image (Isa. 49:26). 'The people who walked in darkness have seen a great light; those who dwelt in a land of deep darkness on them has light shined. You have multiplied the nation; you have increased its joy; they rejoice before you as with joy at the harvest, as they are glad when they divide the spoil' (Isa. 9:2–3). Looking forward to the restoration of the fortunes of Zion, Psalm 126 enlists the harvest image: 'Those who sow in tears shall reap with shouts of joy! He who goes out weeping, bearing the seed for sowing, shall come home with shouts of joy, bringing his sheaves with him' (Ps. 126:5–6).

[22] Although the exact expression used by Mark is rare, the LXX has many references to 'new wine' using a variety of terms. The LXX usually translates *tîrōš* 'new wine' (38 times in the MT), simply using *oinos*, although occasionally in conjunction with *aparchē*. It translates *'āsîs*, 'sweet wine' as *oinos neos* (Isa. 49:26), or *glykasmos*, 'sweetness' (Joel 4:18 [LXX]; Amos 9:13; cf. Acts 2:13, *gleukos*, 'new wine'). Apart from John 2:11, the texts assembled by Jeremias (1963: 118), allegedly showing wine as a symbol of salvation (i.e. Gen. 9:20; 49:11–12; Num. 13:23–24) are questionable.

[23] Jesus probably alluded to this passage in John 4:36.

[24] Cranfield (1977: 113) is uncertain, however, as to the exact original application. Was it a defence of the disciples against those who wanted to confine them by continuing pious practices? He refers to the incompatibility of John's disciples' use of these practices with the recognition of the new situation; the fact that the kingdom of God cannot be confined within Judaism, for the coming of the new must mean the dissolution of the old; the need for new birth, and the fact that it cannot be received without the miracle of the new creation (Hilary of Poitiers: '*Atque ideo et Pharisaeos et discipulos Johannis nova non accepturos esse nisi novi fierent*': 'For this reason, neither the Pharisees nor the disciples of John were about to accept new things unless they were made new [themselves].')

accommodate the old and the new together. 'The ministry of Jesus is not to be regarded as an attempt to reform Judaism; it brings something entirely new, which cannot be accommodated to the traditional system' (Dodd 1961: 88). Jesus has not come to join a system whose rules and regulations could speak only of sinfulness, uncleanness, sickness, mourning, decay and death. 'It is clear that the opposition between life and death is fundamental to the whole ritual law ... Death is the great evil, and everything suggesting it, from corpses to bloody discharge to skin disease, makes people unclean and therefore unfit to worship God' (Wenham 1995: 77). Jesus has not come to be absorbed by this religion of tears. He is the bridegroom, bringing the great time of last days' feasting when the shroud of death is finally cast away once and for all.

Let the new wine flow! Let the eschatological salvation flow out from Israel to the nations and issue in a whole new creation!

The sabbath as gift (2:23–28)

This new creation is also hinted at in the third story (2:23–28), when Jesus again finds himself in trouble with the religious over allowing his disciples to pluck grain on the sabbath day. Jesus told them: 'The sabbath was made for human beings, not human beings for the sabbath. So the Son of Man is Lord even of the sabbath' (vv. 27–28). He reminds them that the sabbath was gift. God gave it for the benefit of human beings. The weekly sabbath was meant to be a foretaste of the great sabbath at the end of time.[25] Their religious rules had made them slaves to a calendar, and obscured the glorious vision of the kingdom of God, towards which their weekly rest should have pointed them. Jesus was now announcing that this kingdom had drawn near (1:15).

Jesus has already made the enormous claim that the divine prerogative to forgive sins has been given to him (2:10), but now he makes another enormous claim about himself. As the Son of Man he is Lord of the sabbath; that is, he is the one who will preside over that

---

[25] Shead 2002: 19: 'The institution of the Sabbath day had an eschatological edge from the first.' Barth comments that, despite the fact that Israel did not see it this way, the weekly sabbath 'is the immutable sign, set up in and with the creation of time, of the particular time of God to which all other times move' (*CD* III.2: 458; cf. III.1: 218–219, 228; III.4: 47–57, esp. 56–57). When Jesus healed on the sabbath, 'He did so deliberately and gladly because His own coming meant that the seventh and last day, the great day of Yahweh, had dawned, and healing was the specific Word of God that He had come to accomplish on this day'; *CD* IV.2: 226. In doing so, Jesus therefore fulfils the role for which humanity was created; Dumbrell 1994: 195.

great sabbath rest at the end of time (Shead 2002), entered through the resurrection from the dead. The one who will be the great Son of Man is already in their midst, and they accuse him of breaking the sabbath day, which, in the end, points towards him and his coming kingdom.

Life and death on the sabbath (3:1–6)

The fourth and final story (3:1–6) brings this cycle of conflict to a head. In this scene, we watch the Lord of the sabbath acting consistently with the sabbath. On the day that was made for humanity, he cures a man with a withered hand. Before he does so, he asks the religious: 'Is it lawful on the Sabbath to do good or to do harm, to save life or to kill?' (v. 4, ESV). But they make no reply. Jesus' question reveals his perspective on his miracles: Jesus does good; he brings life where there is death. By doing so, he points towards the future, towards eternal life in the kingdom of God.

But when he cures this man, in response to this marvellous gift of life the religious leaders immediately join forces with the politicians to plan how to destroy him (3:6). From this point on, the shadow of Jesus' cross falls across the narrative. This deliberate plot to kill him stands in the background of everything that happens from now on. On the sabbath that is made for human beings, his opponents seek to kill him for breaking their rules. Jesus brought life to a world under the shadow of death,[26] and, because of this, he will be put to death – by the representatives of religion.

What is it that provokes such conflict? There is an integral link between this conflict with religion and the coming of the bridegroom. He brings something entirely new; something that cannot be squeezed into the old wineskins; something that cannot patch up the old, failed system. And when the bridegroom is taken away, the time for 'religion' will come to an end.

Jesus and the abolition of religion

Religion exposed

Although it will be the cross that will ultimately do away with religion, Jesus is in conflict with religion from beginning to end. He critiques religious abuses (7:1–23); he warns against a corrupt

---

[26] Cf. Moltmann's (1974: 60) insight into the evils of religion: 'Jesus was also rejected by inhuman persons because of his love for those whom they had dehumanized.'

leadership that had brought Israel to ruin (e.g. Isa. 3:14; Mic. 7:1–4), and exposes the hard heart that is at the core of Israel and Israel's leadership (3:5; 7:1–23; 10:1–5).[27] It is not an explicit part of Mark's story to show Jesus' attitude to Greco-Roman religion,[28] but if he was so clearly disturbed at the abuses within the religion of Israel, it does not require much imagination to guess at his attitude towards the abuses associated with the idolatrous practices that existed outside Israel (cf. Acts 17:16). By demonstrating Jesus' critique of the religion of Israel, how much more does Mark portray his critique of non-Israelite religion.

But Jesus does more than simply expose the abuses of first-century Judaism. Jesus is not just a reformer of a basically good system that is in need of repair. He is the Messiah, and his arrival spells an entirely new stage in God's plans and purposes for the world. The bridegroom has come, bringing something radically new

[27] Mark exposes religion as having multiple faults. It had teaching that lacked authority (1:22–28). It had allowed the *daimonic* into its core (1:21–28). Mark shows that the Jewish religion had rules that excluded people from their own homes in the interest of cleanliness (1:40–45), and rituals that could pronounce that people had become clean, but could not do anything to make them so (1:44). It grumbled over potential blasphemy (2:7) while committing the greatest blasphemy of all time, the destruction of the Messiah. It fostered a judgmental spirit, in which rules were placed above relationships. It displayed an inability to offer real help in the face of human suffering. When somebody died, religion could provide the professional mourners and the rules to ensure that the corpse did not pollute, but could do nothing about the problem of death itself and the grief under which it forces human beings to live. Obsessed with status and position, the religious leaders could miss the miracles in their midst (6:1–6) while demanding miracles more in keeping with their own desires (8:11–13). They nullify the Word of God in order to keep the human traditions (7:1–13), and have the appearance of being scrupulous about the things of God, but in reality have hearts that are rotten to the core (7:14–23). The religious miss the coming of the Messiah, while the condemned Gentiles rejoice that he is in their midst (7:24–30; 8:31–37). They argue about divorce, ignoring the fact that the very presence of the divorce provisions in their law testify to the problem of their hard hearts (10:1–12). They teach that eternal life is achieved by what a person does, and yet cover over the human reality that none of us can do enough (10:17–31). Their obsession with importance and status leads them to exclude the sick and the young. They allow God's house to become a den of robbers, and demand payment for services, even if this is the ruin of the poor widow, whom they were meant to protect. They plot to kill the Messiah on the sabbath (3:6), and later pay his 'friend' to betray him, and collaborate with the national enemies, the Gentiles. They use deception and politics to destroy him. They occupy the Messiah's seat, and yet refuse to give it up when he arrives. They destroy him, and then gloat over the demise of their enemy. See also Marshall 1989: 180–182, for a list of the evils of Jesus' opponents.

[28] This is not to say that the Gospel itself does not offer a critique – which, I would argue, it most surely does. Mark's story severely undermines the assumptions of the Roman imperial cult, for example, even utilizing some of its associated language to this end. See further Bolt 2003.

that could not simply be squeezed into the old wineskins. The age of fulfilment has arrived, which means that the 'good things' of which the old covenant was just a shadow have finally come (cf. Heb. 10:1). He fulfils the law in order for the law to be surpassed and the shadow to be left behind. It could never ultimately deal with the problems of this world. The old religion had failed – as indeed, in God's plan, it was destined to do.

Religion abolished

The shadow had been an elaborate teaching aid, which always pointed towards life. It was, however, impossible for sinful human beings to fulfil the old covenant in order to find that promised life (Acts 15:10; Gal. 3:10–14; Rom. 7). As a consequence, the system that was revealed by God to bring Israel life manifested death instead (Rom. 7:8–10; 2 Cor. 3:6–7). Even though it was the Gentiles who were 'far off' (Eph. 2:13, 17) and the Jews were 'the people near to God' (cf. Ps. 148:14), God's revelation to Israel ultimately had the effect of showing them that sinful human beings could not come close to the holy God.

And so the radical newness brought by Jesus spells the end of Judaism – not just first-century Judaism, with its various abuses, but the Old Testament system of life set down by God's own law. The coming of the bridegroom abolished even God's own religion.[29] The religion of the Old Testament was an elaborate system that effectively taught that God kept his distance from sinners. Even though Israel rejoiced at the presence of God among them, that presence was paradoxically, at one and the same time, a reminder of God's distance.[30] The coming of Jesus abolishes this distance, and so, in another of God's great paradoxes, the Messiah's fulfilment of the law (cf. Matt. 5:17–18)[31] means that Old Testament religion is superseded.

[29] Cf. 'The passages at Mark 10:45 and 14:22ff. illustrate the stress in Mark on the positive significance of the death of Jesus. This is more closely connected with the idea of mercy and self-sacrifice, the creation of a new rather than the rejection, condemnation, and destruction of the old Israel. The latter idea is necessarily involved, but it is as a consequence of the former'; Yates 1963: 233.

[30] For example, notice how the Shekinah, perhaps the supreme token of God's presence with Israel, also demonstrated that God dwelt in both 'unapproachable light' (1 Tim. 6:16; cf. Exod. 13:21–22; 24:15–17) and in deep darkness (Exod. 14:20; 1 Kgs 8:12, cf. vv. 10–11). Whatever image is used, it taught the distance of the present God.

[31] These two verses must be read together. Jesus did not come to abolish without fulfilment. Instead, he came to fulfil every jot and tittle. By the end of the Gospel, this will be done and the new era for the world will have dawned.

This will become clear at the end of the story when Jesus casts out the money-changers and merchants from the temple (11:15–19).[32] This is not a 'cleansing' of the temple, as if some more legitimate purpose for it will rise from the ashes. This is a signal of the end of the old system. At his trial, the false witnesses will speak words of truth, even if they do not know it (14:58), for Jesus' death will do away with 'the temple made with hands', and another temple 'not made with hands' will arise in its place. At the moment of Jesus' death, the veil of the temple will be torn from top to bottom (15:37–38), a dramatic demonstration that the old Jewish religion is abolished when the bridegroom was taken away.

That is why the appropriate response to Jesus is not more religion, nor is it the construction of a new religion. The proper response to Jesus is something completely non-religious. With the coming of the bridegroom, along with the abolition of religion, comes *faith*.[33] But before turning to faith, I shall glance at 'religionless Christianity'.

The abolition of religion and 'religionless Christianity'

After being used by Karl Barth, the phrase 'the abolition of religion' sparked several twentieth-century theologians, in their own diverse ways, to promote what they called 'religionless Christianity'.[34] Perhaps the one who created the biggest storm in the 1960s was John Robinson, in his book *Honest to God* (J. A. T. Robinson 1963), which drew upon the writings of Dietrich Bonhoeffer and Paul Tillich. In recent times, 'religionless Christianity' has been actively promoted, to the great joy of the media, by Bishop John Spong.[35]

When Barth used the phrase, he wished to show that human religion was swept away before God's revelation, for God's revelation

---

[32] The action in the temple was the immediate cause of Jesus' opponents' seeking to arrest him (11:18); see Lightfoot 1950d: 61.

[33] This touches upon huge issues concerning the nature of the relationship between old and new covenants that cannot be fully discussed here. Even though faith does make an appearance in the Old Testament, most notably with Abraham (Rom. 4), and the 'heroes of faith' of Hebrews 11, Paul could still speak of the climactic arrival of faith in the world (Gal. 3:23), and it is in this sense I am speaking here.

[34] For discussion, see Morris 1964. Morris refers to Tillich, Bonhoeffer, John A. T. Robinson and Alex Vidler. Neither Tillich nor Robinson defined religion. For Bonhoeffer, it was individualistic, metaphysical, one department of life; God is *deus ex machina*; Morris 1964: 9–10.

[35] Spong is consciously continuing the project of John Robinson's *Honest to God*. See Spong 1983: 28–29; 1998: xvii–xv, xviii, 131, 213, 237 n. 6; (ed.) 1999: ch. 10; 2001: x–xiii, xvii, xviii, xx, 214, 247 n. 2.

THE CROSS AND THE ABOLITION OF RELIGION

is met only by faith.[36] For the advocates of 'religionless Christianity', however, it meant that human religion was to be swept away before ordinary life. This 'religionless Christianity' does not call for repentance,[37] for it tends to endorse individuals in whatever state of life they are already in, and so requires no change at all. Not surprisingly, 'religionless Christianity' finds no place for the atoning death of Christ.[38]

This is not the 'abolition of religion' that we find in Mark's presentation. The coming of the bridegroom brings a new vision of all of life. Jesus began his ministry with a call to repent and believe, in the light of the declaration that the time is up for this world and the kingdom of God is near (1:15). This was a call to see the world in a radically different way. Jesus urged his followers to cease looking at the world from a human point of view and to begin to see it from God's point of view (8:33). He invited them to leave the ordinary security structures of human life and to follow him through the cross to the kingdom.

This leads to radical changes of life in all its aspects. Faith is reliance upon God alone for security in this world, not upon the security structures of secular life, and not upon the security offered by religion – not even those provided by God himself before the new wine began to flow.[39] The coming of the bridegroom does not abolish religion and confirm ordinary human life in the position it happens to be in already. When the bridegroom appears, human beings are invited into something entirely new. Not a new religion, but a new vision of *life* has been revealed. The only response to this new vision is faith. Far from having no need for the atoning death of Christ, it is

---

[36] Barth, *CD* I.2: 280–361. It is misguided to blunt the edge of Barth's critique by 'contextualizing' his views by comparison with reactions to Nazi immanentism, as does Richmond (1963: 38), cited with approval by Morris (1964: 67–68). Barth's comments, once again, raise the question of the Old Testament depiction of faith as a response to God's revelation, but, for our purposes here, this question does not need to be addressed. The theological discussion at issue addresses religion in its most basic sense, of what human beings do with respect to God.

[37] Morris 1964: 73–74, 88–91. Morris uses the term 'penitence' instead of 'repentance'.

[38] Morris 1964: 71: 'If Christianity is to be "religionless" then what place is there for an atoning act? As Bonhoeffer states the case men are not asked to repent and seek their salvation in what God has done for them in Christ. They are simply to rise to their full secular stature.' See, for example, Spong's sustained attack on the atonement in his writings, e.g. 1998: 84, 88–89, 92–94; (ed.) 1999: 236–237; 2001: 2 ('not just naïve, but eminently rejectable'), 10–11, 120–125.

[39] Phil. 3 shows that Paul systematically rejected the old security structures of Old Testament religion (not just of first-century Judaism) when he discovered Christ.

exactly when the bridegroom is taken away that religion is abolished and the need for faith is established.

After the coming of Jesus provokes conflict with religion in the first narrative movement, Mark's second main movement (4:35 – 8:26) will show Jesus acting to establish faith.

Jesus and the establishment of faith

We shall gain an overview of Mark's second main section by examining its first scene – the 'storm at sea' (4:35–41). This scene functions to structure the reading of the entire section that follows. Therefore, even though 4:35 – 8:26 makes no explicit reference to the cross, it provides an important part of the framework in which the cross can be understood and its benefits grasped.

The structuring role of 'the storm at sea'

This scene contains three questions. When the storm whips up, the frightened disciples wake the sleeping Jesus with the words, 'Teacher, don't you care that we are perishing?'[40] We can label this 'the existential question', for their very existence was in jeopardy. Jesus deals with the storm, and then asks his disciples what we can call 'the faith question': 'Why are you afraid? Do you not have faith yet?'[41] This fills them with even more fear, and, in their panic, they ask each other 'the Christological question': 'Who then is this, that even the wind and the sea obey him?' (4:38–41).

The trouble with questions is that, once heard, they do not leave the hearers alone. They are asked of anyone who hears them, whether their subject is properly their business or not. Questions in a narrative are therefore extremely important for the reader of the narrative as well as for the original hearers. As we read this account, the disciples' questions become our questions. Once these questions are asked, we too want to hear the answers. And since these questions are asked within the narrative, we, the readers, expect to find the answers as the narrative continues. In this way, these questions structure our reading experience, for, as we read on into the next section of Mark's story, we are looking for the answers to these three questions.

[40] Although some English translations particularize the situation with the phrase 'that we are drowning', the verb is more general (*apollymetha*) and should be rendered so.

[41] The use of *oupō* 'not yet', shows that the issue is not simply that they lack faith, but that Jesus expects them to have faith some time in the future. This question therefore opens a 'gap' that the story will seek to fill by showing how the disciples came to faith.

At this point we should underline what we have already noted, namely, that there are *three* questions here, not just two. The importance of the Christological question and the faith question for the subsequent narrative has often been noticed.[42] Unfortunately, the importance of the existential question for the subsequent narrative is usually overlooked.[43] But the three questions are interrelated. If the disciples truly knew who Jesus was, and had faith in him, they would not have been in fear of their lives. The kind of faith Jesus desires is faith in him – properly understood – even in the face of death. So these are the questions that we shall take with us as we read on in the story. These three questions will structure our reading experience, guiding us as we keep moving towards the climax of the story in the cross.[44] For convenience we can deal with them one at a time, and we shall deal with them in reverse.

The Christological question

The Christological question has, of course, already been on the agenda from the beginning (cf. 1:1). Practically every scene in the Gospel contributes to Mark's presentation of Jesus. Characters within the story are asked to form an opinion of him, and this is also on the agenda for the reader. As well as being part of the very fabric of the narrative, however, on several occasions the Christological question rises to the surface by being asked explicitly within the story. As explained before, this means that the reader cannot help but be confronted with this question as well.

Perhaps the most famous example comes from the next narrative movement, Mark's third and central section, where Jesus will take his own opinion poll and receive answers similar to those in 6:14–16: ' "Who do people say that I am?" And they answered him, "John the Baptist; and others, Elijah; and still others, one of the prophets." He asked them, "But who do you say that I am?" Peter answered him, "You are the Messiah" ' (8:27b–29, NRSV).

The Christological question continues to be on Mark's agenda (cf. 11:27–33; 12:1–12) until the climactic scene portraying the cross. When the Gentile centurion provides his own answer, which agrees exactly with Mark's point of view – 'Truly this man was the Son of

---

[42] Marshall (1989: 213–214) is representative in his insistence that 4:35–41 has two themes, Christology and faith.
[43] I have explored this more fully in Bolt 2003.
[44] For reading as an 'experience', see Iser 1972.

God!' (15:39, ESV; cf. 1:1) – the Christological question is finally answered.

The faith question

The faith question travels hand in hand with the Christological question throughout Mark's narrative. Once again, this is a question that is raised implicitly by practically every scene,[45] but from time to time it is also raised explicitly.

The vocabulary of faith

Mark makes extensive use of the vocabulary relating to believing and faith,[46] and also utilizes many related metaphors and images. People within the story – and, through them, the readers – are called upon to 'see', to 'hear', to 'understand', to 'leave', to 'come after', to 'follow'. These are all part of Mark's rich theme of faith.[47] In addition, those of Jesus' miracle stories that depict him giving the gift of sight or hearing, or those in which the response is to follow him, have a direct contribution to this theme.

Faith and the disciples

The need for faith is raised, in particular, with respect to the disciples. In the storm at sea, Jesus asks them, 'Do you *not yet* (*oupō*) have faith?', implying that he expects that they will move towards that position as time goes on. Mark's second main section keeps returning to this question. These men, who are privileged to watch Jesus from close quarters, seem to take so long to realize whom they are following. Jesus is amazed that, just like the people of Nazareth (6:1–6) and even the Pharisees (7:18), the disciples do not seem to see, or to understand, or to believe. The two feeding miracles (6:30–42; 8:1–10) seem to be performed as a teaching aid purely for their benefit, and yet their unbelief and hardness of heart continue (cf. 6:45–52). In the last of the three sea-crossings, Jesus forces them to reflect upon the two feedings, and he expresses utter amazement that

---

[45] 'There is limited abstract reflection or even direct teaching on faith in the gospel; Mark's theological perspective is implicit in the way he tells his story – both the single overall story about Jesus, and the component episodes or stories which make up the larger narrative'; Marshall 1989: 226.

[46] The fact that 'believing' is also a significant theme in the spurious longer ending of Mark (*pisteuō*: 16:13, 14, 16, 17; *apistia*, 16:14) indicates that its writer has recognized this major theme in Mark. The Freer logion also sets Jesus' ministry against the backdrop of 'this age of lawlessness and unbelief'.

[47] For discussion of this theme, see in particular Marshall 1989.

34

they still do not see, or hear, or understand; that is, they still have no faith (8:14–21). Since faith has been discussed using the metaphor of sight, the cure of the blind man at the end of the section holds out some hope (8:22–26). If Jesus can open the eyes of the physically blind, perhaps he will be able to open the eyes of the disciples, so that they can truly see the one they are following.

Despite their obtuseness, however, the disciples do not present an entirely bleak picture. Some of their other features demonstrate what faith looks like in reality. In a controversy with his opponents, Jesus will later say that, just as the coin bearing Caesar's image belongs to Caesar, so too, human beings, who bear the image of God, belong to him and owe him their whole lives (12:17; cf. 12:29–33; R. H. Smith 1973: 331 n. 14, 332). As Mark's story unfolds, we find that the disciples have given their whole lives to following Jesus. They have left their homes and professions to follow him (1:16–20; 2:13–17). Later on, Peter will say that they have left everything (10:28). This is exactly what Jesus has asked of them, and what he will ask of others as the story proceeds (8:34–38; 10:21; 10:49). Jesus calls them to reject all the things that bring security and identity to normal human life, so that they may find their security and identity in following him wherever he may lead.[48] In so far as they have heeded this call,[49] they demonstrate the life of faith.

Faith and the opponents

By contrast, Jesus' opponents provide the negative picture of unbelief. By quoting Isaiah 6:9–10 in his explanation why he teaches in parables (4:10–12), Jesus indicates that nothing has really changed about Israel since Isaiah's day. They see but do not perceive, they hear but do not understand; that is, they are still afflicted with unbelief. Jesus' ministry through parables has the same role as Isaiah's ministry, namely hardening Israel further, so that God's purposes of judgment might be fulfilled. But, at the same time, there will be a holy seed, a remnant, raised up from among Israel, who hear, and see, and understand. Hearing the word with acceptance,

[48] 'Conversion is marked by the spontaneous forsaking of all existing forms of security, and faith consists in embarking on a lifelong relationship of believing trust in Jesus involving material dependence, reliance on him for eschatological salvation, and a submission to a process of learning and personal transformation'; Marshall 1989: 139.

[49] Disciples 'detach themselves from family ties and traditions, the main source of identity for first century Palestinians' (Marshall 1989: 137, referring to Kee 1977: 153f. and Lohfink 1985: 39, 44). For family ties in Mark, see now Barton 1994.

this remnant will be the seed that enters the coming harvest of the kingdom of God.

But this remnant of believers will be raised up against the backdrop of the general unbelief of Israel. The people of Nazareth provide an example of the unbelief of Israel. Well aware of Jesus' mighty works, they nevertheless fail to believe, because he is just too familiar to them (6:1–6). After the transfiguration, Jesus will describe the Israelite crowd as an unbelieving generation (*apistos*, 9:19). In this same scene, one Israelite, a father troubled by his spirit-afflicted son, emerges from the crowd as someone who recognizes his problem and wants help to overcome it. He cries out, 'If you can do anything, help us, after having compassion on us.' Jesus replies, 'If you can? All things are possible to the one who believes.' And the father responds, 'I do believe. Help me in my unbelief' (9:22–24).

But it is the leaders of Israel, both religious and political, who provide the major paradigm of Israel's unbelief (Marshall 1989: ch. 6). They are the ones who are set in opposition to Jesus from the beginning. They question his actions (2:16; 2:18; 2:24; 3:2), accuse him of blasphemy (2:7; 14:64), and align him with Beelzeboul, the prince of the underworld (3:22). They question his authority (cf. 1:22; 2:7; 11:28), because they refused to believe that John the Baptist was sent from heaven as his forerunner (11:29–33).

Jesus indicts them for many things, but his parable of the tenants best summarizes their overall problem (12:1–12). The parable canvasses the history of the unbelief of Israel (R. H. Smith 1973: 331), but is particularly targeted at Israel's leadership. Jesus is simply reissuing the parable from Isaiah 5, and, as in Isaiah's assessment, the vineyard of Israel is in ruins because of the leadership, who have devoured it (Isa. 3:14). Even though they have been placed in their position to care for God's people, they want the vineyard themselves, and do not wish to give God his dues. Even when he sends his final messenger, his own beloved son (12:6), they decide to kill him so that the inheritance can be theirs.

On this occasion, the religious leaders immediately recognize that Jesus is speaking against them (12:12), and so they set about to fulfil his words! They long ago joined forces with the politicians in plotting to destroy him (3:6), and now they actively seek a way of doing so (11:18; 12:12; 14:2), set traps for him to fall into (3:2; 11:18; 12:13–34), and eventually pay one of his closest companions to betray him by stealth (14:1–2, 10–11). They use false witnesses at his trial, find him guilty of the charge of blasphemy, but hand him over to the hated

Romans on a more political charge designed to get him killed (15:2). Even when he is dying, they show their basic inhumanity by standing at the foot of the cross gloating over their victory and pouring their mockery upon the head of their dying victim (15:31–32). They call upon him to come down from the cross, for then they would see and believe (15:32). But, by this stage in the story, we know that they will never see, and their destruction of the king of the Jews is the ultimate act of unbelief.

The opponents provide a foil for the disciples' journey towards faith. Throughout the story, the disciples are torn between two leaders. They are definitely following Jesus, but they also share the unbelief of Israel. In the storm at sea, Jesus asks why they do not yet have faith (4:40). In the second sea-crossing, they still do not believe, suffering from the same hard heart as the leadership (6:52; cf. 3:5). In a controversy with the Pharisees, Jesus reveals that, as in Isaiah's day, Israel's heart is far from God (7:1–23), and then, when the disciples fail to understand, he asks them, 'Then are you also lacking in understanding?' (*houtōs kai hymeis asynetoi este?*, 7:18; note the *kai*); that is, 'Are you just like the rest of Israel and its leadership?' By the final sea-crossing they have made little progress (8:14–21). Jesus warns them that the leaders, both the Pharisees and Herod, are like leaven. The disciples should not follow these leaders, who are like Ezekiel's evil shepherds who only plunder the flock (cf. Ezek. 34 – 36). Rather, the disciples should throw in their lot with the 'good shepherd' who feeds them with the food that will bring them to the kingdom harvest, the future resurrection from the dead.

Faith and the suppliants

Throughout Mark's story a range of characters appear in the story, encounter Jesus, and then disappear again.[50] These minor characters have been described as foils for the disciples,[51] because they often exhibit the faith towards which the disciples are journeying. If the opponents show us what is *not* commended, the minor characters show us what *is* commended. From among these minor characters, a group of thirteen can be separated out and labelled 'the suppliants'.[52] Mark pays greater attention to these 'suppliants', giving each of them a whole scene when their story is told. These are the ones who come to

---

[50] See Marshall 1989: ch. 4; Williams 1994; Bolt 2003.
[51] Rhoads, Dewey & Michie 1999: 133; Marshall 1989: 77.
[52] For a sustained treatment of the role of the suppliants in Mark's narrative, see Bolt 2003.

Jesus with a need for healing or exorcism, which Jesus meets. These are the ones who exhibit faith and are often explicitly commended for their faith. When Jesus saw the faith of those who carried the paralytic, he declared his sins forgiven (2:5). The bleeding woman and Bartimaeus are both told, 'Your faith has saved you' (5:34; 10:52).[53] The father of the boy cries out, 'I believe; help my unbelief!' (9:24, NRSV), and Jesus deals with his problem.

This group of thirteen suppliants shows us a slice of life in the first-century world: a man with an unclean spirit (1:21–28); a woman with a fever (1:29–31); a leper in his uncleanness (1:40–45); a paralytic (2:1–10); a man with a withered hand (3:1–6); a man with a legion of demons who lives among the tombs (5:1–20); a synagogue official, Jairus, whose twelve-year-old daughter is dying (5:21–23) and then dead (5:35–43); a woman who had been bleeding for as long as the girl had been alive (5:24–34); a Greek woman whose daughter was troubled with a demon (7:24–30); a deaf man with stumbling speech (7:31–37); a blind man who lived in Bethsaida (8:22–26); a father and son, severely afflicted by a spirit that had troubled the boy since childhood and had often tried to kill him (9:14–29); another blind man, by the name of Bartimaeus (10:46–52). Despite their variety, together they illustrate a world in great need, a world under the shadow of death. They also show that the Jewish religion was completely unable to help them in their need. In fact, it probably even made their situation worse by excluding them as unclean and so making God seem even further away. By coming to Jesus, this group shows the reader that faith means turning to Jesus Christ in the midst of real physical needs in this world under the shadow of death, and being prepared to follow him into the kingdom.[54]

This is perhaps best illustrated by the story of Jairus. His daughter is at the point of death when he first asks Jesus to come home and help her (5:23). Jesus is delayed by the interchange with the bleeding woman. Just as Jesus was telling the woman that she was saved by her faith, a group come from Jairus' house and tell him that his daughter has died, so there is no point troubling Jesus any more (5:34–35). By this time, Jesus had a reputation as a healer; but what can he do now that the girl is dead?

[53] The noun also occurs at 11:22 in the phrase *pistis theou*, which should be rendered 'the faithfulness of God'. See my discussion of this verse in ch. 3 below, pp. 88–89.

[54] 'Given the unbelief of the world, suffering is a necessary prelude to glory. Faith, however, is itself already a victory, seizing ahead of time in the midst of darkness the outstretched but veiled hand of the Father, refusing to be swerved from the path of trust and service'; R. H. Smith 1973: 338.

Jesus has an important lesson in store for the synagogue leader. Overhearing the conversation, Jesus says to Jairus: 'Keep on only believing' (*monon pisteue*, 5:36). This is the only place in the New Testament where we get the good Reformed expression *sola fide*, or at least its Greek equivalent: *'monon pisteue'*, 'only believe'. Even in the face of death, Jairus must continue to believe. Demonstrating his amazing power, Jesus raised the girl from her deathbed and sent her back into ordinary life.

Jairus is named only at the beginning of this account (5:22). The rest of the time he is referred to by his position as 'the synagogue ruler' (5:22, 35, 36, 38), as well as once by his relation to the girl (he was her father, 5:40). Despite his position, the Jewish religion could provide absolutely no help for this father who had lost his beloved child. He sought out the Galilean preacher who was being opposed by the officials of Judaism. In his despair, he was called upon only to have faith, even in the face of death. He discovered that Jesus was by no means impotent, even when faced with humanity's last and greatest enemy. Jesus could even defeat death.

Faith and the reader

Jesus' initial announcement of the nearness of the kingdom is accompanied by a call to 'repent and believe in the gospel' (1:15, NRSV). This is addressed generally to all his hearers, and, because of its position in the narrative, is assumed to underpin his entire ministry. Because of its generality and its prime position, it is also addressed to the reader of Mark at the beginning of and so throughout the Gospel. Through his story of Jesus, Mark is moving his readers towards faith, even under the shadow of death. He does this by presenting an interlocking network of relationships between the characters, in which each character group contributes to the promotion of faith in the reader. 'Mark's gospel is more than a string of isolated units; it is one unified narrative in which the individual pericopae are no longer experienced by the reader or hearer as separate tales but as cumulative scenes in a single coherent story' (Marshall 1989: 227). By being engaged in the complexities of this story, the readers are moved towards faith in Jesus Christ. In the story, Jesus is presented entirely positively and he draws the readers towards faith in him. The disciples move towards faith, and sweep up the reader in this journey. The unbelief of the opponents repels the readers, thus strengthening the commendation of faith (Bolt 1993: 43–49).

The suppliants – those thirteen characters who come to Jesus for healing or exorcism – have a particularly important role in connecting the story with the readers.[55] They are the readers' entry point into the narrative. They are portrayed sympathetically, as real human beings in need. As such, they are a slice of life in the real world. First-century readers would know of such people; they knew this kind of world. The readers are drawn into the story by being aligned with these characters, see Jesus act on their behalf, and recognize that the proper attitude towards Jesus is faith. Thus, through the dynamics of the narrative, the readers are moved to put their faith in Jesus as well. As in the story of Jairus, this is also faith in Jesus, even in the face of death; for these readers are situated in a particular life setting that is evoked by the disciples' existential question.

The 'existential' question

Faith and fear

In the middle of the storm, the disciples cry out for their lives, and Jesus says that this shows that they do not yet have faith. In Mark, faith is the opposite of fear. Those without faith, whether disciples (4:40–41; 9:32; 10:32) or others (5:15; 6:20; 11:18; 11:32; 12:12), are regularly said to be afraid.[56] By contrast, those who are afraid are urged to have faith (5:36).[57] The mention of emotion in a narrative, especially perhaps such a primal emotion as fear, immediately draws the reader into the story. Even if we have never been caught in a storm at sea, we have all been afraid. The disciples' fearful question easily becomes our own. But we should notice that the disciples' fear was very specific, namely the fear of death (cf. 4:38).

The fear of death

Once again, their fearful question easily becomes our question. The fear of death is a basic human fear that underlies all other fears. The writer to the Hebrews tells us that it is this fear that holds us in slavery

---

[55] I have explored these narrative dynamics at length in Bolt 2003 or, more briefly, in 1993: 43–49.

[56] We can also note the fear of the 'arch-unbelievers' of the story, Jesus' opponents: 11:32; 12:12; cf. 14:1–2 and 15:10.

[57] The situation is more complex in the case of the bleeding woman and the women at the empty tomb. Were they afraid because they did not have faith at that stage? Or, given the association with the notion of 'trembling' (5:33: *hē de gynē phobētheisa kai tremousa*; 16:8: *eichen gar autas tromos kai ekstasis: kai oudeni ouden eipan: ephobounto gar*), are they caught up with a 'holy awe' that is a product of their faith? Marshall (1989: 107) denies that this is the case.

all our lives (Heb. 2:14–15). Thinkers ancient and modern have recognized this to be so. Even though we now live in a society that has worked hard at suppressing any conversation about this most basic of all fears, this was not the case in the ancient world, where death was an obvious, everyday reality. The fear of death constantly occupied the lives of the general populace. Writing to his friend Lucilius at some time between AD 63 and 65, the Roman Stoic philosopher Seneca said, 'Most men ebb and flow in wretchedness between the fear of death and the hardships of life' (*Epistle* 4.6).[58]

Because of this basic concern, philosophers also realized that it was one of their major tasks to try to help people to live under the shadow of death. Socrates said that a philosopher had no business speaking about anything else (Plato, *Phaedo* 64A). Thoughtful people realized that the fear of death was not a peripheral concern in life, but that it actually ate away at all aspects of life, and led to all kinds of other evils. To deal with the fear of death was to deal with all the problems of life.

The fear of death and the problems of life

Lucretius (c. 99 – c. 55 BC), who expounded the philosophy of Epicurus with the aim of dispelling the fear of the gods and the fear of death,[59] is one famous example of someone who linked the fear of death to the problems of life. As Jung would say of many modern anxieties,[60] Lucretius evaluated the worries of Roman aristocrats as 'the symptoms of a "sickness" whose primary cause is an unrecognized fear of death'.[61]

The fear of death and the quest for security

The fear of death is the most basic of all fears. It introduces a profound anxiety into human existence. This existential anxiety provokes us to undertake a quest for security. Lucretius echoes what we find in the Scriptures, that human beings seek after greatness,

---

[58] About the same time (AD 61), after the initial success of her revolt against the Romans, Boudicca, queen of the Iceni in East Anglia, spoke of their oppression by the Romans, saying that they lived with a hatred of the present and a fear of the future (Dio Cassius 89). See further Bolt: 1998c.

[59] See Lucretius, *De rerum natura*.

[60] 'Jung suggests that a good many of the people who go to psychotherapists in the twentieth century are really suffering from the lack of any strong moral or spiritual conviction; and that older people, especially, are troubled essentially by the fear of death. If people were troubled for similar reasons in the Ancient World, they had no shortage of would-be therapists, especially for the treatment of the fear of death'; Gill 1985: 325, drawing upon Jung 1936: 120ff.

[61] Gill 1985: 322, referring to Lucretius, *De rerum natura* 3.31–116, esp. 105ff.

status, importance, possessions, friendship, pleasure – all in the vain attempt to bring some security to an existence that is constantly undermined by the grave. The wealthy manage to find some security in this world, even if their wealth will ultimately fail to ransom them from the grave (Ps. 49). The powerless have none. In Mark, the fact that it is the powerless who put their faith in Christ[62] whereas the rich man goes away disappointed illustrates how difficult it is for the rich to enter the kingdom of God (10:17–27).

This quest for security is an issue of faith. We seek a ground on which to stand. We seek some trustworthy foundation for life. Despite the many attempts to find this in the structures of this world, the only real and proper place to stand is on Christ by faith. As Moltmann puts it, 'Only the crucified Christ can bring the freedom which changes the world because it is no longer afraid of death.'[63]

Faith in the one who cares for the perishing

Mark especially brings this out in the cycle of miracles that immediately follows the story of the storm at sea. Each of them shows Jesus confronting death. He deals with the man who lives among the tombs (5:1–20), and a woman who had been bleeding for twelve years (5:25–34). Both can be regarded as among the living dead. And then, in the case of Jairus' daughter, Jesus deals with someone who has actually died (5:21–24, 35–43). In this scene, we come to the heart of the narrative's concerns. Like the disciples during the storm at sea, Jairus is struggling with the most basic fear of all, the fear below all fears; that is, the fear of death. Even in the face of this fear, Jesus urges him to 'keep on only believing' (5:36). When Jesus conquers death by raising Jairus' daughter to life, the disciples' troubled question, 'Who then is this?' is brought into sharp relief. Fear of death is answered by faith in the one who can raise the dead.

Faith in God with us

In biblical tradition, only one person can ask for such faith. Who is this who can even raise the dead? If the first sea-crossing raises the

---

[62] See Marshall 1989; Lee-Pollard 1987.

[63] 'Only when men are reminded of him, however untimely this may be, can they be set free from the power of the facts of the present time, and from the laws and compulsions of history, and be offered a future which will never grow dark again ... Today the Church and Theology must turn to the crucified Christ in order to show the world the freedom he offers.' This leads to reform of the church and the society: 'What does it mean to recall the God who was crucified in a society whose official creed is optimism, and which is knee-deep in blood?' Moltmann 1974: xvii, xx.

question of Jesus' identity (4:35ff.), the second (6:47–52) provides the answer in the greatest terms of all. The various miracles in Mark's account, each in its own way, show Jesus doing the deeds of God. This comes to a head when Jesus walks across the sea. In a context that has all the signs of a theophany, Jesus says to his disciples, 'Be courageous; I AM, be not afraid' (*tharseite, egō eimi: mē phobeisthe*, 6:50). Using the same designation for himself as God used to Moses at the burning bush (Exod. 3:14), Jesus encourages his terrified disciples. There is no need for fear, because God himself, the great 'I AM', has come near.

Once we see where the story goes, we can return to our parable and ask: what does it mean for Jesus to speak of himself as a bridegroom in the midst of a wedding? Although the New Testament pictures the Messiah as a bridegroom on several occasions (cf. John 3:29; 2 Cor. 11:2; Eph. 5:23; Rev. 19:7; 21:2), and the rabbis sometimes used the imagery of a wedding feast to refer to the messianic era (Lane 1974: 110), it is difficult to find an instance of the Messiah's being called the bridegroom either in the Old Testament or in extrabiblical material.[64] Jesus' use of the image therefore appears to contain an incredibly bold claim. The Old Testament prophets had regularly used the image of a bridegroom for God himself, for YHWH.[65] So, for example, when Isaiah spoke of the great future time of salvation, he pictured desolate Jerusalem becoming the bride of YHWH (Grayston, 1990: 170), and God as the Bridegroom rejoicing greatly over the bride (cf. Isa. 62:5). This bold claim is reinforced by the remainder of Jesus' saying. The first words in verse 20 invoke an Old Testament stereotypical expression, in which YHWH is always the speaker: 'Days are coming, declares the LORD.'[66] When Jesus begins, 'Days are coming ...', his hearers would have automatically completed the sentence for him. Here we have Jesus speaking words that hundreds of years of biblical tradition had placed upon the lips of YHWH. Small wonder that he can demand a person's whole life, or

[64] Grayston 1990: 170. However, Gundry (1993: 136) points out that Qumran may have thought of the Aaronic Messiah as a bridegroom (see 1QIsa on Isa. 61:10; Brownlee 1956–7: 205) and that John the Baptist (cf. John 3:22–30) may have played a role in the development of this title. See also Ziesler 1972–3.

[65] Hosea, *passim*; Isa. 50:1; 54:5ff.; 62:4f.; Jer. 2:2, 32f.; 3:1, 14; 31:32; Ezek. 16:8. Does the use of the figure reflect a consciousness that he was Son of God? For the use of the image in the New Testament, see Matt. 22:1–14; 25:1–13; John 3:29; 2 Cor. 11:2; Eph. 5:22–32; Rev. 19:7, 9; 21:2, 9; 22:17.

[66] When the expression 'days are coming' is used in the Old Testament, YHWH is always the speaker: 1 Sam. 2:31; 2 Kgs 20:17; Isa. 39:6; Jer. 7:32; 9:24 (EVV 9:25); 16:14; 19:6; 23:5, 7; 30:3; 31:27; 31:31; 33:14; 48:12; 49:2; 51:47; 51:52; Amos 4:2; 8:11; 9:13.

claim to forgive sins, or claim ownership of the eschatological sabbath, or do things that only God can do. Small wonder he can ask for faith, even in the face of death.

In this parable, Jesus is gently but firmly stating a momentous truth about himself. The bridegroom, God himself, has now arrived among Israel in preparation for that great wedding day at the end of time, promised by the prophets. This makes mourning thoroughly inappropriate at the moment. But there will be a time of mourning in the future, when the bridegroom is taken away.

Jesus, faith and the reader

Through the stories of the various characters interacting with Jesus, the Gospel of Mark promotes faith in its readers. It calls upon readers who live in this world under the shadow of death to put their trust in Jesus – in the same way that it is appropriate to put their trust in the living God.

It could be argued that Mark contains very few passages in which faith is directly linked to the death and resurrection of Jesus. This would, however, involve a failure to read Mark's narrative sensitively. The stories about belief and unbelief are all part of a complex interaction that comes to a climax in the crucifixion. Thus it is true to say that 'Mark indicates that faith placed in the earthly Jesus is structurally the same as faith placed in the crucified and risen Jesus, and within the story it receives in an anticipatory way the saving benefits secured by Jesus' passion and resurrection at the end of the story.'[67] From the beginning, Jesus is the bridegroom who will be taken away, so faith in him is faith in the one who will die as the servant of the Lord.

Faith is related to the apocalyptic notion of seeing the world from God's point of view (cf. 8:33). The entire Gospel shows Jesus bringing the perspective of the coming kingdom to bear upon all of life. This is especially true at the cross, where Mark contrasts two ways of seeing:

[67] Marshall (1989: 232), notes that 'with the exception of 15.32, Mark does not explicitly associate faith with the death and resurrection of Jesus. We have found, however, that an implicit relationship is insinuated in those faith stories which contain forward linkages to the fate of Jesus at the end of the story.' He lists as 'forward linkages' to the cross 2:1–12; 5:21–24, 35–43; 9:14–29; 10:46–52. Marshall also draws attention to the 'forward linkage' provided by passages on unbelief. These represent what will happen at the end, and so they also foreshadow the cross: 2:1–12 and 3:1–6 (p. 188); 6:1–6 (pp. 190, 195); 11:27–33 (p. 208).

the seeing of unbelief, which remains wedded to human notions of rule and power, and the seeing of faith, which perceives in apparent powerlessness the hidden, saving power of God. Faith alone can penetrate the ultimate paradox of the gospel: that the kingly power of God is manifest in the suffering and death of Jesus on the pagan cross, transforming the cross into a power that is infinitely greater than any human power (Marshall 1989: 207–208).

The entire Gospel moves the readers towards a position of faith in the crucified king.[68] Despite the long-standing approach to sociology that downplays the importance of belief,[69] sociologist Rodney Stark (1997: 14–15) has demonstrated that belief – and so doctrine – was an 'essential factor'[70] in the rise of early Christianity. Early Christianity's focus on the centrality of belief was a radical departure in the ancient Greco-Roman world (Brooten 1994: 472, 475, 479), where 'religion' was about practice and ritual, not belief and behaviour. The corresponding focus upon words, with preaching, teaching and discussion on the one hand, and hearing, teaching and persuasion on the other, which was such a trademark of the early churches, aligned them – as it had, to some extent, aligned Judaism before them[71] – more with a philosophical movement than with traditional religion.[72]

---

[68] For further elaboration of how this is achieved, see Bolt 2003: ch. 8.

[69] Some historians react badly to discussions about how doctrines shape social factors, because they are 'too much influenced by out-of-date, and always absurd, Marxist claims that ideas are mere epiphenomena'; others, because they wish to avoid a 'triumphalism' in which Christianity succeeds due to having 'better' doctrines; Stark 1997: 209. He mentions Adolf von Harnack, L. Michael White and Jaroslav Pelikan as being disparaged for this latter 'crime'.

[70] Stark 1997: 4. To give one example, Stark shows how the well-known initial influx of women into the early Christian movement 'resulted from Christian doctrines prohibiting infanticide and abortion'; p. 95.

[71] Harnack 1904: 14. There were, of course, ample Old Testament antecedents for the focus on Word, preaching and teaching, even if it was so easily buried under human ritual and tradition (cf. Mark 7:1–23). With its temple in Jerusalem and its famous eccentric practices (sabbath, pork avoidance, circumcision and, perhaps, distaste for 'leprosy' – see Bolt 2003: 95–97), Judaism was, nevertheless, clearly a religion in Roman eyes – in fact, a *religio lictia*.

[72] Cf. Judge 1980a: 6: 'The meetings which had first assembled in the wake of Paul's preaching would hardly have been recognised by their contemporaries as religious societies.' Cf. Judge 1980b: 209, 212–217; 1960. Perhaps this is one reason why Christianity made such a great impact upon the intellectual classes from the beginning: Ramsay 57; cf. 133–134, 146–147; cf. Judge 1980b: 209, 212–217; 1980a. As a cult movement, sociologically speaking, it is to be expected that the greatest success was among the middle and upper classes; Stark 1997: 45 (summing up the arguments of ch. 2).

As part of this movement, Mark's Gospel proclaimed the story of Jesus, the bridegroom who was taken away, after demonstrating that he cared for those who were perishing.[73] This ought to have been good news for the Jews. Their long-awaited Messiah had arrived. As we have seen (above, pp. 26, 28–30), the paradox of Old Testament religion was that, at one and the same time, it made God present with the people of Israel, and also preserved his distance. The Old Testament attests to the longing for the day when God, by his Spirit, would be close to each and every one of his people (e.g. Num. 11:29; Jer. 31:31–34; Joel 2:28–29). Mark's Gospel took its place in the Christian mission by declaring that the Messiah had arrived, the one who fulfilled the Scriptures and to whom Old Testament religion ultimately pointed. The bridegroom had come, fulfilling Old Testament religion in order to leave it behind (see e.g. Harnack 1904: 61–62, 64).

The message of Jesus would also be good news for the Greco-Roman world. Rodney Stark suggests that the 'immense popular appeal of the early church' needs to be explained by reference to 'how the message of the New Testament and the social relations it sustained solved acute problems afflicting Greco-Roman cities'. He reconstructs a portrait of these cities as places filled with 'urban disorder, social dislocation, filth, disease, misery, fear, and cultural chaos'. He argues that these circumstances 'gave Christianity the opportunity to exploit fully its immense competitive advantages vis-à-vis paganism and other religious movements of the day as a *solution* to these problems'. Christianity acted as a 'revitalization movement that arose in response to the misery, chaos, fear, and brutality of life in the urban Greco-Roman world' (Stark 1997: 147, 149, 161).

In this world, the prevailing religious systems – whether those of the traditional gods or of the expanding imperial cult – failed to bring any real transformation to the world. For sure, there were the various philosophies that sought to offer answers to the problem of death, but they were unable to demonstrate any real power over human mortality. The mystery religions provided their initiates with some comfort in the face of death, but, once again, the world still struggled under the shadow of death. Many Gentiles found in the Israelite religion some obvious attractions (despite its equally obvious eccentricities) over against paganism, and yet, even with some portions of Judaism (most notably, the Pharisees) holding to a hope

[73] In Mark, Jesus' 'overarching opponent is death itself'; Wegener 1995: 78. See also Bolt 2003.

of resurrection, it is not clear that Gentile proselytes actually shared in these promises for the future.[74] In the face of death religion had not helped at all – not even God's religion! In fact, religion could never help human beings living under the shadow of death. Mark's Gospel proclaims that the coming of the bridegroom has fulfilled, and so abolished, religion. Life is now to be lived by faith in the crucified Christ as the one who opens the door to eternal life.[75] The Old Testament law could not do this, nor could the pagan gods, who 'offered no salvation' and did not 'provide an escape from mortality' (Stark 1997: 88). But faith in the one who cared for the perishing transformed individual believers and, in time, the world (Stark 1997: 80, 36).[76]

Within his apocalyptic perspective, Mark portrays the cross as an event that changed the world (A. Y. Collins 1993: 20). The bridegroom has come, bringing the last days. When he was snatched away, religion was abolished and faith established. Faith is a whole new way of seeing the world, which leads to radical change for all of life. Religion at worst (in paganism) is an idol, and at best (in Old Testament religion) keeps God at arm's length. Religion places God at a distance. But in the moment when the bridegroom was taken away, a new deal came. Religion is abolished and faith established, because, in that cross at such a distance from our present world, God came close.

[74] Harnack (1904: 15) thinks that this is 'very doubtful'. Cf. Eph. 2:12.
[75] Sociologically speaking, this can explain the 'success' of early Christianity, even among the upper classes. See Stark 1997: 35–37.
[76] See the evidence and argument of Stark 1997: ch. 4; 1992. See also Bolt 2003: ch. 8.

Chapter Two

The necessity of the cross

The cross of Jesus Christ changed the world. After he died, his disciples began to speak about his death. The new movement spread across the ancient world like a tidal wave.[1] This book seeks to understand what Mark has to say about the cross of Christ. Why was this event so significant back then? Why does it remain significant today?

The cross in Mark's central section

The third and central major narrative section in Mark (8:27 – 10:52) is divided into three subsections each introduced by a prediction of Jesus' death (8:31; 9:31; 10:32–34).[2] Because Jesus follows each passion prediction with some reference to the implications for those who follow him, this part of Mark's narrative is often said to be about discipleship. The recognition of this discipleship material, however, should not be permitted to overshadow the fact that Mark's story is about Jesus, and this is still a major movement within a story with a clear focus upon Mark's major character. By repeatedly foreshadowing his death, this section propels Jesus towards the cross.[3] In the process, it also explains why he *must* die.

Four elements occur in each passion prediction: (1) the Son of Man (2) will be killed and (3) after three days (4) he will rise. This common ground sets up a very clear expectation for what lies ahead. The differences between the three predictions are also important, however, for they advance the thought significantly as the reader moves

---

[1] I owe this image to my reading of Adolf Deissmann. Unfortunately, I have not been able to locate the source in which he used it. James Moffatt uses a similar image in his Translator's Preface to Harnack 1904: vi.

[2] To be precise, they are actually predictions of both Jesus' death and his resurrection. Cf. Grayston 1990: 4; N. T. Wright 2003: 620.

[3] Evans (2001: 30), following Gundry 1993: 434, agrees that discipleship plays second fiddle to Christology here.

from the first prediction to the last. We shall therefore examine the special contribution of each prediction in turn.

Prediction 1: the Son of Man must suffer and die (8:31)

Must

Jesus' first prediction takes place immediately after Peter's famous confession of Jesus as the Christ (8:27–29). Jesus stressed that Son of Man *must* (*dei*) suffer.

> Then he began to teach them that the Son of Man must undergo great suffering, and be rejected by the elders, the chief priests, and the scribes, and be killed, and after three days rise again (8:31, NRSV).

According to God's will

This 'must' (*dei*) is often labelled the 'divine necessity', for it expresses what is according to the divine plan, the divine will (A. Y. Collins 1999: 401). Mark portrays Jesus as being committed to doing God's will. Throughout his ministry, Jesus displays the sense that he is following the divine purpose for his life. Once he was designated the servant of the Lord by the voice from heaven at the baptism (1:11), he embarked on a journey to the cross from which he did not turn aside. Even on the night before he died, in Gethsemane, the final struggle with his destiny as the servant would end with the famous words, 'not my will, but yours, be done' (14:36). Jesus would go to his death because of his commitment to do God's will.

According to the Scriptures

Because the divine will was embedded in the Scriptures, this 'must' is also equivalent to 'according to the Scriptures'.[4] This raises the question which particular scriptures lie behind the passion predictions. Clearly, they do not depend on any one verse, but they powerfully combine a number of significant Old Testament passages that find their fulfilment in the person of Jesus. To say the least, these predictions show us that Jesus thought of his coming death in terms of

---

[4] R. H. Smith (1973: 332) states that Mark's *dei* is equivalent to 'according to the Scriptures', and is echoed in Mark's Old Testament allusions and quotations.

Daniel's son of man (Dan. 7:13)[5] and Isaiah's suffering servant, and the mention of the Son of Man's rising after being killed echoes Daniel 12:1–2, which promised the glorious day of resurrection at the end of time.

... suffer many things

Jesus went on to say that the Son of Man must suffer many things. Although he is associated with the suffering saints, Daniel's son of man is not specifically said to have suffered.[6] Instead, he is a victorious figure, appearing in a vindication scene in which he receives the kingdom of God, which he then shares with the suffering saints. Instead, the note of suffering probably derives for the most part from the notion of the 'suffering righteous one', found in the Psalms but reaching its apex in Isaiah's servant of the Lord. This reference to suffering is not the only item identifying Jesus as the servant, for the narrative has already clearly designated Jesus as this figure. When Jesus was baptized in the Jordan, the voice from heaven quoted Psalm 2:7 and Isaiah 42:1, declaring Jesus to be the Son of God who would also be the Spirit-anointed servant (Bolt 1991b). Once Jesus took on the role of the servant, suffering was inevitable, and the passion predictions now make that explicit.

... and be rejected

The means of this suffering is now made more specific. The Son of Man must suffer many things, *and be rejected* by the elders and the high priests and the scribes.

The word used here for the Son of Man's rejection (*apodokimazō*), although infrequent, is almost always used in the Septuagint for God's rejection of Israel and as an equivalent for his wrath (Jer. 6:30; 7:29; 8:9; 14:19; on the individual level cf. Wisdom of Solomon 9:4).[7]

---

[5] Some have seen the reference to the Son of Man as a corporate reference, but a comparison with the Son of Man figure in *4 Ezra* 13 and the Similitudes (*1 Enoch* 71), who is conceived as a figure distinct from the community, shows that a corporate dimension is not a necessary conception in the passion predictions. See Schaberg 1985: 216–217.

[6] Schaberg (1985: 208) follows Hooker 1979: 166 in proposing that the suffering of the son of man is implicit in the relationship between the son of man and the saints. 'Whether or not the author of Daniel intended his readers to draw this implication, the framers of the NT passion-resurrection predictions did draw it, apparently recognizing structural patterns and repetitions in Daniel 7 – 12 which open the figure of the one like a son of man to such an interpretation as Hooker proposes.'

[7] The only other passage, apart from those mentioned in this paragraph, is Sirach 20:20, where the proverb of a fool is rejected.

It is also used in the context of the promise of the new covenant, to remind Israel that God will never ultimately reject them (Jer. 31:37 [LXX 38:35]). If these connotations are here, its use in the passion predictions may hint that Jesus is being treated as one who is rejected by God, that is, placed under his wrath.

The Septuagint also uses this verb once for a rejection by human beings. In Psalm 118 [LXX 117]:22–23 we read of the stone that was rejected by the builders only to become the cornerstone of the temple. Since Jesus later applies this verse to himself (12:10), it seems likely that it may also lie behind this portion of the first passion prediction (Grayston 1990: 174). Psalm 118 may also provide a bridge to the mention of the Son of Man's rising again after he is killed, for it contains the confident statement that the Lord 'has not given me over to death' (Ps. 118:17–18, ESV). Jesus predicts that his rivals, who are already established in the positions of power, will crush him. This will not prevent him, however, from being exalted to the place of chief importance. The leaders of Israel will put him to death, but, in this passion prediction, Jesus also reveals his ultimate destination. Through suffering he will enter the kingdom of God, inaugurated by the resurrection.

After Jesus' first passion prediction, and the discussion that followed, Mark then reports Jesus' transfiguration (9:2–13), followed by the dramatic exorcism of a young boy at the foot of the mountain (9:14–29). After this, we come to Jesus' second passion prediction.

Prediction 2

Entering the kingdom

The second subsection (9:30 – 10:31) in Mark's central movement begins to deal with the theme of entering the coming kingdom. In 9:1 Jesus said that the kingdom would come with power before some of his hearers died. If it is now so close (9:1; cf. 1:15), then nothing could be more important than entering it. But how does a person enter the kingdom?

This section will show that entry to the kingdom does not depend on being one of the great ones of the world, but comes simply through receiving the kingdom like children. As the least in society, anything children have comes simply through receiving it (10:13–16). A rich man provides the negative example. He wants entry to the kingdom, but he cannot renounce the security given by his wealth, and so he misses out on the kingdom (10:17–31). When Jesus explains that it is difficult for the rich to enter the kingdom – and, in fact, for anyone to do so (10:23–25) – the disciples wonder how anyone can ever be saved. Jesus replies that what is impossible with human beings is possible with God (10:26–27). God will provide the way into the kingdom.

Into human hands

Returning to the beginning of this subsection, we find Jesus and his party moving on from the foot of the mount of transfiguration to pass through Galilee (9:30). At this point, the second passion prediction is introduced (9:31).

> For he was teaching his disciples and was saying to them, 'The Son of Man is being handed over into human hands, and they will kill him, and, after being killed, after three days he will rise.'

The fact that Jesus will be killed is stressed by repetition ('and they will kill him, and after being killed'; *apoktenousin auton, kai apoktantheis*). There are two new features here: first, Jesus will be 'handed over'; and secondly, this will be 'into human hands'. These features stress the means by which he is to be killed.

Handed over

The word used here for 'handed over', *paradidōmi*, which will be repeated in the final passion prediction (10:33), appeared earlier in Mark, when John the Baptist was 'handed over' (1:14; cf. 6:14–29; 9:13; 11:27–33) and when Judas was introduced as 'the one who betrayed him' (3:19). The passion narrative will use this word to describe how the Jewish religious leaders handed over Jesus to Pilate (15:1, 10), and how Pilate then handed him over to be crucified (15:15). The word also underlines Jesus' role as the suffering servant. In the Septuagint,[8] Isaiah 53:6 spoke of the Lord's handing over the servant 'for the sake of our sins' (*tais hamartiais hēmōn*), and when Isaiah 53:12 promised that the servant would be vindicated, *para-didōmi* occurs twice in regard to his death: 'For this reason he will inherit many and divide the plunder of the strong, instead of whom his soul was handed over into death, and he was reckoned among the

---

[8] Sapp (1998) has demonstrated that the Septuagint actually downplays the servant's death, whereas the Hebrew more clearly supports vicarious atonement theology.

lawless, and he himself bore the sins of many, and because of their sins was handed over.' The servant's death was vicarious, in that he was handed over to death for the sake of the sins of others, for a sin offering (cf. *anēnenken*). Because of his willingness to die in this way, he would be vindicated by God.

Jesus' use of this word, and Mark's subsequent use of it in the passion narrative, may therefore gently remind the alert reader that the servant's death was on behalf of others, for the sake of their sins, and a sin offering.

Into human hands

Jesus predicts that he will be handed over 'into human hands' (cf. 14:41).[9] This is a fairly ready expression for being delivered over to an executioner,[10] but it is also rich with meaning when read against the Old Testament usage of this and similar phrases.

The idea of being handed over to the enemy is fairly common in the Old Testament.[11] When God is the one handing people over, the expression has overtones of divine judgment (e.g. Ezek. 39:23), sometimes explicitly paralleled with a reference to the wrath of God (Judg. 2:14; Ps. 78 [LXX 77]:61, cf. v. 59; *Baruch* 4:6; see also Rom. 1:18ff.). The exact phrase 'into human hands', however, occurs only three times in the Septuagint. When threatened with judgment after numbering the people of Israel in an illegal census, David said that he would rather fall into the hands of the Lord, whose mercies are great (*polloi hoi oiktirmoi autou sphodra*), than into human hands, for, by implication, human beings are not known for their compassion (1 Chr. 21:13). This situation is echoed in Sirach, where those who fear the Lord cry, 'Let us fall into the hands of the Lord and not into human hands, for as is his majesty, even so is his mercy (*eleos*)' (Sirach 2:18). The picture of the unmerciful human being is reinforced

---

[9] The phrase 'into the hands of sinners' is not found elsewhere in the Greek Bible (apart from the Matt. 26:45 parallel). If we can take a lead from a similar expression in 2 Macc. 14:42 (*eugenōs thelōn apothanein ēper tois alitēriois hypocheirios genesthai*), to die at the hands of sinners is equivalent to being handed over to the Gentiles, and is set in opposition to a noble death. For discussion of noble death, see A. Y. Collins 1994; Seeley 1990; Pilch 1995: 69–70.

[10] Cf. Chaereas in Chariton, *Chaereas and Callirhoe* 4.3.10: 'I was handed over into the hands of the executioner' (*dēmiou chersi paredothēn*).

[11] Israel's enemies are given into his hands (Deut. 21:10; Josh. 10:19; 21:44; Judg. 3:28); Saul is given into the hands of David (1 Sam. 24:4); Israel is given into the hands of his enemy (for the threat: Lev. 26:25; for the actuality: Judg. 16:23–24; 1 Kgs 21:10–16; Esth. 14:6, LXX; *Odes of Solomon* 7:32 = Dan. 3:32, LXX = *The Song of the Three Holy Children* 9; Pss. 41:2 (MT 41:3; LXX 40:3); 78 (61 = LXX 78:61). Cf. Judith 8:33.

by God's warning to Egypt: 'I will deliver Egypt into human hands (*paradōsō Aigypton eis cheiras anthrōpōn*); harsh lords and harsh kings will lord it over them' (Isa. 19:4; cf. Mark 10:42). Thus, on each occasion, the phrase signifies the harshness of human beings, as opposed to the mercy of God.

Because this is all according to the divine plan, God is ultimately behind this handing over. Human hands are instruments of his judgment, his wrath. The harshness of human beings without mercy makes this instrument of wrath bitter indeed.

God is ultimately also behind the handing over of Jesus, because his death is part of the divine plan, and because it is governed, in particular, by the prophecies relating to the suffering servant. The servant was handed over by God himself, not for his own sins, but for the sins of others. Jesus is well aware of the harshness of human power (cf. Mark 10:42), and he predicts that the Son of Man will be handed over into the hands of these people who are without mercy, who lord it over their subjects. The identity of these people is not specified here, but the previous passion prediction had indicted the Jewish authorities, the elders, the chief priests and scribes. The dreaded Romans, known for their brutal justice,[12] also stand ominously in the background. The third passion prediction reveals that they too will become the instruments of divine wrath.

Prediction 3

Jesus' forthcoming death is the major item in the third subsection, which brings Mark's central section to a climax. After the opening passion prediction, the narrative moves into a discussion in which Jesus refers to his death several times, utilizing Old Testament imagery and phraseology (10:35–45). By the end of this discussion, Jesus will have explained the meaning of his coming death.

This final passion prediction shows many of the details associated with the normal process of crucifixion.

'We are going up to Jerusalem, and the Son of Man will be delivered over to the chief priests and the scribes, and they will condemn him to death and deliver him over to the Gentiles. And they will mock him and spit on him, and flog him and kill him. And after three days he will rise' (10:33–34, ESV).

---

[12] For a view of Rome 'from below', see the discussion in Wengst 1987.

Detailed crucifixion process (10:34)

Crucifixion normally involved a fairly drawn-out process of abuse and humiliation before the victim was fixed to the cross. This consisted of passing sentence, scourging (cf. Plato, *Republic* 362A), being led outside the city,[13] and carrying the cross-beam[14] all in the context of mockery and abuse.[15] The humiliation also involved varying degrees of what our world would call sexual abuse.[16] In Jesus' case we know, for example, that he was stripped naked inside the Praetorium and then again at the cross (15:17; cf. 20; 15:24). It was quite usual to taunt and mock the condemned, especially in the case of someone who was a pretender to kingship, as we shall see when we turn to Mark 15, where the Roman soldiers mock and abuse the one who was called 'the king of the Jews'. Jesus therefore predicts that his humiliation will consist of mockery, spitting and the dreadful scourging, which was often so severe it could tear the flesh off the victim's back, even causing death in some cases.[17]

[13] Cicero *In Verrem* 5.66; Heb. 13:12; cf. 1 Kgs 21:13 and Acts 7:58. Cf. Plato, *Republic* 362a: 'The just man will have to endure the lash (*mastigōsetai*), the rack (*streblōsetai*), chains (*dedēsetai*), the branding-iron in his eyes (*ekkauthēsetai tō ōphthalmō*), and finally (*teleutōn*) ... he will be crucified (*anaschindyleuthēsetai*).' This could be simply a list of disparate punishments, but *teleutōn* (Loeb Classical Library edn, 'finally') may indicate that all of these may be applied in the one case.

[14] John 19:17; Plutarch, *De sera numinis vindicta* 554A; Artemidorus, *Oneirocritica* 2.56 (Artemidorus refers to the practice in explanation of a dream in which a wrongdoer dreams he is carrying an underworld god: 'It signifies that he will carry a cross. For the cross is like death and the man who is to be nailed to it carries it beforehand'); Chariton, *Chaereas and Callirhoe* 4.2.7; *Bereshit Rabba* to Gen. 22:6; cf. Mark 15:21. Some suggest that the victim was nailed to the cross, or the cross-beam, on the ground first (e.g. Wheaton 1962: 282), but Chariton's account seems to indicate that the crosses were upright before the victims were affixed. When Mithridates sent to save Chaereas, 'they found the others already hanging on their crosses, and he was just mounting his (*arti de ekeinon epibainonta tou staurou*). From far off, they each shouted appeals: "Spare him!" "Come down (*katabēthi*)!" "Do not hurt him!" "Let him go!" So the executioner stopped his work, and Chaereas descended from the cross (*katebaine tou staurou*)'; Chariton, *Chaereas and Callirhoe* 4.3.6). Also, when Chaereas writes to Callirhoe, he says (4.4.10): 'Because of you I have ascended the cross' (*kagō gar epi stauron anebēn dia se*).

[15] For an exploration of the abuse associated with crucifixion, see Tombs 1999.

[16] See further, Tombs 1999 and Hengel 1977, and, to a lesser extent, Pilch 1995: 65.

[17] Cf. Jesus ben Ananias, who was beaten by the Jewish authorities and handed over to the Roman governor, who then ensured that he was 'flayed to the bone with scourges' (Josephus, *Jewish War* 6.300–309). Evans (2001: 177) lists the parallels between Jesus ben Ananias and Jesus of Nazareth. A description of scourging is also found in Polycarp, *Philippians* 2.2 (Stevenson [ed.], 1957: 18). In AD 422/423, Augustine petitioned Alypius to repeal a law that allowed for scourging, on the grounds that it could so easily result in death. See Augustine, *Epistle* 10.4.3, in Divjak 1981: discussed by Judge (1986: 112).

Here the two previous passion predictions come together. Verse 34, in particular, spells out what was meant by 'suffer many things', that is, all the cruelties involved in the crucifixion process. The subsequent passion narrative will show us these details fulfilled to the letter. When it is read against various passages in the Old Testament, both in the Psalms and in Isaiah's servant material, these details also have theological significance. We shall examine some of these when we turn to the mockery of Jesus in the crucifixion account in chapter 4 below. But for now we shall confine ourselves to the statement that he will be 'handed over to the nations'.

Handed over to the nations (10:33)

The new item in verse 33 is that, after the Jewish authorities condemn Jesus to death, they will hand him over to the nations, that is, to the Gentiles. Commentators are often content to observe that these are predictions of the events that will be described in the passion, or to provide historical explanations of why Jesus would envisage that his death would involve more than the Jewish authorities.[18] Thus the theological backdrop of this phrase, 'handed over to the nations', is rarely if ever examined. A clue to its importance, however, can be gained from the fact that early Christian preaching seemed to treat this detail as significant (Acts 2:23, *dia cheiros anomōn*, 'through the hand of those without the law', i.e. the Gentiles; 3:13; 4:27–28; 1 Tim. 6:13).[19] An examination of this phrase in the Old Testament shows that it does not simply refer to the way things will happen, but that it is a theologically loaded term.

The horror of this action should be apparent to all who are familiar with Old Testament history. To hand someone over to the nations (Gentiles) is equivalent to handing someone over to God's wrath. For example, early in their history the people of Israel were warned that, if they broke the covenant with YHWH, they would be scattered among the nations as an outworking of God's wrath. God told them:

[18] Seccombe (1986: 143–144), for example, suggests two reasons why Jesus imagined that the Romans would be involved. First, their involvement would minimize the risk of a popular uprising, given the size of the crowds and their favour towards him. Secondly, it would cast the odium of Deut. 21:22–23 on him and so reduce the impact of his Messianic claims (cf. Acts 5:30; and Philo, *De specialibus legibus* 3.151). This latter reason introduces a theological motive, but casts it as a historical reason why the Jews would hand him over.

[19] The importance of this item can also be seen from the parallels in the other synoptics. Matt. 20:19 has Jesus being handed over with this explicit purpose (note *eis to* . . .). Luke 18:31ff. drops the Jewish involvement altogether, allowing the focus to fall on the handing over to the Gentiles alone.

'I myself will devastate the land, so that your enemies who settle in it shall be appalled at it. And I will scatter you among the nations, and I will unsheathe the sword after you, and your land shall be a desolation, and your cities shall be a waste ... And you shall perish among the nations, and the land of your enemies shall eat you up' (Lev. 26:32–33, 38, ESV). At a later time, the northern kingdom of Israel was threatened with the same fate (Hos. 8:10, LXX), and eventually succumbed to Assyria. As for the southern kingdom of Judah, she did not learn the lessons from her northern neighbour, and eventually went into exile in Babylon. This was a devastating time, when the Jews had to reflect upon the fact that, just as he had warned them, their God had cast them off in his wrath, and in his fury had thrown them out of the land to serve the nations. When they later reflected upon this period, this is the lesson that was repeated:

> Then the anger of the LORD was kindled against his people,
> and he abhorred his heritage;
> he gave them into the hand of the nations,
> so that those who hated them ruled over them.
>
> (Ps. 106[LXX 105]:41, NRSV)

From the days of our fathers to this day we have been in great guilt. And for our iniquities we, our kings, and our priests have been given into the hand of the kings of the lands, to the sword, to captivity, to plundering, and to utter shame, as it is today. (Ezra 9:7, ESV)

After the devastation of the exilic period, the threat of falling into the hands of the nations was still feared between the Testaments: 'You were sold to the nations, not for destruction, and because you angered God; you were handed over to your enemies (*paredothēte tois hypenantiois*)' (*Baruch* 4:6).

The Maccabean struggle was against the Gentile nations who had overrun the land (1 Maccabees 3:51–52; cf. Ps. 2). This was regarded as a period of great wrath (1 Maccabees 1:64; 3:8; 2 Maccabees 5:20; 7:38; 8:5),[20] permitted by God only because the people of Judah had

[20] In Maccabees, anger is often attributed to the enemies of the Jews (1 Macc. 2:44, 49; 15:36; 2 Macc. 4:25; 4:40; 3 Macc. 5:1, 47; 6:22–23, echoing a similar theme in Dan. 3:13; 8:6). The early texts (1 Macc. 1:64; 3:8) are therefore ambiguous as to whether this is a period of human or divine wrath. The writer of 2 Maccabees, however, solves the ambiguity, clearly referring to the wrath of the Almighty that is later removed in his mercy (2 Macc. 5:20, cf. vv. 17–20; 7:38).

THE CROSS FROM A DISTANCE

sinned; but it would be only a temporary period because of God's mercy (2 Maccabees 5:17–20; 8:5).

When Judas Maccabeus and his followers recovered the temple, they offered sacrifices and implored God that 'they might never again fall into such misfortunes, but that, if they should ever sin, they might be disciplined by him with forbearance and not be handed over to blasphemous and barbarous nations (*kai mē blasphēmois kai barbarois ethnesin paradidosthai*)' (2 Maccabees 10:4, NRSV; cf. 1 Chr. 21:13 and Sirach 2:18). When the Jews heard that Antiochus V Eupator (164–162 BC), son of the infamous Antiochus Epiphanes, who persecuted the Jews so terribly, was marching towards them in order 'to show the Jews things far worse than those that had been done in his father's time' (2 Maccabees 13:9), Judas ordered the people to turn to God day and night to pray that he would not let 'the people who had just begun to revive fall into the hands of the blasphemous Gentiles (*tois dysphēmois ethnesin hypocheirious genesthai*)' (2 Maccabees 13:11). About three years later, one of the zealous Jews, named Razis, attempted suicide 'rather than to fall into the hands of sinners' (2 Maccabees 14:42; cf. Mark 14:41).

One of the recently published Qumran scrolls also illustrates this fear, in a prayer put into the mouth of the patriarch Joseph after he was placed by his brothers 'into the hands of strangers'. Sounding very much like Jesus' own cry of dereliction on the cross, Joseph cries: 'My Father and my God, do not abandon me to the hands of the nations' (4Q371–372, Vermes 1962: 530).[21]

In this final passion prediction, Jesus states that he will be handed over to the nations. This is tantamount to being delivered over to the wrath of God. Just as Israel was once delivered over to the nations, under the wrath of God, so the Son of Man, the suffering servant, the Christ, will be handed over into the hands of the nations by Israel's leaders.

The promise of resurrection

Although usually called 'passion predictions', each of the sayings also promises that the Son of Man will rise from the dead. What would this have meant to the disciples? Because of Jesus' own resurrection, later ages automatically tend to think in terms of a solitary resurrection of an individual. For first-century Jews, however, it is more

[21] It may also lie behind the Jews' fear that the Romans may come and take their nation away because of the trouble caused by Jesus (John 11:48).

58

likely that the mention of resurrection would have evoked the expectation of the general resurrection at the end of time, perhaps with the added notion of the Son of Man presiding over the kingdom introduced by that great event.[22]

After three days

Three times Jesus predicted that the Son of Man would be killed and that he would then rise from the dead, 'after three days' (*meta treis hēmeras*). This phrase can simply refer to 'a short period of time', but, from other texts such as *4 Ezra* and Daniel, it appears that the phrase is eschatologically loaded. In the first-century AD text *4 Ezra*, 'after the third (period)' became a way of referring to the beginning of the eschatological signs (5:4; cf. 14:11–13). More particularly, given the allusion to Daniel already inherent in the reference to the Son of Man and to the resurrection, the idea of 'after three days' may allude to Daniel's reference to 'time, two times, and half a time' (Dan. 7:25; cf. Rev. 11:2–12; Schaberg 1985: 209), in which case it would carry 'the eschatological associations of that text. It is referring to the period immediately preceding the end, the resurrection of "many" and final reward and punishment' (Schaberg 1985: 215; cf. Dan. 12:2). Using a similar phrase, the third day of Hosea 6:2 actually becomes, in the Targum, 'the day of resurrection', that is, the day of general resurrection (Cavallin 1980: 119).

He will rise

By mentioning resurrection, the passion predictions evoke Daniel 12:2, which promises the future resurrection.[23] In the flow of Daniel's story, the son of man receives the kingdom of God (7:13–14), which is then shared with the suffering saints (7:22ff.). By the end of the book, it seems clear that the kingdom of God will be entered at the end of the age by means of the resurrection from the dead. Given these connections, it is most likely that, when Jesus referred to the rising of the Son of Man, he would have been understood as saying that the Son of Man would rise as part of the

---

[22] N. T. Wright (1992: 320–334; 2003: 181, 628) argues that 'resurrection' for the first-century Jew would have connoted the general resurrection that would happen to all the righteous at once.

[23] Schaberg 1985: 211–211: 'There may be an allusion to Dan. 12:2 in the mention in the predictions of resurrection (Mark 8:31; 9:9, 31; 10:34; Luke 18:32; 24:7, 46: *anastēsetai*; in Matt. 16:21; 17:9, 22; 20:19; 27:63; Luke 9:22: *egerthēsetai*', and, with J. J. Collins (1977), 'in 12:1–3 (as in 7:13–14, 18, 7:22, 27) Daniel looks beyond the suffering and judgement to describe the eschatological kingdom.'

general resurrection of the dead, even if he will be the one presiding over it (cf. John 5:25–29).[24]

The passion and the kingdom (9:9–13)

The transfiguration and descent

Let us now return to the scene on the mountain in subsection 1. Immediately following the first passion prediction and the related discussion, we read of Jesus' transfiguration. We shall deal with the transfiguration more carefully in our final chapter. For now, we shall examine Jesus' conversation with his disciples on the way back down the mountain (9:9–13). This is a very important scene for understanding the meaning of the cross.

The disciples' debate (9:10)

After their 'mountain-top experience', Jesus charged the disciples to tell no-one about it until after the Son of Man had risen from the dead (9:9). Unfortunately, the English translations of verse 10 often obscure the significance of the disciples' response. The Greek of verse 10 reads: *Kai ton logon ekratēsan pros heautous syzētountes ti estin to ek nekrōn anastēnai.* To be fair, translation of this verse is tricky.[25] A proper translation of the verse requires choosing from several pairs of options. For convenience, the exegetical decisions that are required can be listed. (1) What is the meaning of the verb *krateō*? (2) what is the meaning of the participle *syzētountes*? (3) Does the prepositional phrase *pros heautous* modify the preceding verb or the following participle? (4) What was the exact topic of discussion?

Several respectable translations and commentators[26] endorse the translation, 'They kept the matter/saying in mind',[27] which is usually related either to what they had seen in the transfiguration[28] or to

---

[24] This would also be how Jesus meant the expression. Subsequent events, however, would show that Jesus' own resurrection, which was the 'firstfruits' of the general resurrection, would be separated in time from the rest of the resurrection harvest (see 1 Cor. 15). This gives the classic 'now but not yet' tension to the Christian era.

[25] The coverage of v. 10 in the commentaries could be described as bare to none.

[26] Swete 1909: 192; V. Taylor 1966: 394; Evans 2001: 42; RV, RSV, NRSV, ESV, NIV.

[27] Reference can be made to Dan. 5:12 (Theodotion), where *krateō* is used in relation to things being kept secret. Gundry (1993) argues that this rendering takes *pros heautous* as 'a characteristically Marcan Latinism'; i.e. the disciples place the saying in their memory, (*memoria*) *tenere*. He offers a sevenfold critique of this rendering.

[28] It is generally now agreed, however, that the rendering of *logos* as 'the matter' is definitely non-Markan.

Jesus' command to silence.[29] There are, however, several problems with this rendering, and unfortunately it has tended to obscure the drama and significance of this scene on the mountain.

The first two questions can be answered together: *krateō* and *syzēteō* both have a strength about them that should be retained. Although capable of an occasional milder rendering, *krateō* usually denotes some display of strength and power,[30] as almost always elsewhere in Mark.[31] This should be conveyed by translating Mark 9:10, 'They seized upon the saying.'[32] By the same token, *syzēteō* also has vigorous connotations in classical usage, the New Testament itself and beyond. This is the language of energetic and often hostile debate, of dispute;[33] and the fact that this is exactly the sense of the word in every other occurrence in Mark (1:31; 8:11; 9:14, 16; 12:28) indicates that it almost certainly has this sense in 9:10 as well.

The evidence also seems to be persuasive for taking *pros heautous* with the following participle.[34] Whereas there is no analogous use for this prepositional phrase with *krateō* (Swete 1909: 192), the New Testament itself, including Mark's own narrative, supplies several analogies for *syzēteō pros* (Mark 1:27; 9:14, 16; Luke 22:23; Acts

[29] E.g. Gundry 1993: 463; France 2002: 357. The contradiction that is created between the two halves of the verse is presumably solved by saying that the disciples did not speak openly, but discussed among their closed circle.

[30] This so classically, in the Septuagint, the New Testament, the papyri, and in early Christian literature. See LSJ, s.v.; Michaelis 1981; MM 358.

[31] It is used for the seizure, the 'arrest', of one person by another (3:21; 6:17; 12:12; 14:1; 14:44, 46, 49, 51; cf. Acts 24:6) and the seizure of the hand of a sick person during dramatic healing (1:31; 5:41; 9:27). Even the usage of 'holding to' the traditions (7:3, 4, 8; cf. 2 Thess. 2:15), which has been used to bolster the milder translation of 9:10 (see Cranfield 1977), has a strength about it, for, in the context, the Jews tenaciously and ruthlessly hold on to the traditions. The strength conveyed by the verb elsewhere in Mark has led some to suggest that 9:10a indicates that the disciples did damage to Jesus' word (Schreiber 1967: 111–112, 'violent seizure'; Edwards 2002: 273, 'quashed').

[32] So Hooker 1991: 219; cf. NASB, 'they seized upon that statement'; Mann 1986: 362, 'they fastened on this saying'. Even the notion of 'guarding' the saying/command (France 2002: 357) is inadequate, and, besides, surely *tēreō* would be the choice for this activity.

[33] Cf. Acts 6:9; 9:29; Luke 22:23; 24:15. See LSJ, s.v.; Schneider 1971; MM, 607. This is a much rarer word. A search of the TLG database yielded only 10 occurrences prior to the first century, and a further 24 in the first century, including 10 in the New Testament itself.

[34] With Victor and Syr[s]. Most recent commentators so construe the phrase: Mann 1986: 362; Hooker 1991: 218; France 2002: 356–357; Gundry 1993: 483; Edwards 2002: 273 (although his 'sought among themselves' is rather odd, construing *syzēteō* as if it were *zēteō*).

9:29).[35] Thus, the verse should be rendered: 'They seized on this statement, debating among themselves ... '

As for the final exegetical decision, what was the topic of this excited discussion? Since Jesus looks forward to the time when the Son of Man will rise from the dead, and since Christian interpreters are familiar with the fact that Mark ends with the report of Jesus' own resurrection (16:6), this verse is often explained with a narrow focus upon Jesus' own resurrection – or, at least, that of the Son of Man.[36] By analogy with the later occasion, when the disciples failed to understand Jesus' second passion prediction and were afraid to ask (9:32), this verse is said to be another example of silence after incomprehension, but this time with respect to Jesus' forthcoming resurrection.

This, however, assumes a fair amount of detachment from the issue on the part of the disciples. In a short time, Mark will show that two of the three who were with Jesus on the mount of transfiguration were personally interested in the question of resurrection, for they were looking to secure the best positions when the resurrected kingdom arrived (10:37). It seems likely that their expectation of the coming kingdom may have been sparked by what they saw on the mountain, and they had been jolted into asking after their own place in that future resurrection harvest. The clause *ti estin to ek nekrōn anastēnai* sounds much more general and should be translated, 'what rising from the dead will mean' (Aichele 1994: 87). Given my previous comments upon the disciples' probable understanding of resurrection,[37] it appears that the disciples were having a heated discussion about what it would be like to be a part of the promised future *general* resurrection: 'They seized on the statement, debating with one another what it might mean to rise from the dead.'

[35] This represents exactly half of the New Testament occurrences. None of the 24 extrabiblical occurrences from the eighth century BC to the end of the first century AD is accompanied by *pros*.

[36] Gundry (1993: 463) argues this from the presence of the article: *the* resurrection must be the one already mentioned, namely, that of the Son of Man. Some Western MSS 'clarified' the text in this direction; cf. *hotan ek nekrōn anastē*, D W *f*[1.13] lat.

[37] This is actually confirmed by Martha's reply to Jesus' promise that her brother Lazarus will rise again. The only conception that she had was of the general resurrection at the end of time (John 11:24). Commentators regularly note that this general expectation would have caused some difficulty for the disciples on hearing Jesus' statement about the Son of Man. See e.g. Van Iersel 1998: 298; Donahue & Harrington 2002: 271.

The eschatological timetable (9:11–13)

They then ask Jesus a question, which presumably arose from this discussion as well as from what they had seen on the mountain (v. 11): 'Why do the scribes say that Elijah must come *first*?' This raises the question: 'first' – before what? The answer from the context appears to be: first – before the coming of the kingdom (9:1), or, to say the same thing in other words, first – before the coming resurrection day (9:10), which will usher in the kingdom.

In answering his disciples, Jesus first agrees with the scribal exegesis – naturally enough, because it simply restated Malachi 3:22–23, LXX (EVV 4:5–6). But he then proceeds to pose his own question: 'How is it written concerning the Son of Man that he might suffer many things and be treated with contempt?' (v. 12).[38] Once again, Jesus combines expectations surrounding the suffering servant with those of the Son of Man. This interchange between Jesus and his disciples reveals an eschatological timetable, consisting of a short series of expectations. Before the resurrection day and the coming of the kingdom, the scribes (and Jesus) say that Elijah must come first. But Jesus then adds a second preliminary event: the Son of Man must also suffer many things.

In verse 13, Jesus informs his friends that Elijah had, in fact, already come. The readers recognize that here he is referring to John the Baptist (cf. 1:2–8; made explicit by Matthew, Matt. 17:13). 'And they did to him whatever they wished' (*kai epoiēsan autōi hosa ēlthon*). This expression suggests the exercise of extreme power over a person. It is, therefore, something of an analogy to the 'mockery' that was promised for the servant of the Lord (Isa. 50) and would be a feature of the crucifixion narrative (Mark 15:16–20, 27–32). Jesus' words evoke the memory of John's contemptuous treatment at the hands of Herod (6:14–29).

Now if Elijah has already come, in the person of John, this means that only one of the preliminary expectations in the eschatological timetable is left unfulfilled. The coming of the kingdom of God has been on the agenda since the beginning of Jesus' ministry, and it has been getting closer. Initially, it had drawn near (1:15); then Jesus promised it would come suddenly, interrupting ordinary life (4:26–29,[39] 30–32). After the first passion prediction, just before the

---

[38] Mark 9:12 may allude to Dan. 4:17, 'raises up over it the lowliest (*š'l*; Theodotion, *exoudenēma*) of human beings'; Schaberg 1985: 215.

[39] There may be a hint of death and resurrection in this parable also, since the same verb (v. 27) is used in Dan. 12:2 (Theodotion). N. T. Wright 2003: 620.

transfiguration, Jesus had revealed that the coming of the kingdom was so close that it would occur in the lifetime of his hearers (9:1). Now, as he comes down the mountain, Jesus discloses that there is only one thing left to happen before the resurrection day and the kingdom arrives: the Son of Man must suffer many things and be treated with contempt.[40] In this way, this scene reinforces Jesus' first passion-resurrection prediction. He must die, not only because that accords with the divine plan, but because his death is the necessary precursor to the coming of the final resurrection and the kingdom of God.

If the kingdom of God is just around the corner, the question of entering the kingdom becomes urgent. How is it possible to find eternal life?

The impossible possibility

Humanity's impossible situation

Human beings are in an impossible situation. The grave will swallow us up in the end. There is no way we can escape our mortality. In the century before Christ, thinkers began to reconsider the question of immortality, after neglecting it for a long time. According to Dihle (1982: 8), *sōtēria*, which meant the preservation of physical integrity in ordinary Greek, in this period became a synonym for immortality.[41] But how can human beings be 'saved'? Or, to echo the question of Mark's rich man, 'What must I do to inherit eternal life?' (10:17, NRSV).

Mark's thirteen stories of the suppliants – those who came to Jesus for healing or exorcism – provide a slice of life that demonstrates the tragic consequences of living in a world under the shadow of death (see further Bolt 2003). They were the powerless, the poor, the ones at the bottom of society; the least rather than the greatest. There was

---

[40] Grayston (1990: 174) suggests that this prediction of being treated with contempt can be regarded as an equivalent to the rejection of 8:31. But even though they are obviously related, *exoudeneō* should not be regarded as equivalent in meaning to *apodokimazō*. *Exoudeneō* is a New Testament *hapax legomenon*, although the form *exoutheneō* is found elsewhere in the New Testament (Luke 18:9; 23:11; Acts 4:11; Rom. 14:3, 10; 1 Cor. 1:28; 6:4; 16:11; 2 Cor. 10:10; Gal. 4:14; 1 Thess. 5:20). The occurrence of this word in this verse prepares the reader for the mockery at the crucifixion, rather than for the rejection of the Messiah by the Jewish leaders.

[41] Cf. LSJ listings: 'Deliverance, preservation; II. Of things, keeping safe, preservation ... 5. Bodily health and well-being.'

nothing that they, or anyone else, could do to ransom them from the grave.

The rich man was at the opposite end of the scale. He had it all: wealth, status, power, better health, prospects for the future, good connections, and all the other trappings that wealth could bring. But he asked the same question as everyone else: 'What must I do to inherit eternal life?' The rich man shows that it is impossible for human beings to be saved by their own resources. Eternal life is something outside our grasp. We live in a world that is already under the judgment of God, and the judgment of God is death. We live under the shadow of death, and there is no way that we can ever escape our mortality. As Psalm 49:7–9 puts it, 'Truly no-one can ransom another, or give to God the price of his life, for the ransom of life is costly and can never suffice, that one should live on for ever and never see the grave.'[42] As Jesus put it when he alluded to this psalm: 'What can a person give as an exchange (*antallagma*) for his life?' (Mark 8:37) – with the implied answer, 'Nothing at all!'

In biblical thought, since it was God who afflicted humanity with mortality as his judgment on sin (cf. Gen. 3; Rom. 5:12), the only possibility of ransom lay in God's hands (cf. Ps. 49:15). But what exchange could he give that would ransom human beings from the grave?

The coming kingdom of God

As Mark's story has gained momentum, the kingdom of God has drawn ever closer (1:15; 4:3–20; 4:26–29; 9:1). As they came down the mountain, the disciples argued heatedly about its arrival ('what it meant to rise from the dead', 9:10), and Jesus showed that there was only one thing on the eschatological timetable left to happen: the Son of Man must suffer.[43]

With the kingdom of God on their minds, James and John come to Jesus and ask whether they can be the ones to sit on his right and his left when he enters the glory of his kingdom (10:35–37; cf. Dan.

---

[42] *Adelphos ou lytroutai lytrôsetai anthrôpos ou dôsei tô theô exilasma autou kai tēn timēn tēs lytrôseōs tēs psychēs autou, kai ekopasen eis ton aiōna kai zēsetai eis telos, hoti ouk opsetai kataphthoran hotan idēi sophous apothnēiskontas* (Ps. 48:8–10, LXX).

[43] It could be argued, of course, that there may be many things left to happen but that Jesus mentioned only this one. The fact that the disciples mentioned the coming of Elijah and that he added the suffering of the Son of Man indicates, however, that these are the significant events that are charged with eschatological significance. Other events *may* occur, but these *must* occur in fulfilment of God's plan.

7:14).[44] The two brothers are still seeing things through human eyes (cf. 8:33). For them, the coming kingdom affords a unique opportunity to achieve greatness at the Messiah's side. Jesus previously had to intervene when the disciples were discussing who was the greatest (9:33–41), and James and John's question will lead into another conversation about this misguided quest for personal status and position (10:41–45). They had not learnt the lesson from the rich young man, who had status and importance and yet missed out on the kingdom. Nor had they learnt the lesson from the little children, who had no status or importance, yet in that very lowliness were the paradigm for how a person enters the kingdom (10:13–16).

Viewing the world from human eyes makes greatness a thing to be sought after. Human logic is clear: without greatness, how can a person survive? Greatness brings security in this world that lies under the shadow of death. But as Jesus points out in verse 42, a moment's reflection shows that it is the great ones who add to the insecurities of this world. These are Daniel's beasts, raging across human history with their oppression and bloodshed, their unbridled acquisitiveness and tendency to violence in the pursuit of gain. Why should anyone want to be like them?

When Jesus answers their question, he shows that the brothers seriously underestimate the suffering and struggle that lie ahead. He speaks of his death as a cup to be drunk, as a baptism that he must undergo, and finally as a ransom that he is paying. Through this cup, this baptism, this ransom, God will do the impossible.

God does the impossible

The cup (10:38)

Jesus will use the image of the cup twice more before the end of the Gospel, both times clearly referring to his death (14:23–24; 14:36). This suggests that the image has this meaning also in 10:38.[45]

When discussing Jesus' death, many have taken offence at what is called the theory of penal substitutionary atonement. Both aspects of this label have caused difficulty: was Jesus really a substitute for others? And did he really bear punishment? In particular, did

---

[44] Evans (2001: 116) rightly notes that the expression 'in glory' in this pre-resurrection situation refers not to the parousia but to 'the coming kingdom of God on earth'. I would disagree, however, that this is equivalent to 'the restored Israel'.

[45] The cup has nothing to do with the Lord's supper. This is properly denied by Evans (2001: 117), who refers to other literature.

this punishment involve him in bearing the wrath of God in his death?[46]

We have already seen that the wrath of God is implied by the notion of being handed over as the servant of the Lord, and of being handed over to the Gentiles. The image of the cup, too, is a well-established Old Testament symbol of God's wrath.[47] The idea of draining a cup to the very dregs, the bitter leftovers, seems a suitable image to apply to the bitterness of God's inescapable judgment. Whereas Israel may have thought that the nations were the only ones who should drink this cup, the prophets used the image of the cup being passed to Israel too. Moreover, this image is closely associated with Isaiah's servant of the Lord. Just before the final servant song, in which the servant dies a sacrificial death, we read that Israel has drunk the cup of God's wrath to the dregs, and this cup will be handed to Israel's tormentors (51:17, 22). Isaiah's next chapter shows that it is the servant's death that has exhausted the cup of God's wrath on behalf of Israel. Jesus now predicts that, as the servant of the Lord, he will drink the cup of God's wrath.

The baptism

In Mark 10:38, Jesus refers to a baptism yet to come, which he places in parallel with the image of the cup. In non-biblical Greek usage, the verb 'I baptize' was used only very rarely for bathing or washing, since this range of meaning was conveyed by the simplex verb, *baptō*. *Baptizō*, appropriately in view of its intensive ending (*-izō*), was used in such contexts as a person drowning, or for the sinking of a ship; that is, being overwhelmed by a flood of water. It was also used metaphorically for being overwhelmed by a flood of other troubles, as when Jerusalem, on the brink of destruction, was flooded with crowds of people, or for being swamped by taxes, or immersed in debts.[48] Although the Septuagint usually enlists *baptizō* for washings (2 Kgs 5:14; Judith 12:7; Sirach 31[34]:25; Isa. 21:4; cf. Lev. 6:28[21] Al.), the

---

[46] According to Campbell, for example, Christ is not represented in the passion narrative as 'tasting a penalty of the Father's vengeance and wrath because of his offended dignity'; Jinkins & Reid 1998: 142. See also Weinandy 1995: 221–225.

[47] See Pss. 11:6 (LXX 10:6); 75:8 (LXX 74:9); Hab. 2:16; Isa. 51:17, 22; Ezek. 23:31–34; cf. *Psalms of Solomon* 8.14 and Rev. 14:10; 16:19; 17:4–6; 18:6. The targumim use the expression 'cup of death' (*Targum Neofiti I* on Gen. 40:23; *Targum Neofiti I* on Deut. 32:1). The cup of wrath is also found in 1QpHab 11.10–15; *Psalms of Solomon* 8.14–15 and *Martyrdom of Isaiah* 5.13. Cf. Head (1995: 113), who also draws attention to 14:28 (Zech. 13:7) as further evidence that Jesus suffered under God's wrath.

[48] Josephus, *Jewish War* 4.137; Diodorus 1.73.6; Plutarch, *Galba* 21.3. Oepke 1964: 530; Head 1995: 113; MM, 102.

concept of 'being baptized', being overwhelmed by (metaphorical) flood waters, is, of course, found fairly often; and occasionally one of the versions actually recognizes the concept and applies the vocabulary to it as well.[49]

This imagery most probably lies behind Jesus' reference to his forthcoming baptism.[50] It may even be that he drew upon one of these passages, Psalm 69, in particular. In this psalm, the psalmist uses the image of baptism for the overwhelming troubles that he was facing. The image of being overtaken by the flood waters was used in parallel to his dying, the grave, and the wrath of God.

> Save me, O God,
>   for the waters have come up to my neck.
> I sink in deep mire,
>   where there is no foothold;
> I have come into deep waters,
>   and the flood sweeps over me.
>   ... rescue me
> from sinking in the mire;
> let me be delivered from my enemies
>   and from the deep waters.
> Do not let the flood sweep over me,
>   or the deep swallow me up,
>   or the Pit close its mouth over me.
>   (Ps. 69:1–2, 14–15, NRSV)

Here the parallels reveal the reality to which this metaphor is pointing. The psalmist is suffering at the hands of his enemies. Already he endures their mockery, insults and scorn, and, to make it worse, this is because he is zealous for the Lord (vv. 7, 9–12, 19–20). But there is more: he is in fear of his life. As verse 15 shows, the 'baptism', the flood of water, is a metaphor for 'the Pit' (v. 15); that is, the grave.

It is instructive to notice the other metaphors that are associated with his troubles. Because he is in this condition, he believes that

[49] Pss. 9:16 (EVV 9:15; Al. *baptizein*); 42:7; 49:3 (Sym. *baptizein*), 15; 69:2 (Aq *baptizein*); Job 9:31 (Aq *baptizein*); 22:11; Isa. 43:2; Jon. 2:3–6; Isa. 30:27–28; Jer. 38[45]:22 (Aq *baptizein*).
[50] Cf. D. W. B. Robinson 1958: 30: 'When Jesus speaks in the Gospel (Mark 10:39) of His own death-baptism and of our sharing in it, it is more than probably that He has in mind the Old Testament picture of the wave of death which moves upon the victim.'

God has hidden his face from him (v. 17), an expression that is paralleled elsewhere by God's wrath (Deut. 31:17–18; 32:20–22; Pss. 27:9; 88:14–16; 102:2, 10).[51] He asks God to 'draw near', implying that at the moment he is far away (v. 18). God's drawing near will be to redeem the psalmist (v. 18), to bring him salvation (v. 29). In this passion psalm, the Messiah is dreading the baptism of imminent death, in which God has turned his face away. God will remain far away, until he decides to redeem and save.

As the passion narrative narrates the story of Jesus' death, Psalm 69 is explicitly quoted at the dramatic point when Jesus cries out in thirst (15:23, [36]; cf. Ps. 69:21 [LXX 69:22]). This explicit moment of intertextuality invites the reader to hear the story of the crucifixion against the backdrop of this psalm (among other passages); and several other allusions can be easily recognized, such as Jesus' being bereft of friend and family (Ps. 69:8 [LXX 69:9]) and 'hated without cause' (Ps. 69:4 [LXX 69:5]; cf. John 15:25), for his 'zeal for his Father's house' (Ps. 69:9 [LXX 69:10]; Mark 11:15–18, then 11:27 – 12:12; cf. John 2:17), and especially in the mockery that pervades the crucifixion account (cf. Ps. 69:9–12, 19–20),[52] and when the Father turns his face away in the cry of dereliction (Ps. 69:16–18; cf. Mark 15:34). Informed by the psalm, the account of Jesus' death should therefore be read against its primary image, that is, of being overwhelmed by a flood of troubles. His death is his baptism, the moment when God turns his face away and when he is far from him, until he comes to redeem and to save.[53]

Sharing in the cup and baptism

After speaking of his death using both these terms, Jesus asks the two brothers if they are able to drink the cup and endure the baptism (v. 38), after clearly saying that they really do not understand what they are asking. The disciples naïvely claim to be able to do so. However, Mark's narrative will show that, in the end, only one

[51] It also appears with a cluster of other concepts and states of life: forgotten by God, pain and sorrow, suffering at the hands of the enemy, mockery and scorn, shame, and, in particular, in connection with death (Job 13:20, 24; Pss. 13:1; 22:24; 44:24; 69:17; 104:2, 29; 143:7). The exile, which was an act of God's judgment and wrath upon his people, is also a result of his hiding his face (Deut. 31:17–18; 32:20–22; Ezek. 39:23, 29; Tobit 13:6).

[52] Paul uses this psalm to evoke the mockery of Christ at his crucifixion (Rom. 15:3); see below, pp. 124–125.

[53] Cf. D. W. B. Robinson (1970: 749), who refers to the 'baptism' of Jonah (Jonah 2:1–10) and then draws a parallel with Jesus' cry of dereliction (Mark 15:34).

person will drink the cup and endure the baptism.[54] What does it mean, therefore, when Jesus assures them that they *will* drink his cup and be baptized with his baptism (v. 39)?

To answer this question, Psalm 69 once again provides some help. Even though the request for salvation sounds very personal and individual ('Save me, O God', etc.) because the psalm is messianic, there is a clear recognition in it that the troubles of the king affect others (v. 6), and that the salvation of the king is necessary for the salvation of others (vv. 31–32, 35–36). The Messiah is a representative figure whose rescue is essential to the rescue of those whom he represents.

The debate whether Jesus' death is a penal substitutionary atonement often includes discussion of whether Jesus died as a substitute as well as a representative. Bailey (1998: 231–235, 225) has suggested that, since both these terms are now heavily loaded, often with theological prejudice, a way through this debate might be to follow the German usage of the word *Stellvertretung*, or 'place-taking'. The Messiah is involved in both inclusive and exclusive place-taking. He *inclusively* takes the place of Israel, in that he is one of them and shares in their distress in solidarity with them. When the nation suffers under God's wrath, he suffers *with* the nation. But the fate of the nation is also tied up with the Messiah. Just as the tribes of Israel participated 'in David' and benefited from God's promises attached to him and his line (2 Sam. 7) and the blessing that flowed from them (see 2 Sam. 19:41 – 20:2, esp. 19:43 and 20:1), so the people of the Messiah participate in him and benefit from the blessing of God attached to him.[55] In other words, drawing upon this conception of his role as Messiah, when Jesus suffers he takes the place of Israel *exclusively* in that, he, the one, suffers *for* the many, as their substitute so that they do not need to suffer.[56] Jesus will clarify this further when he immediately goes on to speak of his death as a ransom for many (10:45).

To return to James and John, Jesus' promise to these disciples hints at the vicarious nature of his coming death. They were not going to be involved in Jesus' death by any deed they themselves performed,

---

[54] Cf. Seccombe (1986: 147–148), who argues that Jesus called Israel to endure through to the end in order to bring on the resurrection of the dead, but ultimately only one man did so. This is also the thrust of the argument in Geddert 1989.

[55] This is the theological backdrop to Paul's 'in Christ' language.

[56] Bailey (1998: 224) cites a quotation from Iwand 1962: 101, found in Hofius 1996: 115: 'wo kein anderer Mensch an unsere Stelle treten kann' ('where no other human can tread in our place').

THE NECESSITY OF THE CROSS

whether suffering or martyrdom or anything else. In fact, as the hour of Jesus' death arrives, they will prove to be 'failures', for they, along with the rest of the disciples, will desert Jesus, just as he will predict of them (14:26–27; 50). As we shall see in chapter 3 below, there was only one who could endure the suffering of this time, and he endured it alone.

This gives us the clue to how the disciples were involved in Jesus' death. Jesus died for the many; he drank the cup for others; he was baptized on behalf of others. The vicarious nature of his death means that James and John, along with the many, drank the cup that he drank and were baptized with the baptism with which he was baptized.[57] To use Paul's language (cf. Rom. 6), they will die and rise with Christ, because his death will be in their place and on their behalf.

The vicarious nature of Christ's death is brought into sharp focus by Jesus' famous 'ransom saying', to which we now must turn.

The ransom (10:45)

> For even the Son of Man came not to be served but to serve, and to give his life, a ransom for many (ESV).

This saying has been rightly called 'one of the most important in the Gospels' (V. Taylor 1966: 44), for it is 'a large clean window into Mark's thought' (R. H. Smith 1973: 335).

In the classical literature, *lytron* was used for the price of redemption from captivity. In the papyri it refers to the purchase-money for freeing slaves (Deissmann 1995: 327–328; MM, 382–383). In its nineteen occurrences in the Septuagint, it is used in the context of the redemption of the firstborn (Num. 3:12; 18:15–16) and of a forfeit life (Exod. 21:30; 30:12). This latter instance is related to the notion of giving as recompense 'life for life' (*psychēn anti psychēs*; cf. Lev. 24:18 and Deut. 19:21). No ransom was permitted in the case of murder or for someone who had fled to a city of refuge (Num. 35:31–32).[58] We should note especially that it is used in connection with freeing slaves (Lev. 19:20; 25:51–52) and redeeming land (Lev. 25:26), both in the context of the year of jubilee.

---

[57] Rom. 6 therefore becomes the best commentary on this passage. Cf. the hint in Evans 2001: 117: 'Identifying with the death of Jesus (as in Rom. 6) meant something very different [from martyrdom].'

[58] Although it might be permissible, it would be impossible to get a cuckolded husband to accept a ransom (Prov. 6:35).

This connection with the regulations regarding the year of jubilee is interesting, since this offers significant input into the teaching on forgiveness that is so important to the New Testament as a whole (Shead 2002), and Mark's Gospel in particular (Bolt 1998b). This is also by way of the servant of the Lord, who has links with the jubilee. Isaiah 52:1–10 and Isaiah 61 draw upon the jubilee regulations (Lev. 25), chapters that surround and connect to Isaiah 53, the great chapter explaining the servant's death. The servant's death will bring about the forgiveness of sins, the last days' jubilee.[59]

This allows comment on another connection to the language of ransom. The cognate verb, *lytroō*, is frequently associated with the exodus, when God redeemed Israel out of slavery in Egypt (Exod. 6:6; 13:13, 15; 15:13; Deut. 7:8; etc.). Isaiah picks up this language of redemption to speak of the new exodus, which will ultimately be brought about by the servant of the Lord (cf. 35:9; 41:14; 43:1, 14; 44:22, 23, 24; 45:13; 51:11; 52:3; 62:12; 63:9).

At the heart of the ransom idea is the concept of exchange.[60] This is highlighted strongly in Jesus' saying, in which the death of the Son of Man would be a ransom *anti pollōn* – instead of, in the place of, many. This is substitution terminology or, to follow Bailey's suggestion, it is terminology of 'exclusive place-taking'. The Son of Man will go where the many will not go, so that they may never have to go there again.

The Septuagint does not use *lytron* of the servant in Isaiah 53.[61] It is nevertheless fair to say that Mark 10:45 provides a perfect summary of the servant's vicarious death on behalf of many others. The language of ransom does appear in the context (35:9; 41:14; 43:1, 14; 44:22–24; 51:11; 52:3; 62:12; 63:9; cf. 45:13), the concept of ransom is associated with both the original exodus and the servant's new exodus, and the servant's death is clearly a substitutionary,

---

[59] These wider associations are ignored by those who claim that Mark presents a view of forgiveness that does not require the death of Jesus (e.g. Culpepper 1978: 587; Green & Baker 2000: 202). The announcements of John (1:4–5) and Jesus (2:5–10) speak of an era of forgiveness that will be brought about by the death of the servant, as the Old Testament expected and as Mark's narrative will demonstrate has come about in Jesus. See Bolt 1998b; 2001.

[60] The 'sweet exchange', *antallagma*, which appears in Ruth 4:7, 1 Kgs 20 (EVV 21):2; Pss. 54:20 (EVV 55:21) and 88:52 (EVV 89:51); Sirach 6:15; 26:14; 44:17; Jer. 15:13, was praised as early as *Epistle to Diognetus* 9.5, and *antipsychos* (not in New Testament; LXX only 4 Macc. 6:29, 17:21) is used by Ignatius, as noted by Bailey 1998: 229 (TLG shows 15 occurrences).

[61] For a brief summary of the discussion about whether Mark 10:45 draws upon Isa. 53, see Head 1995: 114.

exclusive place-taking exchange. In accordance with Isaiah 53, the Son of Man will give his life as a ransom for many.

When it comes to Mark's Greco-Roman audience, the ransom language would be quite well understood. Confessional inscriptions use *lytron* with 'several layers of meaning, including: ransom from slavery, ransom from captivity, and release from hidden bonds that cause misfortune' (A. Y. Collins 1997: 381). In her analysis of these inscriptions, Adela Collins argues that the person offering the *lytron* does so to ameliorate some bad situation into which he has fallen, in order to restore better relations with the gods. She also notices (ibid.) that, in at least some of the inscriptions, *lytron* is a synonym of *hilastērion*, 'expiation' or 'propitiation', that is, either a sacrifice that removes sin or one that removes God's anger at human sin.[62]

Jesus says that his coming death will be the ultimate act of service. It will be the ransom paid to release the many from their slavery. When Jesus uses this ransom language, what is the situation from which the many are ransomed?

Ransom: from what?

From sin? In the flow of Mark's story, the ransom is integrally connected with the arrival of the long-awaited forgiveness of sins (Bolt 1998b). But to say that the ransom is 'from sin' is potentially misleading; it can be misheard as saying that Christ's death delivers people from the *activity* of sinning, as if they are no longer sinners. Any rescue from sin in the New Testament is in fact rescue from the *consequences* of sin; namely, from condemnation (Rom. 8:1), the judgment of death (Rom. 6:23).[63] So too in Mark, the ransom brings about the forgiveness of sins and so the deliverance from sin's consequences (Bolt 1998b). In this, Jesus' ransom saying is informed by Isaiah 53:12: 'he bore the sin of many, and made intercession for the

[62] A. Y. Collins (1997: 382) concludes: 'the word group *lyō* served to speak of transactions between human beings and gods in which sins were forgiven and offenses expiated, and thus not only in the contexts of the manumission of slaves and the ransoming of captives. The evidence suggests that the notion of the Son of Man giving his life as a ransom for many (Mark 10:45) belongs to the same complex of ideas as the saying over the cup (Mark 14:24), according to which the blood of Jesus was poured out for many. At least from the point of view of their reception among Gentiles familiar with Hellenistic cults, both sayings interpret the death of Jesus by describing it in a metaphorical way as a ritual expiation [or propitiation] of the offenses of many'.

[63] The explicit vocabulary for being 'saved from sin' occurs only once in the New Testament (Matt. 1:21; cf. Jas. 5:15, 20). Other, similar, expressions refer to the status of justification ('justified from sin', Rom. 6:7; 'cleansed from sin', 1 John 1:7), or to the freedom from the grave brought about by Christ ('freed from sin', Rom. 6:18, 22; 8:2).

transgressors' (NRSV). This is sacrificial language indicating that the servant took the divine penalty associated with sin (Evans 2001: 121).

From the devil? The use of *lytron* for the purchase of slaves into freedom misled some of the fathers into seeing Jesus' death as a transaction with the devil. Origen's statement of the logic became authoritative:[64]

> If therefore we were 'bought with a price', as Paul agrees [1 Cor. 6:20; 7:23], then without a doubt we were bought from someone whose slaves we were, and who demanded whatever price he wished in order to release from his power those whom he held. Now it was the devil, to whom we had been sold by our sins, who held us. He demanded therefore as our price the blood of Christ.[65]

To suggest that the ransom was paid *to* the devil probably pushes the analogy too far. Nevertheless, the early parts of Mark's story showed that the arrival of Jesus provoked the underworld to rise up against him. The unclean spirit(s) asked him, 'Have you come to destroy us?' (1:24). When accused of operating by the power of Beelzeboul (3:22–23), Jesus put the counter-proposal that he had come to plunder the strong man's house (3:27). Since Satan is here portrayed as the 'prince of *daimones*', he is occupying the position of the ruler of the underworld.[66] To plunder his possessions is, therefore, to release the dead from under his sway. Jesus' ransom saying moves one step further by informing the reader how this release will take place, because his death will be a ransom for many.

From death? Thus, to speak of ransom from sin and ransom from the devil ends up at the same spot. Jesus' death will ransom the many from the grave (Teselle 1996: 170). His death will bring about the resurrection. To put it in terms of Psalm 49, Jesus' death would be the ransom from death that is impossible for any mortal to pay (A. Y. Collins 1992b: 69).

---

[64] See the discussion in Teselle 1996.

[65] *Commentariorum in Romanus* 2:13, PG 14.911; cf. *Commentariorum in Mattaeum* 13:8–9, *PG* 13.1111–19. See also Origen, *Commentariorum in Matthaeum* 16:8; Gregory of Nyssa, *Oratio Catechetica* 21–24; Augustine, *De Trinitate* 13, 15–22. Gregory of Nazianzus refuted Nyssa's interpretation in *Oratio* 45, 22. For further discussion, see Lyonnet 1970: 79–103, 208ff.

[66] He is the one who, as Hebrews puts it, wields the power of death (Heb. 2:14–15); or, with Paul, he is the 'prince of the power of the air [= another afterlife space]' (Eph. 2:2); or, with Jesus, the one who is 'a murderer from the beginning' (John 8:44; cf. 1 John 3:11–16). For extrabiblical analogies for 'the prince of daimons', see Bolt 2003: 124–127.

From the wrath of God? The story so far indicates that it is a ransom from death and death's shadow. All the sufferings of this world, however, are part of the fallen world, under God's judgment. All such things will be removed in the coming kingdom. The sufferings of this world are the concrete form of the wrath of God. To be ransomed from death – and from life under death's shadow – is to be ransomed from God's wrath.

The faith that follows

Throughout this central narrative movement, the question of faith has continued to be on the agenda. It finds its finale in the healing of Bartimaeus, who is the last of Mark's thirteen suppliants. Bartimaeus is often recognized as the model disciple, drawing together all the threads of discipleship from the story so far. He cries out for mercy. When called by Jesus, he gets up and leaves everything he has, meagre as that is. He is saved because of his faith. He immediately begins to follow Jesus in the way; that is, the way to the kingdom, through the cross.

The necessity of the cross in Mark's world

The central section of Mark stresses the necessity of Jesus' death. Mark's Greco-Roman audience would hear this 'necessity' in the light of a struggle that ordinary people experienced and that thinkers debated. People in the first century saw the course of life unfolding somehow out of the struggle between chance (or fortune) and some kind of fate or necessity.

Chance, fate, and the cross of Christ

Chance

On the one hand, chance/fortune was fickle, changeable and completely untrustworthy. Life in the hands of fortune was a recipe for anxiety and distress. As the first-century Stoic philosopher Seneca put it, 'nothing given by fortune is stable, and all her gifts flow away more fleetingly than air' (*Questiones naturales* 3, pr. 7).[67] The first-century natural historian, Pliny the Elder, agreed:

[67] The fickleness of fortune is a repeated theme in Seneca (see *Epistles* 8.3f.; 13; 16.4; 18.6f.; 48.3ff.; 63.7f.; 72.4; 74.6ff.; 111.2f.; 98; 113.27f.). As a Stoic, he may have had an axe to grind for fate, but his main concern was to ensure the place of the philosopher. For Seneca, fate, the gods or chance ruled the universe (*Epistle* 16.4ff.), but whatever the case, philosophy must be the ultimate guide.

> Everywhere in the whole world, at every hour by all men's voices
> Fortune alone is invoked and named, alone accused, alone
> impeached, alone pondered, alone applauded, alone rebuked and
> visited with reproaches; deemed volatile and indeed by most men
> blind as well, wayward, inconstant, uncertain, fickle in her favours
> and favouring the unworthy ... We are so much at the mercy of
> chance that Chance herself takes the place of god. (Pliny, *Naturalis
> historia* 2.22)

A generation later, the middle-Platonic Plutarch also had no time for
fortune: 'With chance, we are then like blind men, the blind following
the blind' (*De fortuna romanorum* 98AB; cf. Matt. 15:14; Luke 6:39).
A life subject to chance was a life with no real security for the future,
and that meant anxiety in the present.[68]

Fate

On the other hand, if fate or necessity dictated the lot that fell to one
in life, then the best option was that recommended by the Stoics:
resignation before the things one recognizes one cannot change, and
personal detachment from life in an endeavour to be self-sufficient
and so untouched by the pain of this world. To take one famous
example, the Stoic emperor Marcus Aurelius urged his readers to be
content with their lot, because this maintains the order of creation
undisturbed and the human soul untouched (Oates 1995: 28). Such
fatalism is disastrous for rich and fulfilling relationships, for it is 'filled
with self-sufficiency and loneliness'.[69]

In time, both fate and chance as independent forces in the universe
became major enemies for many a Christian. Those who accepted the
message of the cross, which Mark proclaimed, experienced a revolu-
tion in the way they saw the world. The course of life was now in the
hands of the Lord, who had died on their behalf. This radically
changed the way that life was lived, and brought about a serious clash

---

[68] The other major option was Epicureanism, opposed by Stoic and Platonist alike.
Epicurus' teaching that human life was subject to irrational forces and purposeless
events is similar to the view that life is subject to Chance; Farley 1988: 70–71. The
gods existed, but they were not interested in the affairs of human beings. The cross,
however, shows that this is not so. God is interested, for his will, which sent Jesus
to the cross, is directed towards the good of human beings – rebellious ones at
that.

[69] Oates 1995: 29. In particular, he is talking about the 'dark fatalism' of W. E.
Henley's poem 'Invictus', which ends, 'I am the master of my fate: I am the captain of
my soul.'

with the old despots chance and fate, which had held people in such bitter slavery for so long.

In the contemporary world

Of course, these observations of the ancient world can quite easily be seen to be true of our own. There are signs that our own world appears to have forgotten the liberation of the cross and fallen once again into the grip of the old despots. In the nineteenth century, the secularization of fate reached its peak in the historical determinism of Karl Marx (1818–83) and Friedrich Engels (1820–95), which had such a widespread influence in the twentieth century that it became almost axiomatic (Oates 1995: 31–32). Fatalism also deeply entered twentieth-century thinking by way of the scientific determinism of Sigmund Freud, and through him, on into the psychological determinism of contemporary psychology (Oates 1995: 32–34). Politically, we have witnessed the rise of Islam as a force to be reckoned with, and predictions have been made that Islam will be one of the major players in Huntingdon's (1996) future 'clash of civilizations' that will reshape the world as we have known it.[70] Islam's 'kismet' brings another form of fatalism into the mix,[71] a fatalism that has led to the grisly actions of the suicide bomber,[72] who is already restructuring international security and, through its impact on tourism, the global economy.[73]

The other rival in the ancient struggle, chance, is not just a part of our present popular culture represented by our multiplying game shows, in which a person can even win a marriage partner on breakfast radio.[74] Gambling is now an essential part of the Australian economy, and even many conservative functions of mainstream society utilize chance as 'epitomized in the statistical odds associated with disease, accidents, and unpredictable occurrences' (Oates 1995: 28).

[70] This book is a development of his ground-breaking 1993 article 'The clash of civilizations', in *Foreign Affairs* (summer 1993).

[71] Oates 1995: 36. We should note, however, that Islam has its own tensions and nuances in this regard; Bolle 1987: 295.

[72] Suicide bombers respond to a notion of destiny that is far beyond the value of individual human lives; Bolle 1987: 290.

[73] Another form of political fatalism seems common in the politics of both state and church, in which the rhetoric of change suggests that nothing can be reversed once it is decided (like the laws of the Medes and the Persians), no matter how unjust or inhuman those decisions might be.

[74] Sydney radio FM 104.1 has now run at least two of these contests in recent years.

Furthermore, just as ancient people turned to astrology, divination[75] and magic,[76] in search of some little control in a world dominated by forces beyond human control, so too we are seeing an increasing interest in such things in both intellectual and popular culture. 'The future is divined by astrology, various forms of fortune-telling, gambling, computer projection, and poll-taking' (Oates 1995: 28). There are many signs that our world has lost its way. Although the discovery of the gospel of the cross revolutionized western society, it seems that western society is quickly losing touch with its gospel roots. Even if we do not reckon with any notion of divine judgment, this disconnection will only spell further social problems at every level, especially if the 'clash of cultures' scenario for the future proves correct.[77]

The cross as divine necessity

The cross of Christ is no minor matter, simply dealing with individual salvation. The salvation of individuals through the cross of Christ unleashes a revolutionary force that transforms society to its core. The message of the cross is the only force that *can* change the world for the better, and the only force that has actually *proved* that it can do so. It is time for the cross of Christ to be proclaimed once again, loudly and strongly.

Jesus was not crucified by chance.[78] It was all according to plan.[79] But the divine necessity that took him to the cross was not a blind fate that

[75] Although divination often operates with a random method, it has an overarching desire to understand fate; Yusa 1987: 194–195.

[76] Ancient fatalism differed from its modern counterparts in that there was always an element of mystery that opened the door to such practices in an endeavour to understand fate; Bolle 1987: 290–291.

[77] 'Man finds his lasting happiness only in God. Without Him, there is nothing in nature which will take His place; neither the stars, nor heaven, nor earth, nor the elements; not plants ... war, famine, vices, adultery, incest. Since man has lost track of his true happiness, all things appear equally good to him, even his own destruction, though so contrary to God, to right reason, and to the whole course of nature'; Pascal, as cited in Farley 1988: 53 n. 8.

[78] 'The crucifixion of God's Son is no senseless tragedy. A meaningless death is what people still call a bad death, one which threatens to overwhelm and plunge into madness or unfaith. The insistent reference to the Old Testament and the will of the Father shows that Jesus' death, far from being devoid of all rhyme or reason, corresponds with the highest purposes of all: The plan of God'; R. H. Smith 1973: 332. Smith draws parallels for the potential Roman Christian martyrs reading Mark's Gospel.

[79] 'The three Passion predictions, even though they are heavy with the foreboding of death, contain a theology of providence. These sayings declare that it is not merely sinful men who lead Jesus to the cross, but the Father who is working out His predetermined plan'; R. H. Smith 1973: 332.

led to resignation before the pain of human mortality, or to an isolating detachment from human relationships. Jesus went to his death as the climax of the human-centred plans of a loving Creator. Because of the pains of this world, Jesus took on human mortality and, by experiencing the full force of the horrors of our mortal flesh, he brought redemption. Personal identity is now found in following the Saviour to the cross, in the sure hope of the kingdom of God. This journey brings profound freedom: a liberation that comes from having a secure future.

The course of our lives is not determined in a struggle between chance and necessity. Christ's necessity is human-centred and directed towards the coming kingdom of God. His death was the last necessary event before the coming of the kingdom, a ransom for many. The great exchange that will ransom human beings from the grave is impossible for a human being, even a rich human being, to pay. But God has done the impossible. He has supplied the ransom: eternal life in the kingdom of God is opened up by the death of the servant who gave his life as a ransom for many.

Mercy has arrived

Such mercy would eventually take the ancient world by storm. When Bartimaeus heard Jesus passing by, he called out, 'Son of David, have mercy on me!' (10:47–48, NRSV). This was the key to his salvation. He asked for mercy and found it. Just as we can forget that 'faith' was a revolutionary concept of Christianity, so too we can forget how revolutionary Christian mercy was. We must not do so. A brief look at mercy – or at least, at *clementia* – in the first-century world, shows that Mark's early readers would have found Bartimaeus' discovery remarkable.

Greco-Roman religion

The vocabulary of mercy is practically non-existent in Greco-Roman religion. There are a couple of hints of it in the mystery cults – which is interesting, given their greater concern to provide answers to the problem of mortality – but, nevertheless, even here the elements of mercy and compassion and forgiveness of sins are missing (Harris 1986: 94–95). Instead, *clementia* occurs in mainly political contexts.[80]

---

[80] The Greek equivalent was *epieikeia*, 'reasonableness, equity' (LSJ). This word group is rare in the New Testament, used once by Paul, appropriately of a Roman official (illustrating that the virtue of the Caesars was expected of his officials) in Acts 24:4, and once of Christ (2 Cor. 10:1). The adjective is more frequent: Phil. 4:5; 1 Tim. 3:3; Titus 3:2; Jas. 3:17; 1 Pet. 2:18.

Political clemency

Because of its association with Julius Caesar, *clementia* became a constant part of the rhetoric associated with his successors. Julius Caesar had asked for power so that he might practise clemency, *clementia*. Although his policy of clemency was probably an attempt to conciliate the aristocracy (Chilver 1970: 190), through his propaganda, 'a man of the popular party and a man of *clementia* [became] interchangeable ideas' and his clemency soon gained an international reputation (Stauffer 1955: 44). Defining clemency as the ability 'to conquer feelings, to restrain anger, to spare the defeated',[81] he spared the legions of Pompeius as he marched into Italy in 49 BC, and proclaimed, 'Let this be the new way of conquering, that our strength and our security lie in pity and generosity.'[82] He continued to act in the same manner in Africa,[83] and then, when finally victorious, he proclaimed a general amnesty for all who had fought against him.[84] Later, Pliny summed him up by saying: 'Caesar's special and most profound characteristic was his royal clemency, with which he conquered and converted all men' (quoted in Harris 1986: 96).

In 45 BC, the senate resolved to set up a temple to the *clementia Caesaris* (Dio Cassius 44.6), and, in the following year, a coin was struck celebrating this anticipated temple.[85] These coins were 'intended as good tidings, messengers of the man who was filled with the royal passion to have joyful men and a joyful world around him'.[86] Although the temple was never built,[87] Caesar's statues became places of refuge for those who wished to claim protection by the clemency of Caesar (Harris 1986: 96).

Before the temple could be built, the same senate that ordered its construction was complicit in Caesar's assassination on the Ides of March in 44 BC. Caesar had once said, 'I would rather be slain than

[81] Cicero, *Marcellus* 8, cf. 9, 12; Harris 1986: 96. See further Weinstock 1971: 233–242.

[82] This quotation is from Harris 1986: 96 (unsourced): *Haec nova sit ratio vincendi, ut misericordia et liberalitate nos muniamus.* Cf. Velleius Paterculus 2.52; Appian, *Bella civilia* 2.80.

[83] Velleius Paterculus 2.55.

[84] Velleius Paterculus 2.56; Dio Cassius 44.45; Suetonius 1[Julius].75.

[85] Harris 1986: 96–97, referring to Carson 1980: no. 250.

[86] Stauffer 1955: 51. A poem from the last twelve years of his life includes the lines: 'Grief and poverty must come, and joyous with the joyful be. Revenge and grudges all forgotten, enemies forgiven be. Annihilate your book of debts, be with the whole world reconciled! Joy is sparkling in the beakers, in the ripe grape's golden blood'; quoted in Stauffer ibid.

[87] Stauffer 1955: 50; Harris 1986: 96.

feared, and build upon the clemency which I practise.' It was this commitment to clemency that was said to be his downfall: '*Clementia* became the dictator's fate, his generosity became his destruction' (Cicero). When he was mourned, they sang, 'Those whom I saved have slain me.' Even Christians looked back on Caesar's end and declared this to be so. According to the Christian historian Orosius, 'he was destroyed in the effort to build the political world anew, contrary to the example of his predecessors, in the spirit of clemency'.[88]

Since *clementia* was such a feature of Caesar's reputation, it is no surprise that it also became a prominent virtue displayed in the rhetoric of Augustus and his successors. In 27 BC Augustus was voted a golden shield engraved 'by reason of his valour, clemency, justice and piety'.[89] Horace composed a hymn to be sung at the festival of 17 BC, which looked forward to Augustus' reigning with clemency.[90]

Augustan coins did not take up the *clementia Caesaris* theme, but those of Tiberius, Gaius and Vitellius did, and then, after a break, it was picked up by the coins of Hadrian (Harris 1986: 97). In Jesus' day, the coins jingling in people's pockets proclaimed the virtues of Tiberius: 'clemency, moderation, justice, piety, providence'.[91] Such virtues were 'qualities which together if not singly amounted to quasi-divine claims' (Harris 1986: 97).

Clementia was also discussed at the philosophical level. In AD 55, as the young Nero began to reign, Seneca reminded him of this heritage in his essay, *De clementia*. Rulers must display *clementia* because of their office (1.5.2; 19.1), and in a manner worthy of the gods who displayed divine forebearance (1.7.2). But, perhaps more importantly, Nero should remember that, among those to whom he displays mercy, the ruler increases his *securitas* (1.9.12; 13.1) – so there was political mileage in this virtue!

The first-century readers of Mark would understand *clementia*. It 'was on their coins as an attribute claimed by the Roman emperors, it was on the inscriptions they read in the market place and also in the literature read by the educated classes'. But this was the language of politics. 'There was a hardness and political realism about it that left little room for the more humane feelings of pity and tenderness associated with it' (Harris 1986: 95–96, 97). For Seneca, *clementia*

---

[88] Quotations in this paragraph cited from Stauffer 1955: 52.
[89] Augustus, *Res Gestae* 34.2; cf. 3; see also Suetonius 2[Augustus].51.
[90] Stauffer 1955: 84. On Augustus, see also Fowler 1914: ch. 5.
[91] Tiberius issued coins bearing the words CLEMENTIA and MODERATIO in AD 22, although these virtues were not exactly part of the reputation he had earned at this stage; see Shotter 1992: ch. 4.

consisted in 'temperateness of mind in taking vengeance when in power, or the leniency of a superior towards an inferior in determining punishment' (*De clementia* 2.3.1).

This political 'mercy' is far from the kind of 'pity' that draws one towards the suffering person. Stoics such as Seneca were not in favour of such pity, for it entailed the surrender of one's inner peace and so threatened one's self-sufficiency.[92] At the end of the first century AD, Epictetus would counsel the avoidance of such irrational feelings as pity, shown, for example, in mourning the death of one's child.[93] Death was beyond our control, a natural part of life,[94] so why lose our inner peace for something over which we have absolutely no control?

When individuals find mercy

Throughout Mark's story, Jesus is depicted as someone who *does have* control over death (see further Bolt 2003). He demonstrated that he cared for those who are perishing by actively intervening in their suffering. Eventually, he gave his life to ransom many from the grave. On Epictetus' criterion, he therefore has every right to show pity. Because he can *do* something about their problem, he can be moved by these people who are in such need, struggling to live in a world under the shadow of death.

Bartimaeus might be the first suppliant who actually puts this into words,[95] but throughout the Gospel this reaction is exactly what Jesus has been showing. He has acted towards the needy out of mercy. This was not a detached *clementia* like that of the Caesars, but genuine pity that has affected him deeply. It is this mercy, his commitment to bringing life where there was death, that has placed him upon the road to the cross (cf. 3:1–6). He has brought the mercy of God to the world of human affairs. As he says to the man who once had the legion of demons, 'Tell them how the Lord has had

[92] Zeno, influencing Cicero, *Tusculanae disputationes* 3.20; and Seneca, *De clementia* 2.5.4; Harris 1986: 99.

[93] Epictetus, *Discourses* 3.317, cf. 24.2; 4.4; 4.33. Marcus Aurelius (11.34) was fond of quoting a saying from Epictetus (cf. Epictetus, *Discourses* 3.24.88): 'When you kiss your child, you should say, "Perhaps it will be dead in the morning." Ill-omened words these! "Not ill-omened," says he, "but referring to a process of nature. Otherwise it would also be ill-omened to speak of the corn being harvested"' (cf. 7.40).

[94] This ancient Stoic point of view was widely disseminated in the latter twentieth century, especially through the influence of the 'death and dying' movement associated with Elisabeth Kübler-Ross. See Miller-McLemore 1988: ch. 4.

[95] The vocabulary of mercy occurs only rarely in Mark, but, it can be argued, at key narrative moments (5:19; 10:47, 48).

mercy on you' (5:19) – and the man spoke of all that *Jesus* had done for him (5:20). His drinking the cup, undergoing the baptism, dying as the ransom for many, are all the concrete expression of the mercy of God. Edwin Judge (1986) has argued that the discovery of the mercy of God was the force that changed the ancient world. There was nothing like this mercy of God before the gospel of Christ was proclaimed.[96] The closest we have to a discovery of such mercy is that of another person like Bartimaeus, from the late second or early first century BC. In a papyrus discovered in 1975 (*NewDocs* 1: no. 2) the writer praises Isis, the goddess of a popular mystery religion, for the recovery of sight. Although far from a recognition of mercy, this is moving in the direction of a personal response of devotion to an act of salvation from a god (Harris 1986: 95). But when individuals started to grasp the mercy of God in Christ, with its reflex of personal devotion to the Saviour, they began to be remodelled. When one of them was the emperor Constantine (Judge 1986), this eventually led to the dismantling of ancient society.[97]

Bartimaeus was one of the individuals at the beginning of this transformation. He cried out for mercy from the long-awaited Son of David. In doing so, he discovered the mercy of God in this man from Nazareth, who was moving steadily towards the cross. The sufferings of a world under the shadow of death, under God's wrath, made God feel far away. The quest for immortality seemed fruitless. But God, in his mercy, did the impossible: he provided a ransom, and the door to the kingdom of God was thrown wide open to all who believe. In such

[96] This is not the place for a full-blown discussion of the extent to which mercy is found in the Old Testament. It is always a temptation for Christian readers of the Bible to 'smooth out' the two covenants, by reading New Testament concepts into the Old Testament story, and this should be avoided in the interests of hearing these texts on their own terms. Nevertheless, since the merciful God who reveals himself in Jesus Christ also revealed himself to the people of Israel in the Old Testament period, there are clear Old Testament antecedents to the full display of mercy in Jesus Christ. The Septuagint often used *eleos* (and, rarely, *charis*) to translate *ḥesed*, but the exact meaning of the latter term has proved elusive; cf. Andersen 1986. Despite these antecedents, however, it nevertheless seems to be the case that God's mercy was not recognized by the Greco-Romans as a feature of either the Jewish religion or their Scriptures. Although the difference between the mercy of God as displayed in the Old Testament and as displayed in the New Testament needs more elaboration, at the least it must be understood in line with the promise/fulfilment, shadow/reality schema, with the fullness of God's mercy being displayed in Jesus Christ.

[97] 'The powerful no longer rose to a god-like quality, leaving the weak to fall back to a sub-human level. The moral law of the Bible put all back on the same footing. Just as all stood in need of the mercy of God, so none could justly despise or oppress another'; Judge 1986: 118.

a world, under the shadow of death, fate and chance made God seem far away. But according to God's necessity, the Son of Man *must* suffer. And in that moment of suffering – at such a distance from our world – God came close.

Chapter Three

The cross as
'the end of the world'

Mark 13: apocalyptic preparation for the passion

The death of Jesus Christ turned the world upside down. As the message of the cross spread throughout the ancient world, Mark was one of the message-bearers. In this book we are seeking to understand what Mark says about the cross. What made it such a force in this mixed up world?

In this chapter, we shall focus upon Mark 13, which is the last chapter in Mark's fourth major narrative section (Mark 11 – 13). We shall also examine chapter 14, the first chapter in the passion narrative. Jesus is in firm control throughout chapters 11 – 13 and his actions even appear deliberately to provoke his opponents to move speedily towards his cross. At the climax of this section, immediately before the passion narrative begins, Jesus gives the longest speech in the Gospel, his famous 'apocalyptic discourse' (Mark 13).[1] This speech is the last element in the Gospel before the passion narrative begins in Mark 14. Against the tendency to treat Mark 13 in isolation from the rest of the Gospel, it is worth asking whether this location is significant for its interpretation. If Jesus' discourse is just before the passion, is it in fact an apocalyptic preparation for the passion?[2] If so, then the language and imagery

---

[1] For the debate over whether Mark 13 is 'apocalyptic' or not, see Morris 1972: 87–91. This debate is usually conducted on a definition of apocalyptic which arises from the 'sum of the parts', rather than from its distinctive view of history. See further Dumbrell 1975.

[2] I have argued this at length in Bolt 1991a, which is now summarized in Bolt 1995 and assumed in Bolt 2003: ch. 7. Probably because of the location and timing of these publications, there has been little opportunity for published responses as yet. I am pleased that Bolt 1995 has received endorsement from my Old Testament colleague, Graeme Goldsworthy (2000: 175), and that another, Barry Webb (2000: 80–81), moves in a similar direction, dependent upon Kenneth Bailey, but there has been little interaction elsewhere, apart from a couple of brief mentions (Brower 1997: 124 n. 15, 140 n. 65, 142 n. 72; Dyer 1999: 104 n. 1). I have been teaching this view now for about twenty years and have valued my many discussions of it with students and other hearers. Brower agrees with a number of points I made in Bolt 1995 but does not

of Jesus' apocalyptic discourse will help to illuminate Mark's view of the cross.

The arrival of the last days

Jesus' last days

Mark's fourth and penultimate section (chs. 11 – 13) reports the last days of Jesus' ministry before he goes to the cross. This section is carefully structured using a temporal and a geographical schema. The narrative recounts what happened over the course of three days, and on each day there is a journey into Jerusalem from Bethany and out again at evening – although the journey is incomplete on the third day. The amount of material describing each day increases from day one to day three. By gradually slowing down the reading time, this throws attention on to the final day.[3]

Jesus had begun his ministry by announcing: 'The time is fulfilled, and the kingdom of God has come near' (1:15, NRSV). This is now hammered home, for the arrival of Jesus' last days also means the arrival of the last days for Israel.

The last days of Israel

Day one

On day one, Jesus enters Jerusalem in what appears to be a deliberate messianic demonstration.[4] The coming of the last days is the

---

interact with its main thesis. Dyer (1999: 104) is dismissive (my interpretation is 'a brave one, but rather forced'), asking 'where are the details of Mark 13.5–23 to be found within the passion narrative?' As Dyer would be well aware, if the language of vv. 5–23 is taken as *informative* language (i.e. seeking to state facts about the real world; see Caird 1997: 8–12), their details also prove problematic for the 'fall of Jerusalem' position. A more careful reading of my article reveals that this language should be taken as more akin to *performative* (i.e. seeking to move to action; see Caird 1997: 20–25), in which case the critique loses its sting.

[3] For the manipulation of time for narrative effect, see Licht 1978: 96–120.

[4] For further discussion, see Evans 2001: 140ff., who points to the actions being modelled after Zech. 9:9; the unridden colt as a sign of royalty (cf. 1 Kgs 1:32–40; Mishnah, *Sanhedrin* 2.5); the citation of Ps. 118:22–29, which was understood by the Targum to be of David; the Mount of Olives as an appropriate starting point, given Zech. 14:4; the clothing being placed on the road (v. 7) is reminiscent of a coronation (1 Kgs 1:38–40; 2 Kgs 9:13), an action known to the Greco-Roman world (Plutarch, *Cato Minor* 7; cf. the sarcophagus of Adelphia, mentioned by Evans [2001: 144]); the taking of the animal 'may hint at his assumption of political authority, at least on a par with Roman authority' (Evans 2001: 142), for it would be viewed as an act of *aggareia*, 'pressed transportation', which was common enough to enter Hebrew as a loan word,

THE CROSS AS 'THE END OF THE WORLD'

appropriate time for the Messiah to come, riding on a colt (Zech. 9:9), entering the city from the Mount of Olives (cf. Zech. 14:4). It is also the time when, according to Malachi (3:1), the Lord will suddenly come to his temple. After entering the city, Jesus immediately goes to the temple (Mark 11:12a). Since the story has been moving Jesus towards Jerusalem for some time now, and since he made such a fanfare when he arrived (11:1–11), the reader expects that something dramatic is about to occur. Instead, Jesus simply looks around and, because it is late, immediately turns around and goes back to Bethany (11:11b).

After such a build-up of expectation, this is something of an anticlimax for the reader. What did he see when he looked around? It sounds as though he is preparing for something, but what will it be? The non-action of day one leaves the reader in some tension. We shall have to wait until at least the next day for our answers.

Day two

On day two, while returning to Jerusalem, Jesus sees a fig tree in leaf, and, because he was hungry, he sends to see if there are any early figs. When Jesus finds nothing but leaves, Mark draws attention to the oddity of what is about to happen by providing a narrative explanation: 'for it was not the season for figs' (11:13b). Jesus then curses the fig tree: 'Let no-one ever eat from you again' (11:14). This is the first piece of action on day two. The second takes place when he arrives in the temple and proceeds to cast out the money-changers from the temple precincts (cf. Zech. 14:20–21), accusing the temple authorities of making the house of prayer for the nations into a den of robbers (cf. Isa. 56:7; Jer. 7:11). As a result, they step up efforts to destroy him (11:18; cf. 3:6). When evening comes, Jesus once again leaves the city for Bethany.

Day three

Mark's extended description of the events of day three forces the reader to reflect upon the meaning of the two actions of the previous

---

'aggriā (see Judge 1981: 43, commenting on the practice as illustrated in a Pisidian inscription, *SEG* 1392 [AD 18–19]), and this would explain why Jesus used the term 'Lord' (v. 3). Although Evans thinks *dedemenon* is too common to allude to Gen. 49:11, others recognize this allusion here. The fact that Gen. 49:11 is the only place in the Septuagint that *desmeuō* is present with *pōlos* makes the allusion very likely. Various verses in Gen. 49 have, of course, been recognized as messianic prophecies at various stages of Christian history (see e.g. Luther 1966: 246–271). Bóid (2003: 33) suggests that this chapter is among the prophecies, or 'traditional proofs', of the Messiah referred to in the document reproduced in Origen's *Contra Celsum*, which, he argues, goes back to a Samaritan document written between AD 133 and 170 (2003: 35).

day. As they pass by in the morning, the disciples notice that the fig tree is withered from its roots (11:20–26). Jesus replies with a rather enigmatic saying about casting 'this mountain' (i.e. the Mount of Olives) into the sea, and some notoriously difficult statements about prayer, which many scholars have declared to be rather out of place at this point.

Without arguing the case at length, we can deduce that here Jesus is drawing upon Old Testament prophetic material to declare that the last days of Israel have come. The fruitless fig tree is a sign that Israel is fruitless (see Marshall 1989: 160–161), and that it is not ready for the last days' harvest. This, in turn, points to the catastrophic failure of Israel's leadership (Mic. 7). The leaders have made the temple a den of robbers (11:17, 'you'; cf. v. 18). It is the time for Israel's judgment to arrive. This is the time when the Mount of Olives ('this mountain', 11:23) is to be cast into the sea, for, according to Zechariah 14:4, the land of Israel is to be turned into a level plain. Although, once again the English translations are of limited help because of the difficult exegetical decisions involved, Jesus' comments about prayer should also be understood in this specific context: whenever the disciples are praying for the coming day of judgment and the arrival of God's kingdom, they should realize that it is coming to pass right now, in their midst (11:22–24).[5] When they

---

[5] Although these verses require more explanation than I can give here, I can at least outline the exegetical decisions that I have made; cf. Bolt 2003: 245–246. If, in verse 22, *echete* is taken as indicative and *pistis* as 'faithfulness' – yielding 'you have the faithfulness of God' – Jesus is reminding his disciples about God's faithfulness to his promises, as revealed in the Old Testament Scriptures. In particular, he probably has in mind Zechariah's prophecy about the levelling of the Mount of Olives (Zech. 14:4), since the pattern of his daily journey from Bethany to Jerusalem and back again suggests that this is his location (v. 23, 'this mountain'). The request for the Mount of Olives to be cast into the sea is a dramatic way of referring to this prophecy, and basically, Jesus is saying that anyone who is praying for the coming of the judgment day should believe that it will be done for him (v. 23). Jesus then resumes this thought as he begins his dramatic conclusion in v. 24: 'Because of this, I say to you', i.e. because God is faithful and will answer the prayer for the judgment day. In the indefinite clause of v. 23, the two verbs have the imperfective aspect (present tense), indicating that the action is 'going on, in process, without reference to its completion' (McKay 1994: 29). I suggest that Jesus is referring to the disciples' current (and regular) practice, no doubt as pious Jews, of praying for the judgment day to come: 'whenever you are praying and asking'. The imperative of the stative verb, *pisteuete*, 'believe', indicates that this is the state of life that the disciples should adopt (cf. McKay 1994: 77, 79). The content of the urged belief is given simply as *elabete* (so ℵ B C L W Δ Ψ, etc.), in the aorist aspect, which expresses 'an activity simply as an act or event, as action pure and otherwise undefined' (McKay 1994: 30): 'that you have received it'. The final promise is in the future, *kai estai hymin*, expressing 'simple futurity' (McKay 1994: 34): 'and it will be for you'. This is Jesus' momentous conclusion: at the moment of prayer, when they are

return to the temple (11:27–30), the religious leaders question Jesus' authority to do these things, namely to cast out the money-changers the day before. Jesus answers them by asking their opinion of John. If they understood the authority of the forerunner, they would understand about the one who came after him.[6] He then tells them the 'parable of the tenants' (12:1–12). This parable, which is like the Gospel of Mark in miniature, repeats the same lessons.

The owner of the vineyard sends for a share of the harvest, but his messengers are abused by the tenants. As the last course of action open to him he sends 'his beloved son' (v. 6), whom the tenants kill in order to gain the inheritance. This description is reminiscent of the voice from heaven at Jesus' baptism, and again at the transfiguration (1:11; 9:7), making it clear that Jesus is the beloved Son who has come as God's final messenger to Israel, and who is about to be killed by the tenants. Despite his death, the Son they reject will become the chief cornerstone, as it says in Psalm 118:22–23 (Mark 12:10–11).

Jesus' parable echoes one found already in Isaiah, where the vineyard is Israel and it is in ruins because of the failings of the leadership (Isa. 5:1–10; cf. 3:13–15). So too in Jesus' parable, the tenants are the religious leaders. These men recognize that the parable speaks about them, and so, perhaps ironically, they are all the more eager to kill him (12:12).

In the next section (12:13–34) the Pharisees and the Herodians, who have been plotting to kill him from early in his ministry (3:6), hatch a plan to trap him in his words (12:13). First, they ask him about paying taxes (12:14–17). Secondly, they challenge him about the future resurrection (12:18–27). Finally, a scribe asks him to declare which commandment is the most important (12:28–33). This last attempt is their undoing, for when the scribe hears Jesus' answer, he is impressed and commends Jesus for what he said. Since the scribes have been Jesus' opponents throughout the entire story, and since we know that this scribe's question was part of the attempt to trap Jesus in his words so that he could be arrested and destroyed,

---

praying for the judgment day to come according to God's promise, they are to believe that they have received it and it will be so. In other words, his arrival has brought the fulfilment of God's promises; 'the kingdom of God is at hand' (1:15). The difficulty that some scribes found with the aorist may support the view unfolded here. The future (D θ *f*[1], etc.) sought to place the fulfilment beyond the disciples' present time. The reading *lambanete* (A *f*[13] 𝔐) may have also had this intention, if it is 'futuristic', or, by contrast, it may indicate that the reception is occurring as they pray.

[6] John was the messenger sent to prepare the way before the Lord (1:2f.; cf. Mal. 3:1; 4:5), who would bring the great and terrible day of judgment.

it is surprising to hear him praise Jesus' answer. A scribe, one of their own, has effectively changed sides. Mark underlines the 'failure' by noting that, after the scribe had been 'defeated', 'no one dared to ask him any more questions' (12:34, ESV). Plan A has failed. If they are ever going to arrest Jesus, they will need a new plan. Plan B will fall into their lap in a couple of days, when Judas, one of the twelve, comes to them offering to betray Jesus to them (14:1–2, 10–11).[7]

Jesus then goes on the offensive and questions the religious leaders' theology (12:35–37) and practice. He warns the crowds against the scribes, pointing out the latter's faults and declaring that they will receive a greater condemnation (12:38–40). Instead of caring for Israel, they have plundered Israel. This is illustrated with the concrete example of a poor widow (12:41–44), who, in order to support the temple, had given 'her life' (12:44).[8]

Then, as the final event on day three, as Jesus is leaving the city for Bethany, he pauses on the Mount of Olives (13:1, 3). The arrival of the last days for Israel provokes Israel's leaders to kill the Son. As his last days rapidly draw near, Jesus sits down on the eschatological mountain and delivers his last and longest speech, his 'apocalyptic discourse' (13:5–37).

Mark 13 in the context of the Gospel

Interpreters of Mark 13 usually battle over whether Jesus is speaking about his *parousia* (the 'second coming'), about the fall of Jerusalem in AD 70,[9] or about a combination of the two.[10] In this chapter, I shall repeat a position that I have argued elsewhere, without arguing for it fully here.[11] Although this may not fully satisfy my readers, it is my hope that exposure to the conclusions of my argument may, at least, provoke the desire to give the argument itself a good hearing. In a nutshell, it seems to me that Mark 13, when read in the context of the story, is about Jesus' death and resurrection rather than about the

---

[7] For this reading of this scene, see S. H. Smith 1989.

[8] See A. G. Wright 1982; Fleddermann 1982.

[9] Most recently, so N. T. Wright 1996: 339–366.

[10] In a strange kind of catch-all position, some have even argued that the parousia took place in AD 70: J. S. Russell 1999, followed by Feuillet 1964. France (1982: 230 n. 12) critiques Feuillet. Gaston (1970: 483–487) suggests that Matthew read Mark in this sense, and that the parousia occurred in AD 70. For a history of interpretation of Mark 13, see Beasley-Murray 1986.

[11] See further Bolt 1995, which is a summary of Bolt 1991a.

second coming or the destruction of the temple in AD 70.[12] Mark 13 is 'an apocalyptic preparation for the passion', and so this chapter becomes important for our enquiry into the meaning of the cross in Mark's story.

How do we read Jesus' apocalyptic discourse?

Interpreters have regularly missed the importance of this chapter for Mark's story of Jesus, because of the tendency to read it as if Jesus were talking directly about the situation that would prevail after his death and resurrection.[13] On this reading, Mark 13 speaks more about the time of the *reader* of Mark than about the time of the *characters within the story* of Mark.[14] This has made chapter 13 something of a misfit in its own Gospel. Surely the chapter should be read like any other in Mark's story, namely as an integral part of the narrative, making its own contribution to the story in which it is embedded.

The apocalyptic discourse naturally emerges out of the situation of conflict in the previous chapters. Jesus addresses four disciples who are already familiar to the reader and have had a key role in the story so far. The next chapter picks up the action again, with Jesus back in Bethany, as would be expected from the sequence constructed over

---

[12] If the argument from silence can be admitted, it is interesting that some of the apostolic fathers can speak of the last things (the end, the resurrection), including the return of Christ, without referring to the apocalyptic discourse (Clement of Rome 23; 34; *Epistle of Polycarp* 2; *Epistle of Diognetus* 7), and, similarly, the *Epistle of Barnabas* can refer to the destruction of the temple (16), without using any of the apocalyptic discourse material at all, which, if it was about this event, would have been a gift to his argument and his anti-Semitic tendencies.

[13] The usual exegetical grounding for this exploits the final 'all' (v. 37); for instance, Lightfoot 1950c: 50, takes it as an address to the whole church through the four disciples. Evans (2001: 342; cf. Cranfield 1977: 412) concedes that v. 37 may be a later addition to make the warning applicable to all the community, but in the first instance he agrees that it extends the duty of the four who have heard the address (v. 3) to the remainder of the disciples. It is more obvious, however, given the role of the four in the story, that Jesus is instructing them to pass on what they have heard to the other disciples.

[14] At this point it could be asked: how *could* Mark have written about something that would still be in the future to his modern readers? But surely this begs all kinds of questions. Any interpretation of a portion of a text should be justified by being the best reading of that passage within the whole text. The traditional readings also need to justify their assumption that, at this point in the story, the exhortations within the story cease to be addressed to the historical people who heard them, and become primarily addressed to the readers of the Gospel. An analogy may be sought in interpreting the Old Testament prophets. What would justify extracting their predictions of the future, and the exhortations based upon them, from the historical context and applying them to modern readers as if they concerned *our* future, rather than *ancient Israel's* future?

the previous three days. There is really nothing to indicate that this discourse is anything but an address by Jesus to the inner circle of the twelve on the eve of the climactic moment of his ministry. This reading stance makes us ask how the content of his speech relates to this setting on the eve of Jesus' suffering and death.

Since the discourse takes place in a 'pause' in the action, it appears to function as a narrative 'aside'. That is, what the reader learns in the apocalyptic discourse will be significant for the understanding of the passion narrative to follow.[15]

The interpretation of the apocalyptic discourse

The basic movement of the discourse
Before we become immersed in the details, it is helpful to recognize the basic movement of Jesus' speech.

The introductory narrative (vv. 1–4). As they leave the temple, a disciple comments on the magnificence of the buildings (13:1).[16] This is usually taken as an exclamation from an open-jawed Galilean tourist, awe-struck by his visit to the capital city (what Australians might call 'the big smoke').[17] It makes better sense, however, as a word of encouragement to Jesus, based upon Old Testament 'Zion theology', in which the city of Jerusalem was a symbol of God's permanent presence with his people (see e.g. Ps. 48).

Jesus' reply would have taken them by surprise. These buildings do not offer any security; they are part of this fallen creation that will pass away (13:2).[18] His reply intrigues his disciples and, once the four are settled on the Mount of Olives with their master, they ask him a question about it in two parts. Probably presuming that Jesus was referring to the end of all things (cf. vv. 7, 13), they ask when this will be, and they also ask about the sign that would indicate that these things are about to be accomplished (vv. 3–4).

The movements of the discourse. Jesus' apocalyptic discourse addresses both these questions. In verses 5–23 Jesus addresses the

---

[15] This would make it have a similar function to that of Dan. 7 – 14, commenting on Dan. 1 – 6; or Zech. 9 – 14 commenting on Zech. 1 – 8; or even Isa. 24 – 25, commenting upon the historical situation outlined in Isa. 1 – 23.

[16] For the magnificence of the temple buildings see Josephus, *Jewish War* 5.184–226; 5.222–223; *Antiquities* 15.391–402; Babylonian Talmud *Sukkah* 516 and *Baba Batra* 49.

[17] Lohmeyer 1959: 268; Evans 2001: 298, 'an awe-struck tourist'; France 2002: 496, 'touristic awe', 'typical of a Galilean visitor'.

[18] 'Jesus speaks about the transitory character of the great buildings of Jerusalem, even the temple'; R. H. Smith 1973: 332.

disciples' desire for a sign, warning them that this will open them up to being led astray. This world is characterized by many cosmic disturbances (vv. 7–8), but these do not indicate the end: 'the end is not yet' (v. 7, ESV). In such a world, especially in these last days of Israel, the disciples of Jesus will face additional pressures (vv. 9–13), and he warns them: 'watch yourselves' (v. 9, note *heautous*). They need to endure through to the end (v. 13).

The suffering of the last days will culminate in great distress (v. 19) associated with something called 'the desolating sacrilege' (v. 14), and, in the midst of this great time of suffering, as Deuteronomy 13 warned, there may even be people who produce signs to lead away God's elect (v. 22). So the disciples need to keep alert. If they are seeking signs, as their second question indicates is the case (v. 4b), then they are opening themselves up to great danger in these perilous times.

Discouraging them from looking to the temple buildings for encouragement, Jesus then resets the disciples' sights. He tells them that, after the desolating sacrilege has arrived (v. 14), with the associated great time of distress (v. 19), they will see a definite sequence of events (vv. 24–27, NRSV, italics added):

> But *in those days, after that suffering* (*en ekeinais tais hēmerais meta tēn thlipsin ekeinēn*),
> > the sun will be darkened,
> > and the moon will not give its light,
> > and the stars will be falling from heaven,
> > and the powers in the heavens will be shaken.
> *Then* (literally 'And then', *kai tote*), they will see 'the Son of Man coming in clouds', with great power and glory. *Then* (literally 'And then', *kai tote*), he will send out the angels, and gather his elect from the four winds, from the ends of the earth to the ends of heaven.

The three-part sequence at the core of the discourse is clear: a time of great suffering, followed by the coming of the Son of Man, followed by the gathering of the elect from the four corners of the earth.

The discourse concludes with the parables of the fig tree (vv. 28–31) and of the doorkeeper. The doorkeeper parable is especially important. Because the exact hour of the Son of Man's coming is unknown, this parable urges the disciples to keep watching for that hour (vv. 32–37).

The key: the coming of the Son of Man

The coming of the Son of Man is the event that holds the key to the interpretation of this discourse, and so of Mark 13.

Daniel 7:13–14. The 'coming of the Son of Man' is a citation from Daniel 7:13–14. In Daniel's original vision, the prophet sees a series of beasts intent on bloodshed; they are later explained as representing human kingdoms. This is a vision of human history, with kingdom rising against kingdom and nation against nation (cf. Mark 13:7–8). The prophet then sees a vision of the judgment day, with the Ancient of Days taking his seat, the court sitting in judgment, and the books of judgment being opened (Dan. 7:9–10). In this setting, the beastly human powers are stripped of their dominion, and then Daniel sees the only human figure in the vision:

> I saw one like a Son of Man, coming with the clouds of
> heaven.
> and he came to the Ancient of Days and was presented before
> him.
> To him were given dominion and glory and the kingdom,
> that all peoples, nations and languages should serve him.
> His dominion is an everlasting dominion that shall not pass
> away,
> and his kingdom is one that shall never be destroyed.

This language has previously been used in Daniel to speak of the future kingdom that God himself would set up to replace all the human kingdoms so intent on destruction (2:44; 4:34). In chapter 7, the 'one like a son of man' comes to the Ancient of Days in the context of the judgment day, and receives the position of authority in the kingdom of God.

When does this prophecy reach its fulfilment? In Daniel 12, when the prophet asks that very question, he is told that he would not live to see his words fulfilled. His visions relate to the end of days (cf. Luke 10:24; 1 Pet. 1:10–11). There is a long tradition of interpreters stretching from the church fathers down to today that recognizes Daniel 7:13–14 to be a prophecy of Christ's ascension, or, more precisely, of his exaltation to heaven.[19] That was the moment when he received 'all authority in heaven and on earth' (Matt. 28:18, NRSV).

---

[19] For the ante-Nicene Fathers on the ascension, see Davies 1958: ch. 4. When Hippolytus expounds Dan. 7:13–14, he clearly pictures Jesus being brought to the Father to receive power (*Commentary on Daniel* 4.11), even though he does not speak

94

The parousia? Despite this stream of tradition, however, when the same passage is cited in Jesus' apocalyptic discourse,[20] many interpreters have read it of the parousia, that is, Christ's second coming. Until fairly recently, this was probably the commonest interpretation of Mark 13:24–27, and it is still represented among present-day commentators, despite the difficulties this interpretation causes for the apocalyptic discourse – not the least of which is that Mark 13:30 indicates that the coming of the Son of Man would take place in the lifetime of the generation contemporary with Jesus.

The exaltation therefore the fall of Jerusalem? More recently, many interpreters have regarded Daniel 7:13–14 as fulfilled in Jesus' ascension,[21] and have argued that some or all of Mark's citations of this verse should be understood in the same way. Jesus' citation of Daniel 7:13 at his trial (14:62), for example, is now almost universally taken to refer to his coming exaltation.[22] Some interpret Mark 14:62 along these lines, but they do not feel obliged to be consistent when it

---

as if this event is in the past. Perhaps he pictures this occurring before the second coming (cf. 4:15ff.). Cyprian (AD 249) applied the verses to the power that Jesus received in his resurrection (*Testimonia ad Quirinium* 2.26). For discussion, see Davies 1958: 86); France (1982: 211) views this as 'a reversion to Jesus' primary application of Daniel 7:13–14'. Lactantius, another North African, writing at the beginning of the fourth century, continued this view (*Divine Institutions* 4.21). Dan. 7:13–14 is treated as a prediction of the ascension in the second of two ascension sermons attributed to John Chrysostom, but possibly by Nestorius (Davies 1958: 127–128; they are found in *Codex Berolinensis* 77, ed. Baur [1953: 101–126]). Cyril of Alexandria also interpreted Dan. 7:13 of the ascension (*PG* 70:1461). Among later interpreters Dan. 7:13 was regularly taken to refer to a coming to the Ancient of Days, which 'became for many later exegetes a prefiguration of the Ascension of the Son of man to His Father's throne' (Davies 1958: 26), citing Hugh of St Victor (d. 1140) (p. 164 n. 1), Martin, presbyter of Legio in Spain (d. 1203) (p. 166), Peter of Blois (d. 1204) (p. 163) and Gregory Palmas (Metropolitan of Thessalonica in the 1350s) (pp. 153–154). The great Reformation exegete, John Calvin, in his commentary on Daniel, also joined this stream of interpretation, claiming that these verses are 'undoubtedly of Christ ... He had been endued with heavenly power, and was seated at his Father's right hand.' Throughout his exposition, Calvin uses strong language that expresses his conviction: 'This passage, then, without the slightest doubt, ought to be received of Christ's ascension, after he had ceased being a mortal man'; 40, 44; 'This, in my judgement, ought to be explained of Christ's ascension; for he then commenced his reign, as we see in numberless passages of Scripture' (cf. Rom. 6:10, John 16:7; 14:28); (p. 42); '*He now arrives at the Ancient of days*, that is, when he ascends to heaven, because his divine majesty was then revealed' (p. 43); 'He ascended to heaven, and a dominion was bestowed upon him' (p. 44).
[20] Given the paucity of discussion of Mark's Gospel in the early church, it is difficult to find specific comment on Mark's version, so here I refer to comment usually made on Matthew's version.
[21] Davies 1958: 26; Farrow 1999: 20; J. A. T. Robinson 1957; Glasson 1945.
[22] For some discussion, see Beasley-Murray 1986: 300–303; Davies 1958: 36.

comes to Mark 13:26,[23] however counter-intuitive this might seem from a narrative point of view. Others, by contrast, read the two verses consistently, arguing that in both 13:26 and 14:62 Jesus refers to his coming vindication in his resurrection and exaltation.[24]

But this 'new consensus' is not content to interpret these verses solely of the ascension of Christ. Taking Jesus' words that there will not be 'one stone left upon another' (13:2) as a specific prediction of the temple's destruction in AD 70, they argue that the authority Jesus gained at the exaltation is expressed in a great act of judgment several decades later, when the city of Jerusalem and its temple fell at the hands of the Romans.[25] Thus the coming of the Son of Man quickly becomes a prophecy of this famous Jewish political disaster,[26] sometimes even cutting out the middle-man and ignoring Jesus' exaltation altogether.[27] This interpretation solves the problem of the timing of verse 30, since AD 70 was within the generation of Jesus' hearers; but it introduces other problems, not the least of which is the implication that an event in Jewish political history takes on a greater theological significance than Jesus' resurrection from the dead.

The exaltation, full stop. Why have a two-stage fulfilment when one will do? The strength of the position described previously is the recognition that the coming of the Son of Man is fulfilled in the event

---

[23] Davies (1958: 36–37), who assumes 8:38 and 13:26 to be about the second advent. He also states that 'the presence of the title "Son of Man" in Mark must be regarded as evidence of a belief in the Ascension' (p. 38), and the transfiguration is a foreshadowing of the ascension (pp. 39–40, although discussing Luke's account). France (2002: 502) observes that this argument has now been widely accepted for 14:62, and so, for consistency's sake, should be accepted for 13:24–26, where its acceptance has been somewhat slower.

[24] Farrow (1999: 20) takes 8:38, 13:26ff. and 14:62 to refer to the ascension, given the specific allusion to Dan. 7:13–14. The modification in Matt. 26:64 and Luke 22:69, *ap' arti* and *apo tou nyn*, supports this understanding; Davies 1958: 37–38. See also Glasson 1945; J. A. T. Robinson 1957; France 1982.

[25] This is said to be consistent with the apocalyptic 'end of the world' language being used in the Old Testament of political disasters, 'not the collapse of the physical universe and the end of the world'; France 2002: 500; with N. T. Wright 1996: 339–366.

[26] For argument, see France 1982: Appendix A; 1990: ch. 4; 2002: *in loc.*, followed by many. The 'fall of Jerusalem' argument is not new to France, as he admits (1982: 231 n. 13, referring to Poole (1963: 115–116) and Alexander for older interpreters, and to Kik, Knox and Tasker for contemporary. In Calvin's commentary on the harmony of the Gospels (1545) he mentions that the tribulation (13:19) 'is improperly interpreted by some commentators to mean the destruction of Jerusalem; for, on the contrary, it is a general recapitulation (*anakephalaiōsis*) of all the evils of which Christ had previously spoken' (Calvin 1979: 146). He then interprets the coming of the Son of Man as Jesus' second coming (p. 147).

[27] For instance, Hatina (1996: 48) simply talks as if vv. 24–27 are about the fall of Jerusalem.

of Christ's resurrection, ascension and exaltation.[28] The questions seem to be: why is this great moment of the vindication of the Son of Man deemed insufficient? Why not read Mark 13:26 as referring to the exaltation, full stop?[29]

Mark 13 and the passion narrative

This suggestion is not just an educated guess, but actually appears to arise from Mark's narrative itself. R. H. Lightfoot (1950c: 50–54) observed that there were enough points of connection between Mark 13 and the following passion narrative to suggest that in some sense it is 'undoubtedly designed by the evangelist as the immediate introduction to the Passion narrative'. He noted that the verb *paradidōmi* is used three times in Mark 13 (of the disciples), and ten times in the passion narrative (of Jesus). Jesus' warning that the disciples must not be led astray (13:21–22) seems to find a counterpart in Judas' betrayal, the disciples' fleeing at the arrest, and Peter's denial. The day or hour that is unknown in Mark 13:32–33 appears to be the hour that, in Gethsemane, Jesus prays might pass, but then declares that it has come. Jesus' climactic saying at his trial (14:62) recalls the one at the heart of the apocalyptic discourse (13:26). Finally, drawing attention to the time references in Mark 13:35 that indicate that the Son of Man might come 'in the evening, or at midnight, or at cockcrow, or at dawn' (NRSV), Lightfoot asked whether they might be a tacit reference to the events of the passion. The last supper takes place in the evening, Gethsemane around midnight, Peter's denial at cockcrow, and the trial in the early morning. He also noted that the

[28] Some argue that the cross represents Jesus' enthronement at God's right hand as his eschatological judge; Jackson 1987: 25, referring to Vielhauer 1965: 212–214; Perrin 1976: 91–94; M. Smith 1981: 364–365; Radcliffe 1987. Despite a general sympathy with this position, Mark's account of the death and burial of Jesus contains a number of devices that encourage the reader still to seek the fulfilment of Jesus' words beyond his death, namely, in the resurrection/exaltation.

[29] Surely it is easily demonstrable from other parts of the New Testament that Christ's lordship over the nations began with his resurrection and exaltation to heaven. Is this not what happened when the Son of Man came to the Ancient of Days? This understanding also helps to explain why there is hardly any Son of Man language in the rest of the New Testament. It is also interesting that Son of Man language is not used anywhere else of the second coming. Luke-Acts provides an excellent test case, because the Gospel speaks of the coming of the Son of Man before the exaltation, and Acts then uses Son of Man language to refer to the exalted Christ (7:56), but never when speaking of the parousia. The two occurrences of the Son of Man in Revelation can also be read of the exaltation. In 1:7, the apostle John sees Daniel's Son of Man prophecy fulfilled in Jesus' being enthroned in heaven, as the visions of chs. 4 – 5 will clearly show; and in 14:14 the exalted Christ is doing exactly what is expected of the Son of Man after his exaltation, namely gathering the nations.

last hours of Jesus' life are reckoned in three-hourly intervals, just as in 13:35. He concluded that, if these parallels are legitimate, 13:30 becomes less difficult, for 'a first fulfilment at any rate was not far off, which was itself regarded as a sign, a seal or assurance, and a sacrament of the ultimate fulfilment' (p. 54).

Perhaps because Mark 13 has often been treated in isolation from the rest of the Gospel, these clues have been largely overlooked; but, in this new day of treating the Gospels holistically, the climate is ripe for interpreters to take them more seriously.

Lightfoot's observations on the parable of the doorkeeper, which concludes Jesus' apocalyptic discourse (13:32–37), particularly deserve more attention. Because the hour of the coming of the Son of Man is unknown (13:32), it is necessary to keep alert and watch for its coming. The parable then attaches the expectation of the hour of the Son of Man's coming to the various watches of the Roman night: will he come in the evening, or at midnight, or at cockcrow, or at dawn? If the disciples take this seriously, their expectation of the coming of the Son of Man will become focused upon each of these moments of time as it occurs. As one moment passes without the Son of Man's coming, a heightened expectancy will be transferred to the next moment of time listed here.

After hearing this parable, the disciples are to watch for the coming of the Son of Man. After we readers have heard the parable, we too begin to watch, but the watching in which we engage is not unmediated. We watch the disciples watching. We watch them *within the story*, waiting to see whether – and when – they see the coming of the Son of Man.

The significant thing that Lightfoot noticed was that the events of Mark's passion narrative seem to be structured around these very same time references: the last supper in the evening; the trials in the garden of Gethsemane at midnight; the trial and Peter's denial at cockcrow; and both the trial before Pilate and, we might add, the resurrection at dawn.[30] In this way, the flow of the story shows that the expectations of Mark 13 find their fulfilment in the details of the passion narrative. Since Lightfoot, a small but steady stream of interpreters has recognized such connections,[31] and has attempted to

---

[30] Lightfoot did not highlight the resurrection as the fulfilment of Jesus' words, but I would argue that this is a failure to follow Mark to the conclusion that the narrative itself encourages.

[31] See e.g. Stock 1982: 175–180; Gaston 1970: 478–479; Cousar 1970: 321–325; Marshall 1989: 145. Other interpreters both before and after Lightfoot have also felt the pull in this direction. See e.g. Barth, *CD* III.2:501, Cullmann 1956 (on Mark 9:1), and

understand the apocalyptic discourse as some kind of 'preparation for the passion narrative'.[32] To come closer to our enquiry, this perspective on Mark 13 means that, as R. H. Smith (1973: 333) acknowledged, Mark 13 'affords a framework within which to ponder the crucifixion of Jesus. Jesus' suffering is not just the suffering of one more martyr in a long history of martyrdom. Ch. 13 indicates that His death has universal significance, ultimate power, cosmic sweep. His death is itself precisely that event which ushers in the last times, inaugurating eschatology.'[33] Or, to use the words of the title of this chapter, it ushers in the end of the world.

The cross as the great distress

The death of Jesus in apocalyptic perspective

The clear sequence in the discourse places the coming of the Son of Man immediately after the arrival of the 'desolating sacrilege' (13:14), which is associated with the 'great distress' (13:19). If the coming of the Son of Man is Jesus' exaltation, then these must be two apocalyptic descriptions of the cross. What can they tell us about the death of Christ?

The desolating sacrilege

In verses 5–8, Jesus speaks of the normal upheavals of a world gone wrong: wars, rumours of wars, earthquakes and famines. These are

---

N. T. Wright 1992: 393: '[Mark wants to say that] the glorious expectation of Israel ... has been fulfilled, paradoxically, in the death and resurrection of Jesus, and is to be further fulfilled (or, perhaps, has recently been further fulfilled) in the destruction of Jerusalem'; and, again, 'It is only in the light of chapter 13 that the sense Mark wishes his readers to obtain from the court scene in chapter 14, and from the crucifixion scene in chapter 15, can be grasped. Mark 13 is not simply about something *other than* the life, trial and death of Jesus; it is the line through which those earth-shattering events (let the reader understand) must be viewed. To put it the other way around, it invests those earthly events with their heavenly significance' (italics original). Given the second quotation, I wonder why it is still necessary to propose a referent in the fall of Jerusalem (as in the first) at all – especially since Wright reads Jerusalem semi-symbolically anyway, stating that Jerusalem has become Babylon.

[32] There are also a number of interpreters who prefer to call Jesus' discourse his 'farewell discourse' or even his 'last will and testament'; e.g. Hatina 1996: 47; Dyer 1999. It is therefore surprising that they do not allow this position on the *genre* of the discourse to have an impact upon the interpretation of the *content*. If it is his farewell discourse, is it not logical that he may be speaking about his forthcoming death?

[33] Smith heads his discussion of ch. 13 'The Beginning of the End'. He concludes: 'Thus ch. 13 is instructive concerning the eschatological dimensions of the cross of Jesus and of the sufferings of His disciples' (p. 335).

merely the beginning of the birth pangs, and do not signal the end (v. 7). But in verse 14 he changes his tone. The desolating sacrilege appears to be the one thing that does signal the end (v. 14, *bdelygma tēs erēmōseōs*).

This is a phrase lifted from Daniel,[34] as is indicated by Jesus himself when he says, 'Let the reader [i.e. the reader of Daniel], understand' (13:14).[35] The phrase has been variously translated: the abomination of desolation (ESV), the desolating sacrilege (NRSV), the awful horror. The two basic ideas of the underlying Greek and Aramaic are that this is a sacrilege, an abomination to God, and that it is destructive.[36]

---

[34] The phrase occurs in Dan. 12:11, LXX (without the article in Theodotian) and 11:31, LXX (Theodotian, *bdelygma ēphanismenon*). Both Septuagint and Theodotian have *bdelygma tōn erēmōseōn*, and in Dan. 8:13 both have *hē hamartia erēmōseōs*. In all but the last, the original phrase is *šiqqûṣ šomēm*, 'a detested thing which desolates', or perhaps 'appals'; France 2002: 523. In all cases it applies to the desecration of the temple and – as is usually assumed – to the *cessation* of the daily sacrifice. (Lust [2001: 682–684, 687] proposes that it is a *replacement* sacrifice imposed on the Jews, and/or its altar.) No other use has survived except 1 Macc. 1:54, referring to the abolition of the cult in 167 BC, and to the altar – usually considered to be to Zeus, on a deduction from 2 Macc. 6:2 – erected on top of the altar of burnt offering (cf. 1:59). It is interesting to note, however, that when specific rites are mentioned they are Dionysian (under Antiochus Epiphanes, 2 Macc. 6:7; under Nicanor, 2 Macc. 14:33; under Ptolemy Philopator, 3 Macc. 2:29). The commonly stated notion that a statue was erected is not found in any source earlier than a lost work of Porphyry (third century AD), quoted by Jerome (*PL* 25:569); see discussion in Lust 2001: 677–678. Note that when the sanctuary lay profaned the priests mourned (1 Macc. 3:51), and that this was a symbol of the Gentiles' being arrayed against Israel (vv. 52–53). Note also that Judas, once winning the battle, went back to restore the sanctuary (164 BC). When they arrived, 'they saw the sanctuary desolate, the altar profaned, and the gates burned' (1 Macc. 4:38), and immediately they tore their clothes and mourned (4:39–40). They restored the sanctuary and dedicated it on the same day that the Gentiles had defiled it (4:54, *kata ton kairon kai kata tēn hēmeran en hēi ebebēlōsan auto ta ethnē*). This brought great joy (v. 58), for the reproach brought by the Gentiles was removed (*apestraphē oneidismos ethnōn*). Later, Antiochus heard that 'they had torn down the abomination that he had erected on the altar in Jerusalem' (1 Macc. 6:7, *katheilon to bdelygma ho ōikodomēsen epi to thysiastērion to en Ierousalēm*).

[35] This is explicit in Matt. 24:15, but, in Mark, interpreters have often taken it as an address to the reader, which would constitute a *metalepsis* in the narrative (see France 2002: 523). Some argue for similar asides in 2:10; 3:30; 7:3–4, 19. On this view, the abomination of desolation becomes a puzzle that requires thought – or explanation – to understand. Despite this opinion, the parenthesis reads quite naturally as an arresting word of emphasis from Jesus about the importance of understanding that Daniel is about to be fulfilled.

[36] Those who argue that the coming of the Son of Man is the parousia would regard this desolating sacrilege as a future Antichrist. Those who argue that the coming of the Son of Man is the fall of Jerusalem in AD 70 have a great deal of difficulty in finding an event that corresponds to the desolating sacrilege (France 2002: 520–521). Some have pointed to Gaius Caligula's attempt to install a statue of himself in the temple in AD 40, but this never eventuated and, besides, it is much too early to be a sign of the war (France 2002: 525). Others suggest that it refers to the setting up of the Roman

Jesus alerts his disciples to watch out for something that will be destructive and sacrilegious. Perhaps, too, the phrase hints at a coming time of mourning and great time of trial.[37]

If this is apocalyptic language preparing the disciples for Jesus' coming death, it implies that his crucifixion will be a destructive act of sacrilege. This fits with the rest of Mark's story, for could there be a greater act of sacrilege than the destruction of God's Son in such a horrendous way? Israel's leadership will welcome their long-awaited Messiah by handing him over to the Gentiles; that is, by handing him over to the wrath of God.[38] And if that were not sacrilegious enough, Pilate, the representative of the Gentiles, will receive the Messiah from Israel, and condemn him to death by crucifixion. What right have the Gentiles to commit such sacrilege? If the destruction of the temple of God by Nebuchadnezzar in 587 BC, or the desecration of the temple by Antiochus Epiphanes in 169 BC, was an abomination committed by the Gentiles, how much more is the 'temple of his body' desecrated when the Gentiles destroy the Son of God on their cross? What a time of mourning that ought to be for Israel; what a time of mourning for the world!

Returning to Jesus' discourse, we find that in vv. 15–19[39] Jesus uses

---

standards in the temple during the war, to which the soldiers then offered sacrifice (Josephus, *Jewish War* 6.316) – which the Jews naturally regarded as idolatrous (cf. Pilate's attempt to do so, Josephus, *Antiquities* 18.55–59). The trouble with this alternative is that by the time this occurred it was of little value as a sign of the time to escape the city (France 2002: 525). This was probably also true of the other suggestion, that the desolating sacrilege was the defilement of the temple by the Zealots under John of Gischala (Josephus, *Jewish War* 4.150–157; 196–207). Josephus himself took this as a fulfilment of an ancient prophecy that the city would be taken after 'native hands' had already defiled it (*Jewish War* 4.388).

[37] It is interesting to notice that the phrase was also used in 1 Macc. 1:15–27, where, in response to Antiochus' plunder of the temple in 169 BC, Israel mourned deeply in every community (v. 25); the rulers and elders groaned, young women and young men became faint, the beauty of the women faded (v. 26); and every bridegroom took up the lament while she who sat in the bridal chamber was mourning (v. 27; cf. 1:37–40). Here the desolating sacrilege is associated with the mourning of the bridegroom and bride. If this passage were widely known, and the likelihood is that it was, perhaps Jesus' parable of the bridegroom is also imported into the background of Mark 13:14 through the image of the desolating sacrilege. Here is the time of mourning promised by his parable of the bridegroom (2:20).

[38] Schreiber (1967: 142–144) also made this identification between the desolating sacrilege and the piety of the high priests and scribes, who sought the life of Jesus in the temple.

[39] France (2002: 521–522) finds it baffling to determine exactly who is addressed in these verses: is it the disciples, or those generally in Judea? His interpretation leads to a strange outcome. The discourse is specifically addressed to the disciples in Mark's narrative (13:1–4), but the most puzzling thing, on France's interpretation, is 'the uncertainties about just how the disciples themselves are to fit into the events described'.

fairly common apocalyptic vocabulary and themes to stress how serious this moment will be when it arrives. Once they see the desolating sacrilege, the disciples should flee urgently (vv. 14–16), which they later do in the garden of Gethsemane (14:50).[40] Jesus then stresses the trying nature of the time by utilizing the motif of how difficult it will be for the pregnant (cf. 2 Kgs 8:12; 15:16; Hos. 13:16; and also 1 Maccabees 1:61; 3 Maccabees 1:20; 5:49), or if these events happen in winter (cf. Zech. 14:6). These images reinforce the fact that this will be a time of great distress (13:19).

The great distress

The great distress is also a phrase drawn from Daniel. In the final chapter, Daniel learns that just before the future day of resurrection (Dan. 12:2) there will be time of terrible suffering (12:1).[41] Daniel promises that in that time of distress God's people will be delivered.

Jesus' informs his disciples that this suffering will be 'such as has not been from the beginning of the creation that God created until now, no, and never will be' (Mark 13:19, NRSV: *esontai gar hai hēmerai ekeinai thlipsis hoia ou gegonen toiautē ap' archēs ktiseōs hēn ektisen ho theos heōs tou nyn kai ou mē genētai*). The first phrase echoes Daniel 12:1, in which the suffering is described as 'such as has never occurred since nations first came into existence until now'. By pushing it back to creation itself, Jesus encompasses the entire period of human existence in order to indicate that this coming distress will exceed any suffering that has ever been experienced. 'The tribulation will be so great that it will eclipse all crises of biblical history. This is quite a claim when we remember the flood, the Babylonian captivity, and the wars against Antiochus' (Evans 2001: 322). Jesus adds a statement that broadens the scope of his comparison into the future.

Yet he claims that these uncertainties 'do not affect the main function of these verses within the flow of the discourse as a whole', even while heading for an answer to the disciples' question!

[40] Dismissing my view as 'a brave one, but rather forced', Dyer (1999: 104 n. 1) asks, 'where are the details of Mark 13:15–23 to be found within the Markan passion narrative?' This misses the function of the language here, assuming that it is 'informative' rather than 'performative'; see Caird 1997: 8–12, 20–25.

[41] Although this connection is admitted by France (2002: 527), he counsels against a specific link with Daniel, since this is language frequently associated with disaster (Exod. 9:18; 10:14; 11:6; Joel 2:2; 1 Macc. 9:27; 1QM 1.11–12; *Testament of Moses* 8:1; Rev. 16:18) and 'stock expressions for unparalleled suffering' (i.e. *kai ou mē genētai*, cf. Exod. 10:14; 11:6; Joel 2:2). We should, however, note that the verses listed by France do not use the same expression (*kai ou mē genētai* occurs only in Isa. 65:20), even if there is a similar intent. Ezek. 5:9 is much closer to Mark's expression (*kai poiēsō en soi ha ou pepoiēka kai ha ou poiēsō homoia autois eti kata panta ta bdelygmata sou*).

There 'never will be' (*ou mē genētai*) such suffering again. The suffering he has in view will be worse than any that has been experienced before, and will be worse than anything else to follow.[42]

There is nothing trivial about the suffering of Christ on the cross. His death was the greatest suffering this world has ever known – or will ever know. No suffering will ever surpass what Jesus Christ experienced on the cross.

Mark 14: preparations for Jesus' death

The passion narrative begins

Once the apocalyptic mood is set, it continues on into the passion narrative proper when the latter begins in chapter 14. In this chapter, every paragraph, in its own way, prepares for Jesus' death. The chief priests are glad of Judas' promise to betray his friend (vv. 1–2, 10–11). A woman anoints Jesus' body for burial (vv. 3–9). During his last Passover, Jesus reinterprets this meal in terms of his own death (vv. 17–25). As they leave the city, he warns that he will be struck down and the disciples will be scattered (vv. 26–32). In the garden of Gethsemane, he prays in great anguish that the cup might be removed (vv. 32–42). He is arrested and the disciples flee (vv. 43–52). He is tried before the Jewish authorities and condemned to death, while, outside, Peter denies his master (vv. 53–72). By the end of chapter 14, the Jewish religious authorities have done all they can. They are ready to hand their Messiah over to the Gentiles.

Several passages in Mark 14 are especially important for understanding the meaning of Jesus' death.

The last-supper sayings

Jesus sat down to eat his last Passover meal (14:1, 12, 14, 16)[43] 'when

---

[42] Those who interpret 13:26 of the destruction of the temple generally agree that this period of distress refers to the period of war that preceded; e.g. France 2002: 520, 527. However, Jesus' language sounds rather excessive if this is what is being referred to – despite the fact that France (2002: 521) argues that it 'does not outrun the detailed and lurid description of the siege in Josephus' (*Jewish War*, e.g. 5.424–438, 512–518, 567–572; 6.193–213)'. Evans (2001: 322) is surely right when he says that 'unless we view this statement [i.e. v. 20] as unbridled hyperbole, the warning that the period of tribulation will be so severe that unless shortened it will extinguish human life argues that the prophecy portends more than the Jewish war … [At that time] the fate of the whole of humanity did not hang in the balance.'

[43] It is difficult to decide on which day the meal actually took place. See the commentaries for discussion, and Lightfoot 1935.

evening came' (14:17, *kai opsias genomenēs*). This is the first of the time references placed by Mark 13:35, and so its mention raises the expectation of the coming of the Son of Man. Will it be in the evening?

Before looking at Jesus' words and actions in anticipation of his death, it is important to notice that the significance of this unit can be misunderstood if it is primarily considered as 'the institution of the Lord's supper', as is so frequently the case.[44] Whatever connection this meal may or may not have with later church practice, that is not the main point of this paragraph.[45] This scene is Jesus' *last* supper before he dies, and, in fact, more particularly, it is his last *Passover* meal (14:1, 12, 14, 16). During this last meal with his friends, Jesus reinterpreted the Passover meal, so that it became a pointer towards his own forthcoming death.

The bread and the cup

After Jesus broke the bread,[46] he said to the disciples: 'Take; this is my body' (v. 22, NRSV; *labete, touto estin to sōma mou*). This stark saying is left unexplained until verse 24, when the words spoken over the cup

---

[44] So, e.g., Evans 2001: 379. France (2002: 567) even makes up for items *not* in Mark's account by saying that 'this would have been taken for granted on the basis of regular liturgical experience'.

[45] France (2002: 568) admits that the focus of the account does not fall on liturgical prescription, or on 'memory' as such, but rather on the symbolism of Jesus' death *hyper pollōn* (vv. 22–24) and on the eschatological dimension (v. 25).

[46] This may itself have been an implicit messianic claim. For this discussion, see Evans 2001: 390–391; Daube 2000a; 2000b; Noy 1971; Jastrow 1950: 1: 104. A portion of the bread is broken off at the beginning of the Passover and then consumed by all at the end. It is called the *afikomen*, from Greek *aphikomenos*, 'he who comes', which 'represents the portion of the meal that the Messiah will eat when he returns to celebrate with Israel'. Jesus distributed it and said, 'This represents me.' Daube believes this tradition lies behind a Hillel saying: 'There shall be no Messiah for Israel, because they have already enjoyed him in the days of Hezekiah' (Babylonian Talmud, *Sanhedrin* 99a; cf. 98b). Here 'enjoyed' is literally 'consumed, eaten' (*'ākûl*). Israel had already eaten the messianic *afikomen* in the person of Hezekiah, so further messianic expectation is unwarranted. This may be the AD 300 Hillel, but it may also be the 15 BC Hillel. Melito's paschal homily twice refers to Jesus as the *aphikomenos*: 'This one is he who comes (*aphikomenos*) from heaven to the earth on account of the one who suffers' (*Peri Pascha* 467–468); 'This is he who comes to you (*ho pros se aphikomenos*)' (*Peri Pascha* 642). Is this why the risen Jesus is recognized in the breaking of the bread (Luke 24:30–31)? Is this why early Christian meals are simply called 'breaking bread' (Acts 2:42, 46; 20:7)? Is it why we are to remember the Lord in eating and drinking until he comes (1 Cor. 11:24, 26)? It also suits the notion of 'the coming one' that *ho erchomenos* may have been a Christological expectation; see Cullmann 1967: 26. This interpretation may then give a parallel to 9:13: 'Like Elijah, so too the Messiah has come; like Elijah, so too the Messiah will die'; Evans 2001: 391.

have a flow-back effect. The 'cup word' reinforces the ransom saying of Mark 10:45. Once again, his language echoes Isaiah's prophecy about the servant of the Lord, picking up the vicarious nature of the servant's death (Isa. 53:12).[47] His blood poured out (*to ek-chynnomenon*) not only 'recalls the language of sacrificial atonement (cf. Lev. 4:7, 18, 25, 30, 34)' (Evans 2001: 394), but probably also reflects the Hebrew or Aramaic of Isaiah 53:12 (but not the Greek):[48] 'He poured out his soul to death, and was numbered with the transgressors; yet he bore the sin of many.' This latter phrase, 'on behalf of many', *hyper pollōn* (Evans 2001: 394), as we saw with the similar phrase *anti pollōn* in Mark 10:45, means that his death will be a 'place-taking' death. Once again, it is an *exclusive* place-taking, in that the Son of Man will stand alone in this death, and the death of the one will benefit the many.[49]

His exclusive place-taking death will be the blood of the covenant. This phrase alludes to the sprinkling of the blood at the establishment of the covenant with the nation (Exod. 24:3–8).[50] More importantly, the reference to 'the blood of the covenant' was further developed when the prophets used it in regard to the new covenant. According to Jeremiah 31:31–34, this new covenant is associated with the forgiveness of sins. According to Zechariah 9:11, the blood of the covenant will rescue God's people from the waterless pit; that is, from the underworld.[51] In other words, the blood of the covenant is the ransom that Psalm 49 could not find. Jesus' death will be the ransom that will bring about the defeat of the grave, and eternal life (cf. Ps. 49:7–9).[52] It is no surprise, therefore, to find that this last Passover also points ahead to the coming kingdom of God.

---

[47] V. Taylor 1956: 16–17; Evans 2001: 392; Edwards 2002: 427; France 2002: 570.

[48] For a comparison of the variations between the Hebrew and Greek versions of Isa. 53, see Sapp 1998.

[49] For the language of 'place-taking' and 'exclusive place-taking', see Bailey 1998.

[50] The 'blood of the covenant' was, to the rabbis, a reference to circumcision; but Edwards (2002: 426) sees Jesus' reference as 'vastly different'. It is interesting to note, however, that Paul seems to have equated Jesus' death with 'circumcision' (see Col. 2:11–13).

[51] The Aramaic paraphrase of Zech. 9:11 was apparently read at Passover time: 'You also, for whom a covenant was made by blood, I have delivered from bondage to the Egyptians; I have supplied your needs in the wilderness desolate as an empty pit in which there is no water.'

[52] Bread and cup are also associated with life and immortality in some late Jewish texts (*Joseph and Asenath* 8.5; 8.11; 16.16).

The coming kingdom

Jesus declares to his disciples, 'Truly, truly,[53] I say to you, I will never again drink of the fruit of the vine[54] until that day[55] when I drink it new[56] in the kingdom of God' (14:25). Here Jesus looks ahead to the great messianic banquet in the new age,[57] when the shroud of death will no longer cover the nations, and death will be swallowed up for ever (Isa. 25:6–8). All of this will come about because of his atoning death, because of the blood of the covenant. As Jesus looks ahead to the kingdom of God, this once again reminds the reader of the expectation of the coming of the Son of Man, for, according to Daniel 7, the kingdom will be given to him. But the evening passes without the fulfilment of this expectation.

The striking of the shepherd

After singing a hymn, they once again find themselves on the Mount of Olives (v. 26), presumably around the midnight hour.[58] As they stand for the second time on the eschatological mountain (cf. Zech. 14:4), Jesus delivers what could be called a 'mini-apocalyptic discourse', in which he informs his disciples that they will all fall away,[59] fulfilling the apocalyptic prophecy of Zechariah. Peter disputes this: he will not fall away, even if everyone else does! Jesus tells him that, in fact, this very night he will deny Jesus three times before the cock crows twice (vv. 29–31). The intensely loyal Peter still

[53] The introductory *amēn legō hymin* gives a solemn tone to this pronouncement; cf. 3:28; 8:12; 9:1, 41; 10:15, 29; 11:23; 12:43; 13:30; 14:9, 18, 25, 30.

[54] Cf. Isa. 32:12; Hab. 3:17 – looking forward to God's salvation.

[55] 'That day' is an expression familiar to the Old Testament prophets, which now provides an eschatological feel to Jesus' words (cf. 2:20; 13:17, 19, 20, 24, 32); Edwards 2002: 427.

[56] The mention of drinking it 'new' appears to refer to the new wine to be drunk in the kingdom. Does it refer to the new wine (Mark 2:22)? So Casey 1998: 220–221, 242–243. Is he talking about himself being renewed? Some say that he is, but this relies upon the theory that an underlying Aramaic source has been mistranslated. Evans 2001: 395.

[57] Cf. Isa. 25:6–9; *1 Enoch* 62:13–16; *2 Baruch* 29:5–8; 1QSa[28a] 2.11–22; Matt. 8:11–12; Rev. 19:9; *4 Ezra* 6:52; Luke 13:28–29; 14:15–24; 22:30; cf. Jesus' lifestyle (Matt. 11:19 = Luke 7:34; Mark 2:16). Evans 2001: 395–396.

[58] The exact time is not mentioned, but according to the Mishnah (*Pesaḥim* 10), the Hallel Psalms (113 – 118) were cited at Passover, with Pss. 116 – 118 being sung as a fourth cup of wine was drunk near midnight; Edwards 2002: 423. These connections with the events portrayed in Mark 14 give rise to the usual assumption that Jesus' party moved to Gethsemane about midnight.

[59] *Skandalizō* occurs in Mark at 4:7; 6:3; 9:42, 43, 45, 47; 14:27, 29. The passive sense suggests that 'external factors will act upon them and cause them to [defect]'; Edwards 2002: 428. The disciples stumbled at this point because they failed to watch, as Jesus commanded them in ch. 13.

cannot believe it, and he vehemently declares that he will not deny his master.

The disciples' defection will fulfil Zechariah 13:7, which Jesus quotes as: 'I will strike the shepherd, and the sheep will be scattered' (Mark 14:27, NRSV). The image of shepherd and sheep is a standard one for a ruler and his people in the Bible, ancient Near Eastern culture and Greco-Roman culture.[60] Jesus has already been portrayed by Mark as the good shepherd who cares for the sheep, in contrast to the false shepherds, namely the religious leaders and Herod.[61] The scattering of the sheep is a picture of defeat, and is actually the reverse of what would be expected of the Messiah (Num. 27:17; 1 Kgs 22:17; 2 Chr. 18:16; Ezek. 34:8, 12, 15; Zech. 10:2; *Baruch* 4:26; *Psalms of Solomon* 17.4, 21, 26–28; *Targum* on Isa. 6:13; 8:18; 35:6; 53:8; *Targum* on Hos. 14:8; *Targum* on Mic. 5:1–3). Jesus' promise that he will go before them to Galilee (14:28) implies, however, that he will gather them together after his resurrection (cf. 16:7).

An interesting feature here is Jesus' change in verbal form. In Zechariah, in both the Hebrew Masoretic text and the Septuagint, the verb is in the imperative: 'Strike the shepherd.' Here, however, Jesus uses the first person indicative ('I will strike the shepherd'), which makes it a statement from God himself, consistent with the final clause of Zechariah 13:7, 'I will turn my hand against the little ones.'[62]

With the first-person form clearly identifying God (the Father) as the one who will strike the shepherd (the Son), Zechariah 13:7 is making the same point as Isaiah 53:10 (Edwards 2002: 429).[63]

> Yet it was the will of the LORD to crush him with pain.
> When you make his life an offering for sin,
> he shall see his offspring, and shall prolong his days;
> through him the will of the LORD shall prosper.
>
> (Isa. 53:10, NRSV)

---

[60] I discuss the evidence in Bolt 2003: 192–194.

[61] This is a major theme of Mark's second movement. For details, see Bolt 2003: 190–196.

[62] This yields an interpretation of Zech. 13:7 similar to that found at Qumran (cf. *Damascus Document* 19.7–13), so there may be an underlying textual issue here. Alternatively, Jesus could have provided the true interpretation of the saying, now that its fulfilment was about to occur.

[63] Gundry (1993: 845, 847) says that the subject is undefined to keep God from blame, but France (2002: 575 n. 73) argues that the reader of Zechariah would know that God was the subject. See van Iersel 1998: 429–430.

107

'Awake, O sword, against my shepherd,
against the man who is my associate,'
                    says the LORD of hosts.
'[*I*] strike the shepherd, that the sheep may be scattered;
I will turn my hand against the little ones.'
                    (Zech. 13:7, NRSV, italics added)

This is a most significant observation for our understanding of the atonement. God the Father will be actively involved in striking the Son. In chapter 4 below, we shall explore what this might mean for our understanding of the Trinity, but even now, Jesus' announcement comes as a horrific shock to the reader. Is this not the one who will inherit the kingdom of God? Is this not the bridegroom himself? Is he not the good shepherd, who has already fed the sheep and promised them eternal life? What does Jesus mean by saying that God will strike the shepherd down and scatter the sheep? With this mini-apocalyptic discourse the sky begins to darken. But once again, there is no coming of the Son of Man; no coming of the kingdom of God.

Jesus and his party then move to Gethsemane (14:32) where we shall eventually hear him declare, 'The hour has come' (14:41, NRSV).

The hour has come!

The terrible apocalyptic moment

During the Gethsemane scene, the narrative stresses the fact that the disciples fail to do what Jesus had asked them to do in the apocalyptic discourse: they do not keep watch (13:5, 9, 32–37; cf. 14:32–34, 37–38, 40, 41).

At the arrest, as predicted in the mini-apocalypse (14:27), they desert Jesus: 'All of them deserted him and fled' (14:50, NRSV). Is this because they recognize the great distress is about to arrive and so they flee as Jesus told them to do (cf. 13:15ff.)? Shortly after this, even the great Peter fulfils Jesus' words as he denies three times that he knows him (14:66–72). So much for his earlier protests. Because we are so familiar with Peter's eventual denial, we can too easily dismiss his protest, made when Jesus first warned him of his dreadful future, as 'mock heroics'[64] and direct our scorn, patronizing laughter, or, worse still, our self-righteous judgment towards it. This is not, however, the stance taken by the narrative itself. The text never encourages the

---

[64] Edwards 2002: 429; cf. France 2002: 578, 'brash self-confidence', 'bravado'.

reader to laugh at Peter, or to stand in judgment over him without any sympathy. His protests of loyalty should evoke admiration. He desperately wants to remain loyal to the end, and he commits himself to doing so – even if everyone else should fail.[65] The narrative will show him to some extent achieving this commitment, since he alone of the disciples will follow the arrested Jesus back into Jerusalem (14:54). Yes, eventually even he falls: as predicted, he denies Jesus three times (14:66–72). But since the narrative has given us nothing but positive narrative norms by which to evaluate Peter, displaying great sympathy with him, the effect of his denial is to cause us to join him in his bitter weeping (14:72), as we recognize that a great tragedy has taken place (Boomershine 1987).

Jesus predicts his disciples' fall, not to allow them to be judged for their failure, but to underline the momentous seriousness of this time. *Nobody* can withstand this hour, not even the great Peter, with the best will and strongest commitment in the world.[66] Their subsequent desertion shows that *nobody* can withstand this great time of suffering that is now dawning – nobody, except one man, Jesus, the one destined to die as the servant of the Lord before he comes as the Son of Man to the Ancient of Days to receive his kingdom.

Even Jesus feels the strain. His emotions in Gethsemane are reported by the narrator: 'he began to be distressed and agitated' (v. 33, NRSV; *ērxato ekthambeisthai kai adēmonein*). The reader then hears the same emotion from Jesus' own mouth, in words that allude to Psalm 42:6, 12: 'My soul is sorrowful, even to death' (v. 34; *perilypos estin hē psychē mou heōs thanatou*). With the prospect of his death now so close (*heōs thanatou*), he is overwhelmed with sorrow.

The allusion to Psalm 42 [LXX 41] adds to the pathos. Here the psalmist is taunted in a way similar to the taunting Jesus himself will experience on the cross: 'Where is your God?' they ask him (Ps. 42:3, 10, NRSV; cf. Mark 15:29–32). He has a similar experience of losing touch with the face of God (Ps. 42:2), and cries out in words that are similar to what will be Jesus' final words: 'Why have you forgotten me?' (Ps. 42:9, NRSV [LXX 41:10: *dia ti mou epelathou*; cf. Mark 15:34]). If these overtones are imported by Jesus' desperate words, then it seems that Jesus, even as he considers the prospect of his death,

---

[65] In this he displays the supreme commitment of a disciple, for 'taking up the cross' is a solitary activity (8:34). Barth (1963: ch. 10) meditates upon this lonely position that is essential to Christian discipleship.

[66] Evans (2001: 402–403) also makes some sensible comments in this direction. See also Boomershine 1987; Geddert 1989.

can sense that it will mean some kind of disruption between himself and his Father.

Jesus realizes that it is the great time of trial (v. 38), and he urges the disciples to watch and pray so that they might not succumb to it. This adds to the drama of the scene. Jesus is at one end of the garden, struggling against the great cosmic battle about to be fought, and the disciples are at the other end, struggling to stay awake against the weakness of their mortality. This reinforces the fact that Jesus will face this battle alone.[67] He alone can embrace this hour.

Jesus' struggle to drink the cup

At his end of the garden, Jesus struggled with the prospect of having to drink this cup, the cup of God's wrath. He alone can drink it. It was his destiny. His death will be 'for the many' (10:45; 14:24); that is, it will be *an exclusive place-taking* death. He will go where the many will not go, so that the many might never have to go there at all. In a sober and serious manner, we can even say that the destiny of the many hangs in the balance at this moment. Will he go through with the last event to occur in God's timetable? Will he suffer the wrath of God so that the kingdom of God may come, ensuring the end of all the suffering and pain of this world?

In the apocalyptic discourse, Jesus stressed both the necessity of enduring through to the end (13:13) and the urgent need to keep awake, watching for the coming of the Son of Man (13:35–37). His cosmic struggle takes place at the midnight hour. This was the great time of trial (14:38). Filled with a desperate emotion that we can never fully understand, he falls on the ground and prays: 'Abba, Father' (14:36). The future of the world, the future of the human race – our future! – is wrapped up in this passionate exchange between the Son and his Father.

His desperate prayer is well known. Mark tells us that he prayed that, 'if it were possible, the hour might pass from him'. Jesus' own words repeat the theme, 'Abba, Father, for you all things are possible; remove this cup from me' (14:35–36, NRSV). His faith that God can do the impossible reminds the reader that he has already promised that God will do the impossible by gathering human beings into the kingdom (10:27) through the death of the Son of Man as a ransom for many (10:45). If this is so, there will be no other way; Jesus will have to drink this cup.

[67] Cf. Lightfoot 1951: 114; Geddert 1989. I have explored the implications of this for Mark's presentation of the atonement in Bolt 2001.

110

Once before, he spoke of his death as being a cup that he had to drink (10:38; cf. 14:23), and now the hour has come for him to drink it to the bitter dregs. As the servant, he knows his destiny, but desperately prays for another way. Probably already knowing the outcome of his prayer, he concludes with the words of the faithful servant: 'yet not my will, but yours, be done' (14:36).

Once again, following the pattern of the entire course of his ministry from his baptism in the Jordan until now, the Son consents to do the Father's will. Father and Son are in this together. The Son will go willingly to his death at the Father's command. The Father will lovingly restrain his rescuing hand and allow the Son to suffer it. The many will find their impossible possibility through this great act of God in human history.

And then, his desperate, lonely time of prayer comes to a conclusion. As he wakes his tired companions for the third time, he says, 'The hour has come.'

The hour arrives

The signal is the sight of Judas arriving with a crowd bedecked with the symbols of our violent world – swords and clubs – out to get a revolutionary (14:43, 48). The horror of the betrayal is underlined by the mention that Judas was 'one of the twelve' (14:43, 10, 17, 20; cf. 3:13–19; 6:7–13). What an awful thing it is to watch him using his friendship to betray his master, and to do so with a kiss (14:45)!

This act of betrayal is the first step towards the handing over of Jesus into the hands of sinners. First Judas hands him to the high priests, then the high priests to the Gentiles. Through its properly constituted representatives, all of humanity is involved in this betrayal. The hour when the world will destroy the Messiah has now arrived – the destructive sacrilege, beyond all acts of sacrilege; the great distress, beyond all human distresses.

The arrival of the betrayer indicates that the hour that no-one but the Father knew about (13:32) has now come. 'The Son of Man is betrayed into the hands of sinners' (14:41, NRSV). But here, at midnight, there is still no coming of the Son of Man, no coming of the kingdom of God. Even the account of Jesus' early-morning trial keeps this expectation alive. For Jesus will be condemned for blasphemy, for declaring that he is the Christ, and ' "you will see the Son of Man seated at the right hand of the Power" and "coming with the clouds of heaven" ' (14:62, NRSV).

111

Evening has passed. So has midnight. Peter's betrayal and Jesus' trial took place at cockcrow. The weight of expectation of the coming of the Son of Man now falls on the dawn. Will the Son of Man come at dawn? As we leave Mark 14, we shall have to wait a little longer for that great moment of victory. In the meantime, the apocalyptic discourse has put us in a position to see the passion of Christ in cosmic terms: the cross as the end of the world.

The cross as the end of the world

World security and world anxiety

Our world today hovers between a concern for international security and profound anxiety.[68] We are anxious about our world and its future, and so we seek the security of both. Although the anxieties of the present time may seem more pressing than ever before, this is probably just because they are ours. There is nothing really new in this situation. The world has no doubt always hovered between this concern for security and an anxiety about how things actually are. Kingdom rises against kingdom, and nation against nation. This is the world of the beasts. Their teeth are filled with flesh as they bite and devour one another, bringing more and more bloodshed to our world, always with the promise of more security.

In the first century, the eternal culture of Greece had been taken over by the *Pax Romana*, the peace of Rome, which was won by bloodshed and secured by the irresistible iron fist of Roman justice. The future was guaranteed by looking to the past. Caesar Augustus had won the *Pax*, and his successors maintained the empire that was bequeathed to them. The imperial rhetoric proclaimed that Augustus had brought life to a world teetering on the brink of destruction; he had brought 'salvation'. The *Pax Romana* must now be maintained at all costs, for this was the future of the world; this was the security that would ensure that there was no more need for anxiety.[69]

---

[68] For 'world anxiety', see Körtner 1995: 1–22. This anxiety increased as the world headed towards the turn of the millennium, and has been exacerbated by the terrorist attacks on New York and Washington (11 September 2001), on Bali (12 October 2002), and on Madrid (11 March 2004), and by the 'war against terror' that has been launched in reprisal. See also Kyle 1998.

[69] Augustus himself expressed this hope: 'It has been my endeavour to be described in days to come as the creator of the *optimus status*, and to hope, when I come to die, that the foundations which I have laid will last immovably'; quoted in Stauffer 1955: 99 (without referencing the source). Stauffer renders *optimus status* as 'the best possible state of affairs', and suggests that these words have an Aristotelian sound.

Things did not, however, look as rosy to those who lived under the Roman boot.[70] They had their own dreams of the future, even if they gradually realized that Rome was an irresistible force. The disciple who commented on the magnificent temple stones proclaimed one such 'dream'. Zion is a symbol of God's presence with Israel; as long as Jerusalem stands, there is no need for anxiety. We are secure; our future looks good! It is the tower of Babel all over again. Human culture, whether Roman or Jewish, whether in its political or in its religious form, is no solution for world anxiety, no basis for security, no ground for faith. The only security for this world is found in the coming of the Son of Man, in the kingdom of God that is awarded to him at his exaltation. And before the Son of Man comes, human culture is shown up for what it really is, and is judged once and for all.

The great distress again

The cross was the great distress promised by Daniel before the resurrection day (Dan. 12:1). It was the culmination of all the beastly struggles for power that have afflicted this world with so much pain. The Messiah came into this world, and the Jewish people went out to meet him with the swords and clubs that have so often been wielded in our world as kingdom rises against kingdom. They handed him over to the Gentiles, who received him by ending his life on the cross. This was the reality of the *Pax Romana*: brutally crush any rival to the eternal security of Rome!

In that great distress, the Son of God suffered more than any other human has ever suffered. The suffering of the world was placed upon his shoulders. Anyone and everyone who has suffered in this world of the beasts can know that Jesus understands. He died as part of the pain of this world, in *solidarity* with the pain of this world. But, at the same time, he exposed the world for what it really is. For his death was also the destructive sacrilege.

The destructive sacrilege

Jew and Gentile alike joined forces to destroy the Son of God. There is no greater sacrilege! The one who brings life is put to death as a criminal, as a sinner. That is what Jewish nationalism achieved. That is what the *Pax Romana* achieved. That is what human culture in the succession of Babel achieved.

---

[70] For the 'view from below', see Wengst 1987.

In the cross, human sinfulness is supremely displayed. And, in the cross – the destructive sacrilege – human sinfulness is judged and condemned. Here is the great judgment day, when the arrogant brutality of the beasts is stripped away, when humanity hands the Messiah over to the wrath of God, and, in turn, finds itself condemned.

But there is another side to this great apocalyptic event.

The blood of the covenant

When Jesus died, he shed the blood of the covenant. This horrendous crime in which human sinfulness was exposed and condemned was, at the same time, the event that brought a new deal to the world. Here was the ransom for many. This blood was shed for many. This blood of the covenant brought redemption. The sentence of death that has always hung over humanity has been removed. A ransom from the grave has been paid. Forgiveness of sins can be proclaimed. This great distress has ushered in the resurrection from the dead for all who put their faith in the glorious Son of Man.

The end of the world

This was the end of the world. For those who put their faith in Christ, the future no longer depends on the vicissitudes of human politics or religion. The security of the world is not found within the system of the beasts. Human culture is no answer to world anxiety, because it has no answer to our mortality. The future is in the hands of the Son of Man, and that future is resurrection from the dead and the glorious kingdom of God.

When people began to live by faith in Christ, it led to further clashes with human culture. It always will. Those who believed in the Peace brought by Christ found themselves being opposed by the Peace of Rome. Those who serve the kingdoms of the beasts oppose those who look to the kingdom of the Son of Man.

God in the cross

In the second century, an unknown graffiti artist daubed a picture on a wall at the heart of the empire, in the 'eternal city' of Rome.[71] It depicted a man in a posture of worship, standing in front of a crucified figure who had been given the head of a donkey. Under this piece of mockery obviously directed against the Christian message was daubed the slogan, 'Alexamenos worships his god.'

---

[71] The drawing is reproduced in Stark 1997: 146, among other places.

What kind of god gets himself crucified? The world of the beasts, that is built on power and might, cannot understand. It can only mock. The human culture that committed the desolating sacrilege in the first place continues to mock what it does not understand. But the cross spells the end of that world.

The graffiti artist, ironically, wrote words of sober truth, for there, in the cross, in the greatest suffering of all time, in this destructive sacrilege that spells the end of this world, where the blood of the covenant was poured out for many – there in that cross that is at such a distance from all that our world stands for – God has come close.

Chapter Four

The cross:
where God comes close

The first-century world knew that crucifixion was a horrible way to die. It was so horrendous that it repelled people even to talk about it. This is often illustrated by Cicero's famous words during the trial of C. Rabirius in 63 BC, namely, that 'the very word "cross" should be far removed not only from the person of a Roman citizen but from his thoughts, his eyes and his ears' (Cicero, *Pro Rabirio* 16).[1] And yet, despite the odium attached to crucifixion, the Christians were known for worshipping a crucified God, and their message soon began to attract people in droves.

The Gospel of Mark put this message of the cross into story form. Once again, we can ask: why did such a repulsive message change the world?

The climax of Mark's Gospel

In this chapter we come to the climax of Mark's Gospel, in which Jesus is crucified and, at the very moment of his death, he is declared to be the Son of God (15:39).

There are three basic movements in Mark 15. First, Jesus is tried before the Roman governor (vv. 1–15). Secondly, the crucifixion itself is narrated, sandwiched between two separate accounts of the mocking of Jesus (vv. 16–32). Finally, we read of the death of Jesus and the dramatic events that occurred at that time (vv. 33–39). Thus the chapter moves from the legal decision, through the mockery, to his death.

The events of Mark 15 appear to be narrated without theological embellishment or explanation.[2] I hope to demonstrate, however, that all the details of this account are significant for understanding Jesus'

[1] For discussion, see Hengel 1977: 133–137.
[2] 'The Gospel story [speaks] factually. It does not offer any theological explanation. It says hardly anything about the significance of the event'; Barth, *CD* IV.1: 239.

death aright. The details will help us to perceive what the cross of Christ tells us about God.

The first scene shows the world officially rejecting the Messiah.

The world officially rejects the Messiah

The legal charge

The timing

The trial before Pilate takes place early in the morning (v. 1, *prōi*), the final time reference in the series listed in the parable of the doorkeeper (13:35), which has sustained the expectation of the coming of the Son of Man. With the passing of the previous time notes without the arrival of this event, this final moment is filled with heightened expectation. The chapter will end, however, with these expectations still unfulfilled.

Some have argued that the expectation of the coming of the Son of Man is fulfilled in the cross, which is taken to represent Jesus' enthronement at God's right hand as his eschatological judge.[3] The New Testament, however, consistently speaks of Jesus' exaltation to heaven as the moment when he sits at the Father's hand in fulfilment of Psalm 110. In addition, the narrative of Mark encourages the expectations associated with the Son of Man to continue beyond the crucifixion scene. There is no vindication in this scene. One of the tensions in the account is that Jesus is now declared to be king, but there is no evidence of his kingdom in this tragic moment. At his burial, Joseph of Arimithea is said to be 'waiting for the kingdom of God' (15:43), and, in narrative terms, this continues the expectations the narrative has already set up for the kingdom to arrive with power (1:15; 9:1). If Joseph still waits for it, then it has not yet arrived. This is also reinforced by the fact that the resurrection scene is introduced by a repetition of the final time reference, stressed by several other phrases to indicate that this is the moment of dawn. This time, in the resurrection, the Son of Man comes, and, in his resurrection from the dead, the kingdom of God has come with power.[4]

---

[3] Jackson 1987: 25; referring to Vielhauer 1965: 212–214; Perrin 1976: 91–94.

[4] The resurrection of a man from the dead is the most powerful event of all time. The overcoming of death itself was expected on the last day (Dan. 12:1–2), which would issue in the kingdom of God. With the advent of the resurrection of one man (Jesus), the kingdom of God has come with power into human history. He is the 'first fruits' of the resurrection to come (see 1 Cor. 15).

To return to 15:1, Mark, instead of introducing the moment of the coming of the Son of Man, introduces the destructive sacrilege and the last great suffering before the coming of the resurrection.

The handing over

After condemning Jesus at their own preliminary hearing (14:53–65), the Jewish leaders hold a consultation with Sanhedrin, the highest Jewish governing body in the land, before handing their prisoner over to the Roman governor, Pilate (15:1).

The charge

Pilate's question, 'Are you the King of the Jews?' (15:2, NRSV) dominates the narrative to follow (vv. 2, 9, 12, 18, 26, 32; Lightfoot 1935: 148). This is the charge that will be nailed to the cross, above Jesus' head (15:26), declaring to the world why he had been executed. Historically speaking, Jesus was condemned as the pretended king of the Jews.[5] This shows that Pilate correctly understood the Jewish title 'the Christ', but he presented it in kingship terms to suit Gentile understanding. The Romans were the ones who permitted and refused kingship to those under their domain.[6]

During the trial Jesus makes only one statement, and it comes in response to this question. 'Are you the King of the Jews?', asks Pilate, to which Jesus replies: 'You say so (*sy legeis*)' (NRSV). Since only the Romans could appoint or depose kings, Jesus' reply allows Pilate to decide the case – which he does, for this now becomes the charge nailed over Jesus' head when he is killed (15:26). The representatives of the Jews had tried Jesus for being 'the Christ' (14:61), and now the representative of the nations declares Jesus to be 'King of the Jews', the Messiah. In doing so, Pilate unwittingly declares Jesus to be the king over the nations as well, for, according to Old Testament expectation, that also is the Messiah's role.[7]

---

[5] The historicity of this charge finds support, among other means, in Rome's continued attempt to destroy Jesus' dynasty at later times. See Mastin 1973: 361–362; and, for Hegesippus' report of Domitian's examination of the grandsons of Jude, Eusebius, *Ecclesiastical History* III.20.4–5 (Stevenson 1957: 9).

[6] See Bolt 2003: 257 n. 3.

[7] There was an expectation that the Messiah would conquer the nations (see e.g. Ps. 2), and this expectation contained the seeds of messianic rule over the nations. (Ps. 2 asks the nations to 'kiss the Son'; Isaiah's eschatology has the nations streaming into Jerusalem.)

The sentence

Because Pilate wanted to satisfy the crowd – now whipped up by the jealousy of the religious leaders (v. 10) – even though he appears to declare Jesus innocent (v. 14), he accedes to their demand, and hands Jesus over to that most wretched of all deaths, crucifixion.[8]

The meaning

For those with eyes to see, when read against some key Old Testament passages, the details of the trial reveal some profound theological truths about the meaning of the cross.

Handing over to the Gentiles

As we saw in chapter 2 above, to hand someone over to the Gentiles is to hand them over to the wrath of God. When the Jewish Sanhedrin decides to hand Jesus to the Gentile governor, they are handing the king of the Jews over to divine judgment.

The Messiah given to the wrath of God

Jesus goes to his death as the result of a legal decision made by the properly constituted governing bodies of his day, namely, the Sanhedrin[9] and the Roman governor. This places Jesus' death in a forensic setting. If we can take a lead from Luke in Acts 4:23–28, this scene can be explained as a fulfilment of Psalm 2.[10] Here we see the people of God joining forces with the nations of the world, in an act of rebellion against the Lord and his Messiah. In this scene, the whole world, both Jew and Gentile, officially rejects the Messiah[11] and hands him over to the wrath of God.

This act, in turn, therefore indicts the world for its sin, for 'no-one who lays a hand against the Lord's anointed can remain guiltless' (1 Sam. 26:9; cf. 1 Sam. 24:6, 10; 26:11, 23; 2 Sam. 1:14, 16), and those who do stretch out their hands against the Lord's anointed deserve to

---

[8] The best survey of crucifixion in the ancient world is Hengel 1977.

[9] Similarly, when dealing with the Gospel of John, Ovey (2001: 111) treats the high priests as 'a representative corporate character', drawing justification from John 1:10–11; 'Humanity crucifies its king' (cf. John 19:15).

[10] The person of Jesus has been explained by reference to Ps. 2, if not since 1:1, then certainly from 1:11. It is in the context of the opposition from the world that the declaration of sonship is made; Ps. 2:7; cf. Mark 15:39.

[11] This was also recognized by Schleiermacher (1999: 457–458): 'especially in the last days of His life, He was surrounded by Judaism and heathendom, as political and religious authorities, causing His suffering, and representing the sin of the whole world ... this alliance of the two chief classes of sinners'.

die (1 Sam. 26:15–16). Psalm 2 speaks of this rebellion as being futile, an action that is liable to arouse the wrath of the true king. When read against this backdrop, the crucifixion of Christ by the representatives of both Jews and Gentiles demonstrates humanity's supreme sin and establishes our corporate guilt.

The silence of the servant

Pilate is amazed that Jesus does not defend himself against the many accusations levelled against him (vv. 3–4). This silence is like that of the innocent sufferer in the Psalms, who is silent because of his faith in God (cf. Pss. 22, 31, 69). 'Jesus, like the righteous sufferers of old (Ps. 38:11–15; Isa. 50:5–6; 53:7–9; compare 1 Pet. 2:22–23) faces His torment without snivelling or pathetic efforts at self-defence, without abusing His tormentors, and without complaint to God. His silence means that His attitude is one of trust in the Father' (R. H. Smith 1973: 333).[12]

In particular, his silence shows that he is the servant of the Lord and his death is on behalf of others. Consider Isaiah 53:7 (NRSV):

> He was oppressed, and he was afflicted,
>   yet he did not open his mouth;
> like a lamb that is led to the slaughter,
>   and like a sheep that before its shearers is silent,
>   so he did not open his mouth.[13]

For those with eyes to see, Jesus' silence entails the other aspects of the servant's role: his vicarious, sin-bearing death, which will ransom many; the pouring out of the blood of covenant, which would bring forgiveness of sins and rescue from the grave into the kingdom of God.

The imminence of the kingdom of God

The constant repetition of the term 'king' also taps into the narrative's major concern with the kingdom of God. The suffering of the Son of Man was the last event in God's eschatological timetable that had to occur before the arrival of the kingdom (9:9–13). If Jesus is now designated as the king just as he is handed over to

---

[12] Smith finds in this a model for persecuted Christians.
[13] It is also associated with the fact that justice was being perverted: 'By a perversion of justice he was taken away' (Isa. 53:8, NRSV) – although translating this verse is not without its difficulties.

his suffering, does this mean that the much-expected kingdom of God is about to arrive?

The mockery of the Messiah

We now come to 'the heart of the passion proper'.[14] The report of the crucifixion of Jesus is sandwiched between two scenes in which Jesus is subjected to terrible mockery.

The mockers

His mockers include the Roman soldiers, who ridicule him before he is crucified. After the event, three separate groups add their own particular brand of mockery:[15] the passers-by (v. 29), the chief priests and scribes (vv. 31–32), and even the two bandits who are bleeding at Jesus' side (v. 32).

The mockery

The soldiers mock Jesus with a parody of the kind of treatment that would be given a king (15:16–20). This scene is true to what we know from elsewhere of the behaviour of Roman soldiers with similar pretenders to kingship.[16] The passers-by mock in words reminiscent of a charge at Jesus' trial (14:58): 'Aha! You who would destroy the temple and rebuild it in three days ...!' (15:29–30, NRSV; cf. John 2:19). They demand that he save himself by coming down from the cross. Israel's religious leaders (vv. 31–32a) gloat over their victim in the hour of their victory: 'He saved others; he cannot save himself.'

---

[14] Black 1996: 196, writing on 15:16–41.

[15] Marshall 1989: 206, deems vv. 33–36 to be a mockery scene also, because, 'unable to comprehend the meaning of these happenings, they mockingly twist Jesus' words into a last desperate cry for Elijah's aid and cruelly seek to prolong his life to "see" if Elijah will save the Messiah who cannot save himself. In reality they expect Elijah's appearance as much as the priests expect Jesus to descend from the cross.' In support he cites Best 1990: 101–102; Matera 1982: 29–32, 122–125.

Marshall (1989: 201) notes that each of the narrated events in Mark 15 is followed by a mockery scene, 'representing a sort of "anti-confession" of Jesus' true messianic identity':

Trial (vv. 1–15)	Soldiers mock (vv. 16–20a)
Crucifixion (vv. 20b–27)	Passers-by and religious leaders mock (vv. 29–32)
Darkness and cry of dereliction (v. 34)	Bystanders mock (vv. 35–36).

[16] Cf. the mockery of Vitellius (AD 69) by troops loyal to Vespasian (Dio Cassius 64.20–21) and the Carabas episode in Alexandria (Philo, *In Flaccum* 36ff.). The giving of the vinegar may also be part of the mockery, which would explain why the soldiers permitted the bystander to give it to him; Evans 2001: 508.

They also demand that the king of Israel come down from the cross, adding that this will be the sign that would guarantee their belief. There is great irony here.[17] Jesus' death spells the end of religion, and so, in this sense, it will mean the destruction of the temple – as the torn veil at the moment of his death will dramatically demonstrate (15:38). Three days later, Jesus will rise from the dead as the mighty Son of Man, as the new focus of worship. The Son of Man is the new temple, raised up in three days.

Both the passers-by and the religious leaders demand that he come down from the cross, that he save himself. The religious leaders acknowledge that Jesus has saved others, but of course the second part of the chief priests' mockery is also ironically true: 'He saved others, *but he cannot save himself.*' Ultimately, since Jesus is dying as a ransom for many, he cannot save himself if he wants to save the others (Marshall 1989: 205).

The meaning of the mockery

A study of the vocabulary of mockery (*blasphēmeō*, v. 29; *empaizō*, vv. 20, 31, cf. 10:34; *oneidizō*, v. 32) in the Septuagint proves most illuminating.

Mocking as sinfulness

Mockery displays the sinfulness of humanity. According to the Psalms, the mocker (Ps. 1) is part of the sinful world. Scoffing is associated with arrogance towards God, and is a symptom of a world gone bad. The righteous man has no place for such mockery himself (Ps. 15:3 [Lxx14:3]), but finds that he becomes an object of mockery: for instance: 'I have become an object of reproach to my neighbours' (Ps. 31:11; cf. Ps. 79:4). In this scene, therefore, human beings are once again indicted for their sinfulness; they incur guilt (cf. Lev. 24:14–16) and so are placed under the threat of God's judgment.

The mocking of the servant/Messiah

The reproach of the Messiah. Not surprisingly, the Messiah also suffers such reproach from those around him. The dilemma of the messianic Psalm 89, for example, turns upon the tension between God's promises to David (vv. 1–37) and his rejection of David's line (vv. 38ff.):

---

[17] Marshall (1989: 203) notes the irony in all the mockery: 'Jesus is the temple destroyer; he is the Saviour; he is the Christ; his cross is the sign of faith.' For irony in Mark, see Booth 1974; Camery-Hoggatt 1992.

> But now you have spurned and rejected him;
>> you are full of wrath against your [Messiah] . . .
> All who pass by plunder him;
>> he has become the scorn (*oneidos*) of his neighbours.
>> > (Ps. 89:38–41, NRSV; cf. vv. 49–51)[18]

This can also be illustrated from two of the messianic passion psalms that are important to Mark's passion narrative:

> But I am a worm, and not human;
>> scorned by others, and despised by the people.
> All who see me mock at me;
>> they make mouths at me, they shake their heads
>> > [cf. Mark 15:29];
> 'Commit your cause to the LORD; let him deliver –
>> let him rescue the one in whom he delights!'
>> > (Ps. 22:6–8, NRSV)

The mockery of the Messiah is also a prominent feature of Psalm 69, where it is part of the 'baptism' that he has to undergo (cf. Mark 10:38):

> You know the insults I receive,
>> and my shame and dishonour;
>> my foes are all known to you.
> Insults have broken my heart,
>> so that I am in despair.
>> > (Ps. 69:19–20, NRSV)

Mockery and insults are also part of the suffering of Isaiah's servant of the Lord, even if the Septuagint itself does not use the vocabulary at this point:

> I gave my back to those who struck me,
>> and my cheeks to those who pulled out the beard;

[18] Ps. 88:52, LXX (MT 89:52; EVV 89:51) is interesting, for the Lord's enemies mock 'the exchange of your Messiah' (*to antallagma tou christou sou*). Given that human mortality is a significant part of the problem in the psalm (see vv. 46–48), is this a reference to the Messiah's providing the 'ransom' that Ps. 49 sought (cf. Mark 8:37)? It is also interesting to notice that, where the LXX has the enemies mocking 'the exchange of your Christ', the Hebrew (89:52; EVV 89:51) has *'iqbōt*, 'footsteps' – the word used by the *protoeuangelion* in Gen. 3:15.

> I did not hide my face
> from insult and spitting.
> (Isa. 50:6;[19] cf. Mark 10:34).[20]

Blasphemed by the Gentiles. The word used for the passers-by 'blaspheming' him (v. 29) provides an interesting piece of corroboration for this point. It occurs only rarely in the Septuagint and in the passages that have a Hebrew equivalent, always in a particular context. In 2 Kings 18 – 19, the king of Assyria taunts the people of Jerusalem, saying that their God was unable to save them from the might of the nations. God takes this personally, and declares that the pagan king has blasphemed his name (2 Kgs 19:4, 6, 22). Isaiah recalls this incident in 52:4, before applying the lesson to the Babylonian exile. The rulers of the nations continue to blaspheme the Lord's name (Isa. 52:5), and so he promises to reveal his name anew. This will issue in the announcement of good news on the mountains (52:7ff.), and, of course, it will all come about through the death of the servant (Isa. 52:13 – 53:12). Thus, the nations' mockery of God will provoke God to reveal his name in the sending of his righteous servant.

Hebrews and Paul. Perhaps Mark's mockery scene can be illuminated further by noticing the importance of the mockery at the cross for two other New Testament authors. For the author of the letter to the Hebrews, no doubt it was this theme of mockery, found in the Old Testament material and focused in the actual event of Jesus' crucifixion, that gave rise to the notion of 'the reproach of the Messiah' (Heb. 11:26, *ho oneidismos tou Christou*). According to this author, the reproaches that Christ suffered were part of the shedding of blood by which his people were sanctified (Heb. 13:12–13).

In Romans 15:3, in the context of practical instruction, Paul cites Psalm 69:9: 'The insults of those who insult you have fallen on me' (NRSV). Although Paul's use of this citation at this point has mystified the commentators,[21] taking it as a meditation on the crucifixion of Christ as the fulfilment of Psalm 69:9 adds real depth to his argument.

---

[19] The Septuagint is slightly different: *apo aischunēs emptysmatōn.*

[20] These and similar texts probably gave rise to the expectation in some quarters of a Messiah who would be mocked. Although the evidence for this is slim, recently published scrolls from Qumran, for example, show that the Qumran community expected this of the Messiah. The future priest of 4Q541 is 'depicted as the object of rejection and calumny on the part of his antagonists, much like the Suffering Servant in Isaiah. Yet, he is to atone for all the children of his generation'; Baumgarten 1999: 540.

[21] See e.g. Moo (1996: 868–869), who is surprised that Paul does not refer to the cross at this point.

This interpretation becomes even more probable if he is also meditating upon Isaiah 53:4 in the immediately preceding verses.[22]

Mockery as the wrath of God

The mockery suffered by the righteous in the Psalms can be viewed as the wrath of God (e.g. Pss. 39; 79; 102), as can the mockery suffered by the nation under the judgment of exile (e.g. Pss. 44; 74; 79; 123).[23] This is also true of the mockery endured by the Messiah. As Psalm 89:38 (NRSV) puts it:

> But now you have spurned and rejected him;
> you are full of wrath against your anointed.

On the one hand, the mockery expresses the sinfulness of the world as it pours contempt upon the Creator. On the other, it is utilized by God as an instrument of his wrath (see also Ps. 69).

The death of Jesus

The final scene centres upon the actual crucifixion. There are three great events associated with the death of Jesus. For three hours the land is plunged into darkness (v. 33). Out of this darkness Jesus cries with a loud voice, his great 'cry of dereliction' (v. 34). Then, as he dies, the temple curtain is torn in two (v. 38) and the Gentile centurion confesses him to be the Son of God (v. 39) at the climactic moment of Mark's story.

Darkness

The strange feature of this darkness is that it comes at noon (v. 33), the middle of the day, when the sun is meant to be at its brightest. At midday, darkness descended on the whole land, for three hours. According to Mark 13:24, since this was a preliminary sign for the coming of the Son of Man, this darkness keeps alive the readers' expectations for the arrival of that event.

---

[22] Although Isa. 53:4, LXX, does not use any of the vocabulary of Rom. 15:1–2, the Hebrew could be translated with the words Paul uses here, as is demonstrated by the Greek of the citation at Matt. 8:17. Because the Greek version of Isa. 53 is markedly different from the Hebrew at a number of points, the New Testament authors tended to prefer to allude to the Hebrew, rather than to cite the Septuagint. See further Sapp 1998.

[23] Note that the language of 'wrath' is often replaced by equivalents, such as being forsaken, rejected, put to shame, disgraced by God, etc.

Interpreted by the biblical story, this darkness also becomes a sign of an event with great cosmic significance. It shows that Jesus is subject to the judgment of God. The Old Testament used darkness as an image for judgment, especially for the day of the Lord, or the day of judgment.[24] Way back in Israel's past, darkness was among the plagues inflicted upon the Egyptians by God. Before the final plague, when the angel of death moved throughout the land before that first Passover, when Israel was saved from slavery, darkness fell on the whole land for three days (Exod. 10:21–22). As a sign that the land was under the curse of God, people stumbled around in deep darkness, a darkness that could be felt.

Darkness at noon was a particular image used on several significant occasions to underline the severity of the judgment.[25] When God warned Israel of the curses that would fall on them if they broke his covenant, 'darkness at noon' was one of the images used to convey these curses: 'you shall grope about at noon as blind people grope in darkness, but you shall be unable to find your way' (Deut. 28:29, NRSV). This is the fate of the wicked, according to Job, for 'they meet with darkness in the daytime, and grope at noonday as in the night' (Job 5:14, NRSV).

Then, when Israel does indeed break God's covenant and his judgment falls on them, this imagery is picked up to describe Israel's state of affairs in the exile:

> We grope like the blind along a wall,
>   groping like those who have no eyes;
> we stumble at noon as in the twilight,
>   among the vigorous as though we were dead.
>
>   (Isa. 59:10)[26]

When the Lord saw Israel's groping in the noonday, with no-one to save, he decided to strap on his armour and save them himself (Isa. 59:15b–20), and promises to come to Jerusalem as Redeemer.

The prophet Amos also used the imagery to speak of the great day of judgment (Amos 8:9–10). 'On that day', that eschatological day of the Lord, apocalyptic darkness will fall. No longer will it be a time of

---

[24] This is also an image that is utilized for judgment in the Jewish pseudepigraphal literature; Hatina 1996: 57.

[25] Cf. Jer. 15:9: Jerusalem's 'sun went down while it was yet day; she has been shamed and disgraced.'

[26] The reverse image is found for the salvation beyond the exile, should Israel return to the Lord (Isa. 58:10).

rejoicing, for all feasts will be turned to mourning, and the mourning will be as bitter as that over the loss of an only son (cf. Mark 2:20).[27]

The death of Jesus and the end of religion

When Jesus finally dies (v. 37), the veil in the temple is torn in two, from top to bottom (15:38), signalling that the Jewish religion is now over. Their temple has ceased to operate, for now the Messiah has come (Marshall 1989: 204).

As we saw in chapter 1 above, Jesus' death now spells the end of religion. No rules, regulations or rituals are to be imposed between God and humanity. The distance these created between sinful humanity and the holy God has been done away with from God's side. There is now free access to God the Father through the work of the Son on the cross. God has now come close. It is the event that takes place between the darkness and the tearing of the veil that helps us to understand why this is so: Jesus' famous 'cry of dereliction' (v. 34).

The cry of dereliction

The cry: significant and mysterious

Out of the darkness comes Jesus' terrible 'cry of dereliction'. Quoting Psalm 22:1, he cries: 'My God, my God, why have you forsaken me?' (15:34, NRSV). Earlier in the Gospel, Jesus had been constantly surrounded by people. He has gradually been deserted by the crowds, his friends, Israel's leaders, and even the nations themselves in the person of Pilate. 'The Gospel According to Mark is the record of the steady and relentless forsaking of Jesus and of His being handed over into the darkness and pain of death on a Roman cross' (R. H. Smith 1973: 330). And now, amid the darkness that signals God's displeasure, it seems as if Jesus is absolutely alone, without people and without God: 'My God, My God, why have you forsaken me?'

Nobody doubts that this cry is of immense significance. Despite this, the saying is extremely difficult to understand and explain. Explanations often seem to resort to paradoxical language (cf. Jinkins & Reid 1997), or the language of mystery,[28] or restraint, or even evasion! As Rossé (1987: vii) puts it, whether we avoid speaking about the meaning of this saying, or whether we attempt to do so, 'a

---

[27] In *Assumption of Moses* 10.1–10 the darkness marks the shift from one age to another.

[28] 'Here we are in the very heart of the Christian faith, and it is a mystery, dazzling in its blackness'; Holloway 1984: 57.

certain fear is noticeable'. How can we understand this desperate cry at the climax of Mark's Gospel?

Evading the difficulties

Because of the profound theological problems that are raised by this cry (to which we shall return shortly), several strategies have been mounted to evade them.

Formulating illustrations. It is the temptation of the teacher to try to clarify what seems difficult. Interpreters have often sought to do this by inventing illustrations or proposing analogies for Christ's work on the cross. This is a temptation, however, that should be resisted at all costs. The track record of these manufactured illustrations has not been a happy one; they have been sometimes obscure, often bizarre or inhumane, and usually just plain heretical.[29] Any illustration can get into trouble simply by virtue of the fact that it requires saying God's Word *in other words*, entailing an automatic shift away from God's Word.[30] Although the preacher needs to 'illustrate' the world to which the Word is addressed, the Word itself should probably be permitted to speak for itself. In addition, there are some things that should never be illustrated. As with the Trinity, given the unique nature of the cross, analogies simply do not exist. We understand the cross, not by finding some contemporary illustration that clinches the deal, but by listening carefully to the biblical context in which it makes sense (Weston 2001: 149–150). This may leave us with some unexplained mysteries, but, even so, we shall be closer to the truth when we live with the rough edges of God's Word than when we try to impose the smooth lines of our own fancy illustrations.[31]

[29] Cf. Weston (2001: 148), who critiques the well-used story from Ernest Gordon, *Miracle on the River Kwai* (London: Collins, 1963), in which a soldier sacrifices his life for a comrade in a prisoner-of-war camp.

[30] See Barth, *CD* I.1:345: 'Interpretation means saying *the same thing* in other words. Illustration means saying the same thing *in other words*. Where the line is to be drawn between the two cannot be stated generally. But there is a line. For revelation will submit only to interpretation and not to illustration. If we illustrate we set a second thing alongside it and focus our attention on this. We no longer trust revelation in respect of its self-evidential force.' He is speaking of illustrating the Trinity.

[31] There may, of course, be some scriptural analogies that will aid us in our understanding. Barth himself (1991: 349) draws attention to Rom. 7:24 as something of an analogy for Mark 15:34, in the context of a discussion of natural theology: natural theology cannot lead to God, but 'over against the human possibility in question there still stands the mystery of revelation, the Yes concealed in the No, the Son of God on the cross, dying according to Mark [15:34] with the words: "My God, My God, Why hast thou forsaken me?" The task of a proof of God is to find the analogy in this – only an analogy, of course – on the human side.' The analogy Barth finds is in Paul's 'wretched man' cry in Rom. 7:24, which is answered in 7:25 by 'Jesus Christ!'

Jesus was not really forsaken. Perhaps it was a case of mistaken identity (runs one explanation), and it must have been one of the others crucified with Jesus who uttered this cry. Or perhaps we are listening, not to Jesus, but to the church: this is the voice of the sinful body speaking through her head.[32] Or, if it *was* Jesus, perhaps the bystanders *thought* that Jesus was deserted by God, but, in fact, he was not (Reed 1992: 261). To take this a little further, because he was so distraught, perhaps Jesus himself thought that he was deserted, but in fact he was not.[33] Reed calls this the 'traditional answer', which 'strive[s] valiantly both to present Jesus' full humanity and to preserve his divinity and the unity between Father and Son even in the cry of dereliction.'[34]

It was not a cry of dereliction, but despair at human unresponsiveness. Menzies (1954: 183–184) puts forward the tentative suggestion that 'this cry was wrung from the soul of Jesus by the *unresponsiveness* of men.' Yet although Psalm 22:1, which Jesus quotes, sounds despairing, the psalm actually goes on to express a profound hope of deliverance. Many interpreters have argued that, despite the fact that Jesus cites only the first verse, the entire psalm was in his mind[35] – an entirely reasonable assumption to make, given citation practices at the time. On this view, Jesus' cry is not one of despair, or lack of faith, but a cry

---

[32] Gregory Nazianzus, *Oration* 30.5–6, according to Lyonnet's (1970: 200) summary: 'We were abandoned, but by the sufferings of the impassable, we were assumed and saved. Because he has appropriated our madness and disorder, he pronounced the rest of Psalm 22.' Augustine, *Enarrationes in Psalmos* 54(53):5: 'It is the voice of Christ, but it speaks for the members. "Why has God forsaken the son ..." if not because he recognized the voice of the sinner in the flesh of our infirmity?' (alluding to Rom. 8:3); from Lyonnet 1970: 214. This was Augustine's explanation, with recourse to a sort of *communicatio idiomatum* between Christ and church (Rossé 1987: vii). 'Why, then, do we disdain hearing the voice of the body from the mouth of the head? When he suffered for the church, it was the church that suffered in him, just as when the church suffered for him, it was he who suffered with the church. As we have heard the voice of the church which suffered in Christ: "My God, my God, turn to me your face; why have you abandoned me?", so have we also heard the voice of Christ who suffered in the church: "Saul, Saul, why are you persecuting me?"'; Augustine, *Epistle* 140.18.

[33] Jesus 'felt Himself deserted by His Father, but in reality He was never dearer and nearer to Him than then'; Menzies 1954: 184. 'Although not deserted by His Father, it seemed for a while that He was forsaken by Him'; V. Taylor 1956: 20.

[34] Reed 1992: 342, noting in the cry 'my God' 'the slender connection which remained even in the moment of abandonment'.

[35] Schleiermacher 1999: 460 n. 2, who agrees with J. J. Hess, who 'could not bring himself to regard the passage Matt. 27:46 as a description by Christ of His own state of misery, but only as the first words of the Psalm, quoted with reference to what follows'.

of confident hope.[36] Adopting this point of view, Schleiermacher[37] even claimed that this cry portrayed Jesus as looking forward to his departure from this world with increasing calm and cheerfulness of soul.[38] Although it is appropriate to understand Jesus' cry by reference to the psalm he quoted, however, interpreters should avoid the temptation 'to empty the cry of abandonment of its content by drowning it in the optimism expressed in the conclusion of Psalm 22'.[39]

In the past, some of the strategies for evasion have been partly motivated by a discomfort with divine emotions. Many today, however, find it quite an attractive idea that God is closely identified with human emotions and pain. On this scenario, whatever difficulties might be raised by it, the despair of Jesus' cry is embraced as a thoroughly human cry.

Embracing the difficulties

The cry as a human cry. It is common to hear the cry as an echo of our own cries of forsakenness. We identify with it, since the feeling of being Godforsaken is a common human experience.[40] In its worst manifestation, this identification with Jesus' cry can simply amount to wishing for 'a God who authenticates and justifies their self-pity' (Weinandy 2000: 281). Nevertheless, this perspective contains a very important part truth. As our cry is caught up with his, we realize that he cries out like this because he has entered into our situation in the

---

[36] Jinkins & Reid (1998: 140), explaining Campbell's exposition of the cry of dereliction. See Campbell 1996: ch. 12. Trudinger (1974: 235) supports this argument, insisting that the words must not be read as arising from despair, but in the context of Ps. 22 as a whole, which is 'the confident prayer of One who did not lose faith even in the midst of his aloneness'.

[37] In a sermon preached during the period 1820–23; see Barth 1982: 82.

[38] Barth (1982: 84–85) observes that, in Schleiermacher's hands, 'the word of dereliction loses all its offensiveness and changes into a statement of its opposite once (1) we put alongside it the rest of the Psalm, which Jesus unfortunately did not quote, and (2) we interpret it as peaceably as possible'. Barth also adds that, in reporting Schleiermacher's views, he has refrained from inserting the question marks and exclamation marks that might be inserted after almost every sentence (p. 87).

[39] Rossé (1987: viii) lists several problems with the interpretation that relies on the final victorious component of Ps. 22. First, it ignores the exegesis of many saints and fathers of the church; secondly, it fails to account for the deliberate selection of these words by Matthew and Mark, and to the emphasis given by their isolation; and thirdly, Jesus does not quote the rest of the psalm.

[40] Cf. Lull (1985: 10), who points out the element of 'protest' in the cry, which acknowledges that 'for the sufferer the present seems to be empty of God, so filled as it is with isolation and alienation'.

first place. The most important thing is not that we can identify with him, but that he has identified, in a real way, with us.

Solidarity with suffering humanity (inclusive place-taking). Jesus' cry is often taken as 'a cry of identification with the God-forsaken',[41] expressing his solidarity with human suffering.[42] Although popular, this thought is seldom developed theologically and it is often left unclear how his being 'brother to all souls who are similarly afflicted' (Menzies 1954: 184) is actually supposed to help (Bauckham 1993: 386). One wonders if it is simply an extension of the psychological notion of 'empathy'. If so, the biblical warrant for it would be the letter to the Hebrews' insistence on the Son of God's sympathy; the Son of God has been tempted as we are, and so is able to help us in our hour of need (Heb. 4:15–16). Even then, sympathy is not empathy, and there is more to the help he provides than simply solidarity with our suffering. Hebrews explains that the Son takes on solidarity with our humanity, becoming 'flesh and blood' by taking on a body (Heb. 10:5–10).

Occasionally the notion of identification is linked with the ancient idea of recapitulation, which goes back to Irenaeus (see also Read 1957: 262). By virtue of his incarnation, the Son of God was able to recapitulate the entire human experience, except that he did so with perfect faith as the true human being. In this sense, the incarnation is the crucial factor in our salvation, and the death of Christ is simply the final stage of the incarnation.[43]

The writer to the Hebrews, however, puts this equation the other way round. The Son of God shared in flesh and blood, because this was a necessary condition for his work as the high priest on our behalf in order that he might defeat the one who held the power of death and set humanity free from its fear (Heb. 2:14–15). The incarnation *was* crucial, because the Son learnt obedience through a lifetime of

---

[41] See e.g. Stassen, Tooley & Williams 1992: 347; Reed 1992: 331, 342–345.

[42] Cf. R. H. Smith (1973: 327), who argues that, in the midst of persecution, Christians can utter the same cry.

[43] Read (1957: 262) speaks of Phil. 2:5ff. as an experience of abandonment. Jesus' descent is a 'progressive identification of Himself with sinful man', 'even death on a cross': 'The death of the cross implies more than the physical suffering and the public degradation; it surely speaks of the final horror that awaits mankind – that of separation from God ... This is consistent with the Gospel portrait, in which Christ identifies with man – in the baptism, as the Servant, and as the Son of Man. Christ comes to share all life, to experience every step of the way in which man has gone astray, to know pain, loneliness, abandonment – and to know all this as the Reconciler.'

suffering, even to the point of death. The totality of his life *and death* enabled him to taste death for everyone (Heb. 2:9).[44]

To speak of Jesus' solidarity with us is to speak of Jesus' death as an inclusive place-taking (see Bailey 1998); that is, he entered into human experience in this mortal world. There is a real strength in recognizing that Jesus enters into our experience in this cry. The experience of forsakenness is a fact of life in this world, which is 'under the shadow of death' because sinful humanity has been forsaken by God, delivered over to our sinfulness to live under the wrath of God (Rom. 1:18ff.). It is no surprise, therefore, that human beings feel this objective God-forsakenness in their subjective experience from time to time. When we do, we do not simply read our cry into Jesus' cry of dereliction, for ultimately that would have no redeeming power at all. Instead, we must hear Jesus entering into the experience that lies behind our cry. He has taken up solidarity with our 'flesh and blood'. He knows what it is to live in this mortal world, under the shadow of death.

But there is more to this cry than an expression of Jesus' inclusive place-taking. It is also a messianic cry that signals an exclusive place-taking, because it is the cry of the suffering servant at the end of his ministry. The messianic dimension can already be seen in Psalm 22, for the salvation of the messianic speaker issues in the salvation of the people of God, of the ends of the earth, and, by the end of the psalm, even of the living and the dead and of generations yet unborn. The Messiah is constituted as the representative of others. His salvation benefits others.

Jesus has come to this hour as the servant of the Lord. The cry of dereliction represents the fulfilment of his ministry as the servant. As we have seen, the servant's death is an exclusive place-taking death. As the obedient servant, for the sake of the many, he is forsaken in the wrath of God. The cry of dereliction resonates with similar cries throughout the Psalms, in which the psalmist finds himself forsaken by God, left to endure difficult circumstances without God's saving help; in other words, forsaken in the wrath of God (e.g. Ps. 27:9).

---

[44] Cf. Barth, *CD* IV.1: 215: 'The self-humiliation of God in His Son is genuine and actual, and therefore there is no reservation in respect of His solidarity with us. He did become – and this is the presupposition of all that follows – the brother of man, threatened with man, harassed and assaulted with him, with him in the stream which hurries downwards to the abyss, hastening with him to death, to the cessation of being and nothingness. With him He cries – knowing far better than any other how much reason there is to cry: "My God, my God, why hast thou forsaken me?" (Mark 15:34). *Deus pro nobis* means simply that God has not abandoned the world and man in the unlimited need of his situation, but that He willed to bear this need as His own, that He took it upon Himself, and that He cries with man in his need.'

Even though many interpreters are reluctant to follow this line, can Jesus' experience on the cross be regarded as the wrath of God? In discussing the atonement, there is a tendency to speak of God's wrath as if it were something that can be abstracted from the concrete event of Jesus' death by crucifixion. On such a view, one might ask: certainly he was crucified, and certainly he died, but did he suffer the wrath of God? If we read the details of the event against the backdrop of the Old Testament material, as we have been doing, however, Jesus was most certainly under the wrath of God since, as we have seen, the very historical details of his crucifixion should be interpreted as the wrath of God.

His wrath should not be considered as an abstract idea. This world is already under the wrath of God (Rom. 1:18ff.), and it is felt in the concrete circumstances of everyday experience and the very fibre of our being. Mark's passion predictions prepared us for the concrete circumstances now described in the passion narrative, and, as we have seen, these details are theologically loaded. God is in the details, and he is using them as instruments of his wrath.

Jesus was handed over to the nations. One of the recently published Qumran scrolls uses this language in a prayer that sounds very much like Jesus' own cry of dereliction: 'My Father and my God, do not abandon me to the hands of the nations' (4Q371–372 [Vermes 1998: 530]).[45] As we have already seen in chapter 2 above, this is an Old Testament way of saying, 'handed over to God's wrath'.

Jesus was mocked, again a concrete form of experiencing God's wrath. He had previously spoken of his coming death as a baptism, and as a cup to be drunk; both images refer to God's wrath. Death itself is the manifestation of God's wrath, especially death by crucifixion.

What of the cry of dereliction? Jesus is forsaken, because, like the psalmist, his Father leaves him to endure this affliction rather than saving him out of it. He would not be forsaken if God chose to rescue him.[46] But is this cry of dereliction an extra experience of the wrath of

---

[45] It may also lie behind Caiaphas' fear that the Romans may come and take their nation away because of the trouble caused by Jesus (John 11:48).

[46] Lull (1985: 10) calls it a 'cry of protest': 'Jesus prays for God to do something, to prevent what was about to happen; then Jesus protests when God does nothing. So God could be blamed, at least indirectly, for the crucifixion of Jesus.' The latter 'theodicy', however, should be disregarded. God (Father, Son, Spirit) is entirely responsible for the crucifixion, for it is central to his plans. Lull writes from a perspective akin to process theology, arguing that God is limited by the contingencies of human beings and that he could not prevent the crucifixion. Nevertheless, he accepted it, which suggests 'that God

God, above and beyond the concrete expressions of God's wrath that Jesus has been left to endure?

Often, at this point, the language of 'separation' is introduced to explain the cry. In the Scriptures, spatial metaphors of separation are often used to picture the wrath of God (e.g. Gen. 3:23; Matt. 25:41; Luke 16:26; Rev. 21:27; 22:15). The language of relational separation is also quite frequently employed (e.g. 'far off', God 'hides his face', 'depart from me', 'I never knew you', etc.). In addition, English translations of 2 Thessalonians 1:9 have implied that God's wrath is equivalent to being 'away from the presence of the Lord'. Despite its frequent repetition in commentaries, however, this understanding is almost certainly misguided, and the underlying Greek prepositional phrase ought to be taken as providing, not a further definition of eternal punishment, but the source from which this justice comes, namely 'from the face of God'.[47] Far from implying the absence of God in punishment, this verse therefore speaks of the active *presence* of God in punishment.[48]

Since God's wrath is often pictured as 'separation', this language is often used in popular parlance to speak of the death of Jesus. The only possible support that the rest of the New Testament offers for this interpretation is found in a textual variant of Hebrews 2:9b, which reads *chōris*, 'apart from', instead of *charis*, 'grace', yielding, 'apart from God, he might taste death for everyone'. Although this may be early evidence for the interpretation of Jesus' death as 'separation from God', the reading is probably not what the writer to the Hebrews originally wrote.[49]

---

takes suffering into the divine self' (p. 8) and so that 'God's self is affected by Christ's death' (p. 11). This conclusion is true, but the assumptions behind it and argument that leads to it can be disputed.

[47] Commentaries often draw upon Isa. 2:10 to argue for a spatial separation. The meaning of the sentence, however, derives from the combination of the preposition with its verb. The sense of separation in Isaiah comes from the fact that people were told to 'hide from' the Lord. In 2 Thess. 1:9, the Lord is the one giving justice, and so the preposition refers to the source of the justice. For a recent commentator who interprets in this direction, see G. L. Green 2002.

[48] This has proved distasteful to many, both ancient and modern. See further Bolt 2000.

[49] See discussion in Hughes 1977: *in loc* and Elliott 1972; Elliott accepts the variant, as do Weinandy (2000: 217 n. 6) and Zuntz (1953, following von Harnack). Elliot argues that Jesus is separated from God because he entered death, which, according to Old Testament thought, is a domain in which God is not found. This is true, but this then underlines just how amazing – and scandalous– is the gospel message that proclaims that God not only became not just flesh (John 1:14) but mortal flesh (cf. Rom. 8:3), and not only that the Son of God took on mortal flesh, but that he went as far as dying, even by means of the cross (Phil. 2:5–6).

In view of this fairly common way of speaking about Jesus' death, then before we continue to answer the wrath question, we must ask a more important one. What does this cry say about God? Has the Son has been 'separated' from the Father?[50]

The cry of dereliction and God

The Trinity to the cross

If we take as our starting point the doctrine of the Trinity, two important parameters are set for our thinking about the cry of dereliction. First, there is only one God, and God is one. This affirmation was one of the points that worried the Arians. They asked, 'How can he be the one Word of the Father, without whom the Father never was ... who said upon the cross, "My God, my God, why hast thou forsaken me?"' (see Athanasius, *Apologia contra Arianos* 3.27). Their solution was, of course, to deprive Christ of full deity.

But there is only one God, and this saying cannot be explained in such a way as to threaten this reality. And God is one. That is, Father, Son and Spirit, are united together and cannot be divided or opposed or set one against another.[51] There *is* no separation of the persons. In fact, it is the union between Father and Son that makes the cry of dereliction so terribly profound.[52]

The orthodox discussion of Christology provides a second parameter. The *Gospel of Peter*'s version of the cry has a docetic view of Christ: 'My Power, my Power, thou hast left me!' (5:19). The power that came upon Jesus in his baptism is perceived as leaving him at the

[50] 'Was this Christ actually abandoned by God at this point? – a conception logically irreconcilable with the doctrine of the Trinity; or did He feel Himself to be so abandoned? – a conception scarcely less difficult to reconcile with orthodox Christology. It is clear even in the framing of such questions that we are in an area where the ordinary categories of human thought and logic are hopelessly inadequate'; Read 1957: 261.

[51] 'We must not ... speak of God punishing Jesus or of Jesus persuading God, for to do so is to set them over against each other as if they acted independently of each other or were even in conflict with each other. We must never make Christ the object of God's punishment or God the object of Christ's persuasion, for both God and Christ were subjects not objects, taking the initiative together to save sinners. Whatever happened on the cross in terms of "God-forsakenness" was voluntarily accepted by both in the same holy love which made atonement necessary'; Stott 1986: 151.

[52] 'The experience of Christ is an experience of Godforsakenness, a Godforsakenness given its unique depth *because* of the experience of the union between Jesus Christ and God the Father, an experience of union which forms the eternal backdrop against which the drama of the cross is played out. At the cross we glimpse the mystery of God's differentiation in union and union in differentiation'; Jinkins & Reid 1997: 36–37; cf. 1998: 143; Jungel 1983: 361.

crucifixion. This, too, however, is unacceptable. The Son of God is at one and the same time both God and Man, two natures in one united person. Whatever we say about the cry of dereliction, we must not divide up the Son. It is not as if the human Jesus is crying in despair while the divine Son of God rejoices in his future vindication.[53] This cry of dereliction is a cry from Jesus of Nazareth who was God the Son.

The cross to the Trinity

Such parameters are a definite guide to our thinking about Jesus' last words. However, our task here is to try to understand the cross in Mark's presentation. This means that our direction of travel should not be from the Trinity to the cross,[54] but from the cross to the Trinity. How does Mark help us to understand the cry of dereliction, and so the larger questions about God?

The task of theology is to attempt to provide coherence to the data of God's revelation. This means that the scriptural data limit the kind of theological speculations being made, and it also means that theological thought is always *post hoc*, always after the event of the crucifixion. This requires theologians to live in a degree of epistemological tension, and some have been better at displaying this kind of theological method than others. Barth, for example, concludes: 'It is not for us to speak of a contradiction and rift in the being of God, but to learn to correct our notions of the being of God, to reconstitute them in the light of the fact that He does this' (i.e. acts in Jesus Christ; *CD* IV.1: 186).

In this book I have attempted to adopt this stance, arguing that it is in the very historical details of the crucifixion as recorded by Mark that its theological significance is to be found. In the end, the cross displays 'God with us', but how does it do this?

God with us

The scandal of the cross

Our enquiry begins with the man, Jesus, dying under the wrath of God. Certainly this would be clearly proclaimed by his death upon a Roman cross. To die in such a way was an unambiguous sign to

[53] From scholasticism to modern times, some have explained the saying according to two spheres in the soul of Christ, allowing him to experience abandonment and joy at the same time.

[54] For an exploration from this direction, see Thompson 2004.

anyone in the ancient world, Jew or Gentile, that he had died under the curse of God (Hengel 1977). The Greco-Roman world shuddered at the thought of crucifixion. The fact that the body of the crucified person was so marred probably indicated that his soul was impure as well. The crucified person had no hope in the afterlife,[55] and, being brutally killed without proper burial, ran a high risk of spending eternity as an unhappy ghost with no proper rest for his soul. Someone who departed this world on a cross died under divine wrath.

The Jews agreed. Deuteronomy 21:22–23 taught that anyone who was hanged on a tree was accursed by God. The discovery of 4QpNah among the Dead Sea scrolls has reinforced what we find in the New Testament, namely that, on the basis of this law, to be crucified was regarded as dying under God's curse (Fitzmyer 1998: 136–137).[56]

When the passers-by and the chief priests call upon Jesus to come down from the cross (15:30, 32),[57] they hint at the inappropriateness of a cross for the Messiah. If Jesus died under the curse, he cannot be the Messiah. Alternatively, if Jesus was the Messiah, he would not allow himself to be crucified. But Mark's story has already prepared us for this moment. As we have seen, the details of the passion predictions and the events of the passion narrative themselves, when read against Old Testament expectations, indicate that Jesus, as the servant of the Lord, would be placed under God's wrath.

His Godforsakenness must also be seen as a concrete event in human history. In the Psalms, the experience of being forsaken is aligned with not being saved. If the psalmist is left to endure his suffering, he cries out because God has turned his face away, God is far away, and he is enduring God's wrath. He prays that God will turn his face towards him, that he will come close, that he will save him. In other words, the wrath of God is found in the concrete historical circumstances that cause the psalmist pain.

So, too, with the crucifixion. Jesus endured the cross, with all its

---

[55] Cf. the story of the underworld journey related in a second century papyrus; as a man sat at the shores of ugliness, 'stretched around there lay a vast plain, full of corpses of dreadful doom, beheaded or crucified. Above the ground stood pitiable bodies, their throats but lately cut. Others, again, impaled, hung like the trophies of a cruel destiny. The Furies, crowned with wreaths, were laughing at the miserable manner of the corpses' death'; Page 1941: no. 94).

[56] On analogy, 4QpNahum probably recognizes the wrath of God against the Pharisees in the action of Alexander Janneus, who crucified 800 of their number (Josephus *Antiquities* 13.14.2; cf. *Jewish War* 1.4, 5–6). So Yadin 1971: 10–12, endorsed by Fitzmyer 1998: 132.

[57] In Chariton's story (see above, ch. 2 n. 14), Chaereas was spared at the moment of being crucified (with fourteen others).

humiliation. Throughout his ordeal, His Father chose not to rescue him from any of this suffering. Despite his request in the garden of Gethsemane, because he was the servant, it was the Lord's will to crush him (Isa. 53:10; cf. vv. 4–6). As Jesus had predicted, the Father struck down the shepherd and the sheep were scattered. Throughout the entire process, the Father stays his rescuing hand, so that the servant will endure the wrath of God for the many.

Son of God

The next step in our examination of the details of Mark's story is to notice that, when Jesus of Nazareth is hanging dead on a cross, and so supremely lying under the wrath of God, the centurion declared, 'Surely this man was the Son of God' (15:39). What a paradox this is! The centurion would have known that the same expression was applied to Roman rulers, but, whatever he may have meant, the wider norms of the story cause the reader to hear his words as a confession of Jesus as *the* Son of God.[58]

Ruler

The inarticular expression *huios theou* is regularly applied to Augustus on coins and in other inscriptions and documents. Since Julius Caesar had been divinized after his death, and Augustus was his adopted son, it was logical that Augustus began to use the title 'son of God'. His successors kept the Augustan mythology alive by continuing to proclaim his divine sonship. When the centurion cried, 'Surely this man was the Son of God', this was a remarkable usage indeed. He was taking a revered and exalted title that belonged only to Augustus, and applying it to the crucified man who had just breathed his last there in front of him. He can only be saying, '*This* man, not Caesar, is the Son of God!'[59] – this *crucified* man. In Mark, Jesus is portrayed as a rival to Caesar, and especially to the great Caesar Augustus[60] – the *crucified* Jesus.

[58] 'Whenever it [*huios theou*] is used, it appears to speak of the unique position of Jesus in relation to God and so warrant the use of the definite article'; Bligh 1968–9: 52.

[59] 'It is left to a pagan soldier, a centurion, the backbone of the Roman army, from whom utter loyalty was demanded, who stands looking upward at the lacerated corpse of a Galilean peasant on a Roman gallows, to give the final verdict in the words of [this] imperial title'; Bligh 1968–9: 53.

[60] See Stauffer 1955: ch. 7, which opens: 'The fact that the two most significant figures of history, Augustus and Jesus, appeared in the same generation, was a subject for thought even in the writings of the Fathers. Augustine's *Civitas Dei*, in the last analysis, circles round the foci of Augustus and Jesus. Christian art till the Reformation returned again and again to the same double theme' (p. 90).

Messiah

Dating back as far as God's promises to David in 2 Samuel 7, and mediated through such messianic psalms as Psalm 2, the title 'Son of God' was also a designation of the Jewish Messiah. Peter had declared that Jesus was the Christ (8:29), and at his trial the high priests asked if he was so: 'Are you the Christ?', immediately adding, 'the Son of the Blessed One' (14:61). Jesus was put to death under the equivalent Gentile title, 'The King of the Jews' (15:26). This man under the wrath of God is the Christ of Israel, the Son of God who was the Servant of the Lord, the cursed Christ. But we can go one step further still.

God the Son

The theme of Jesus as the Son of God is a most important one in Mark. At the baptism, the voice from heaven alludes to Psalm 2:7 (Mark 1:11), which sets the scene for this title to be functional, that is, relating to Jesus' role as the Christ/Messiah. There is more to the use of this title, however, for it refers, not just to Jesus' function, his role as Messiah, but also to his person. Of course, Mark assumes that there is only one God, but as the story gets under way he nevertheless portrays Jesus as divine. Jesus explicitly takes divine prerogatives (e.g. he forgives sins, 2:10; and claims to be Lord of the sabbath, 2:28). In many of his miracles he does what only God can do. In the second sea-crossing, he calls himself 'I AM', YHWH's own name (6:50).

But the use of the title 'Son of God' also seems to exceed its functional purpose. It works in concert with the designation of God as 'Father' to describe the warm relationship between the Son and the Father (e.g. 'my beloved son', 1:11, 9:7, cf. 12:6). This relational connection with the Father reaches its climax in the garden of Gethsemane.

Only in Mark's Gospel do we find Jesus actually calling God 'Abba', and he does so on the eve of his crucifixion (see Mark 14:36). Here, at the very moment when God looks to be less than fatherly, Jesus, in calling God 'Abba', acknowledges both that God, despite all appearances, truly is his Father and that, in his obedience to the cross, he is the true Son (see Mark 15:39). This 'Abba', spoken from within the passion, reveals the very depth of the Father's and the Son's subjectivity; that is, that they are who

139

they are only in their complete subjective orientation toward one another. The agony in the garden then supremely illuminates the paternity of the Father and the filiality of the Son.

Now, if 'Abba' can only be spoken in the Spirit (see Gal. 4:6; Rom. 8:15), then it is in the crucifixion that we witness most clearly that eternal bond of love forged in the Spirit between the Father and the Son. Within the crucifixion, at this most severe and radical moment, we behold in time the eternal enactment of the Father being ceaselessly, in the Spirit, the Father of and for the Son, and the Son being always, in the Spirit, the Son of and for the Father (Weinandy 1995: 29–30).

This crucified man, clearly under the wrath of God, is thus declared to be the Son of God, God the Son.[61]

Father, Son and Spirit

The next step is to observe that the Father, Son and Spirit have worked in harmony in leading up to the cross from the beginning of the story. At the baptism (1:11), the Father announced that Jesus was the Son of God and the suffering servant, the Spirit equipped him for his ministry as the servant, and the Son immediately accepted his commissioning as the servant (see Bolt 1991b). From that moment on, the Son sought to do the Father's will, empowered and equipped by the Spirit. Even in Gethsemane, as the hour of apocalyptic darkness began to fall, the Son accepted the Father's will (14:36), strengthened by the Spirit, who was ever willing (14:38). Now, at the death of the servant, the persons of the one God, Father, Son and Spirit, have all reached their united goal. The cross is an act of divine partnership between Father, Son and Spirit (Weston 2001: 153).

The Son of God and God's wrath?

This brings us back to the question of wrath. From our examination of Mark's story of the cross, it seems that we need to bring together two aspects of this cry of dereliction. First, it arises out of concrete circumstances in our world that are instruments of the wrath of God. Secondly, it is a cry from the depths of God. Father and Son and

---

[61] Chronis (1982: 104) points out that the title *basileus Israēl*, ironically on the scoffers' lips in 15:32, is a designation for YHWH in the Septuagint (Zeph. 3:15; Isa. 44:6), but never for the royal Messiah. For an examination of Jesus' divine sonship in the New Testament, see Hengel 1976.

Holy Spirit were in this cry. That is, the cry needs to be heard not only from within the history of humanity, but also from within the history of God himself.[62] The conclusion must be that, in the cross of Christ, God entered into his own wrath. The Judge has been judged in our place (Barth's phrase: *CD* IV.1: 211–283).

In becoming human, the Son 'plac[ed] Himself under the judgement under which man has fallen . . . under the curse of death which rests upon Him. The meaning of the incarnation is plainly revealed in the question of Jesus on the cross, "My God, My God, why have you forsaken me?"' (15:34; Barth, *CD* IV.1: 185).[63] According to Jinkins and Reid (1997: 36), this is a 'strange new step . . . whereby God delivers Godself up to suffering and death at the hands of God's own creatures'. But there is an even stranger new step, because, by delivering himself to his creatures, God delivers himself up to experience his own wrath. Now, what does this tell us about God?

In the cry of dereliction we hear Jesus crying out in solidarity with our own Godforsaken mortality. His death is an inclusive place-taking death, in that he shares the 'flesh and blood' of our mortality. But his death is also an exclusive place-taking death, in that he is the one who dies for the many. In the concrete circumstances of his death, he bore the wrath of God on our behalf, in our place. His death was the ransom that set us free. At the exact moment that he did all this, he was declared to be the Son of God; God the Son, suffering for the many sinners in this world under the shadow of death, in perfect harmony with Father and Spirit; God, experiencing the wrath of God on behalf of the many. If God himself has dealt with his wrath, then the liberation of the sinner will be freedom indeed (cf. Rom. 8:32)!

---

[62] Cf. Jinkins & Reid 1998: 142: 'We should hear this cry of dereliction as a genuine cry of Godforsakenness, in all its terror and radicality, yet that we should hear this cry in the larger context of the full communion of God the Father whose eternal faithfulness remembered from the past and anticipated in the future upholds the forsaken Son in the present (of crucifixion) by the power of the Spirit. When we hear the cry of dereliction, in other words, we hear a cry from within the Trinity, yet a cry grounded in our history.'

[63] It is this view that raises the temptation to propose a conflict in God: 'The more seriously we take this, the stronger becomes the temptation to approximate to the view of a contradiction and conflict in God Himself. Have we not to accept this view if we are to do justice to what God did for man and what He took upon Himself when He was in Christ, if we are to bring out the mystery of His mercy in all its depth and greatness?'

The gods and the crucified God

The traditional gods

By the time of the first century, the traditional gods of Greece and Rome were in something of a decline. The Epicureans had solidly argued that, since the gods were not at all interested in human life, there was little point in worshipping them. Others had realized that the gods could not be relied upon for much help in this world under the shadow of death, and that not even they could overcome the grave and all the problems it caused for the living. We could say that the people felt forsaken by the old gods. The intellectuals, especially, had moved away from the polytheism of the past towards a monotheistic worldview.[64] But this divine monarch was subject to the rational order of the universe. He could not do the impossible. As Pliny put it at roughly the time that Mark's Gospel was entering circulation (AD 60–70; *Naturalis historia* 2.27): 'Not even for God are all things possible ... He cannot cause twice ten not to be twenty, or do other things along similar lines.'

Among these logical impossibilities Pliny also listed another. This was the real problem: 'He cannot bestow eternity on mortals.' Human beings were mortal, and that was that. The traditional gods could not deal with that problem, even if they wanted to do so. Neither could the divine monarch of the Greek intellectual tradition. This was a barrier that could not be crossed, even from the side of the gods. Human beings were forsaken, left to bear the suffering of mortality alone; left to bear the wrath of God that was written into the fabric of our own suffering world.

The newer gods, who walked on earth

With the divinization of Julius Caesar and then Augustus, a new kind of god now walked the earth. Throughout the first century AD the imperial cult was steadily expanding into the Roman provinces, where its civic religion began to structure almost all of life in Caesar's domain. The old gods were domesticated into the new system, often as the Caesar took over the domain of some traditional god or other.

---

[64] Dihle (1982: 3), who points out that the monotheistic tradition of the Greeks goes back as far as Xenophanes (DK B 23–26) and was maintained in classical and post-classical periods (cf. Plato, *Timaeus* 28Aff.; Cleanthes, *SVF* 1:537). Antisthenes (Decleva-Caizzi 1966: fr. 29) taught that there are many gods *kata nomon* ('according to law or custom'), but only one god *kata physin* ('according to nature').

But the Caesars were gods who ruled by force of military might and brutal justice (see Wengst 1987). The Augustan rhetoric proclaimed a new age, life to a world on the brink of death; but in reality Rome left a long trail of blood, and the *Pax Romana* was established and maintained with military muscle; it was 'peace through victory' (Augustus, *Res Gestae* 13).[65] Ultimately, these new gods did not seem to make much of a positive difference to the world under the shadow of death. In fact, the glow of Augustus' new age began to fade even under his next in line, Tiberius. Towards the end of his life a rhyme was composed (see Suetonius 3[Tiberius].59.1):

Caesar, you have changed the golden age,
For as long as you live it will be an iron age.

Despite the rhetoric, the people had been forsaken by the new gods too. As Stauffer comments (1955: 100), 'the dance of death was beginning again, worse than ever before'.

The gods of today's world

The gods of today's world have fared no better. We serve the 'no god' of Money, and yet we still cannot buy our way out of the grave. We run after the god of Pleasure, and yet we know deep down that we 'eat, drink, and be merry' *because* 'tomorrow we die'. We live in a pluralistic, multicultural world, where all the gods must be given a space to live. And yet, as the divine public service multiplies, so does its inefficiency, and people are left forsaken by all of these gods, or any one of them. The civic religion of Rome failed; equally, although western civic religion might appear to be necessary in a secular state, in that state no god really has any power (cf. Judge 1989). Which of them can deliver us from life under the shadow of death?

A Godforsaken world

We still live in a Godforsaken world, where God seems to remain at a distance, unmoved, uncaring, uninvolved, while human suffering continues unabated. The suffering and pain of this world continue to make so many people feel forsaken. Where the symbol of postmodern society is a traffic jam (apparently going somewhere eventually; plenty of people around, but absolutely no personal involvement), loneliness

[65] I note that the 'victory' is in the Latin version, but not the Greek. This text can also be compared with Augustus' boast about the provinces, which 'I reduced to a state of peace' (*eirēnēi katestēsa / flum[inis pacavi]*; *Res Gestae* 26).

and isolation have become a tragic art form. For so many, God seems not to care. And, in fact, this world *is* Godforsaken. Because of our sinfulness, our hardness of heart, our perversity, our strange contradiction in which the creature continues to spurn the loving Creator, we live in a world that is already under the wrath of God (Rom. 1:18ff.). That wrath is all around us in the concrete details of our fallen world. Our mortality reminds us daily that we are reaping the wages of sin, and that we stand under the sentence of death.

But that is why the cross is such world-changing good news! For this is where God has come close.

The cross where God comes close

If Pliny saw that it was impossible for God to bestow immortality upon mortals (*Naturalis historia* 2.27), for him it was equally impossible for the immortal god to become mortal and die. Immortality belonged to the gods and mortality to human beings. But what kind of a god was proclaimed by the Christians? A god who actually died? Worse, a god who died on a cross! Small wonder then that that second-century graffiti artist daubed the walls with his picture of the crucified man with a donkey's head (see above pp. 114–115)! Small wonder that Lucian mocked the Christians as those who 'worship the man who was crucified in Palestine' (*De morte peregrini* 11).[66] What use is a god who allows himself to be put to death, especially death on the cross? Those who mocked Jesus sought to save him this future embarrassment: 'Save yourself and come down from the cross' (v. 30); 'Let this Messiah, the King of Israel, come down from the cross now, so that we may see and believe' (v. 32). That would display his divinity! But to stay there, to die, to become a crucified man? What kind of a god would do that?

But there, on that cross, God entered into solidarity with us human beings in our suffering. In the person of the Son, God took on flesh and blood, and gathered up all our cries of Godforsakenness. And more! He did not simply share our common experience of God-forsakenness in this world under the shadow of death. There, on the cross, in the person of the Son, God himself endured God's wrath – on our behalf! God himself has done the impossible. God paid the

[66] Kern (forthcoming) points out that Lucian probably intends two slights. First, the crucifixion occurred in Palestine and, more particularly, 'Galilean' was an insult – as it most certainly was by the time of Julian, as probably reflected in the forged *Acts of the Council of Antioch* (see Harnack 1904: 97). Cf. Epictetus, *Discourses* 4.7.6, which is often taken to refer to Christians. For the contrary view, see Hengel 58–59. Secondly, they worship a crucified man.

ransom to free us from the judgment of death, and in so doing he bestowed eternal life on us, who are mortal. God poured himself out so that we could be truly free. The hope of resurrection, eternal life in the kingdom of God, is ours!

In the first-century world, conversation about crucifixion generally repelled people. But the message of *this* cross rang out through the ancient world and changed it. In a repulsive cross, which human beings both ancient and modern may wish to put at a distance because of all its shame and horror, God has come close.

Chapter Five

The cross, resurrection and the hope of humanity

Nearly two thousand years ago, Jesus of Nazareth was nailed to a Roman cross. Almost immediately, the new Christian movement sprang into existence, proclaiming a message of 'Christ crucified' (1 Cor. 1:23) and gaining the reputation for worshipping a crucified god. In this book we have been looking at the message of Mark, one of the preachers of that new movement. How did the message of a crucified man change the world?

Mark's denouement: the crucified one is risen

In this final chapter we shall examine Jesus' cross from the perspective of Mark's final scene.

The denouement (15:40 – 16:8) [1]

In terms of Mark's narrative, we have now passed the climax (15:39) and entered the denouement (15:40 – 16:8); that is, the section of the story in which the complications are unravelled and unfinished business is finished. Given the function of the denouement, it is perfectly reasonable that this section will cause us to reflect further upon the climax of Mark's story. In other words, the resurrection ought to inform our understanding of the cross. What do we learn here?

It was most likely on Sunday 5 April, in the year we now know as AD 33, that a group of women, including Mary Magdalene, Mary the

---

[1] There is little doubt that the Gospel of Mark ends with 16:8, despite the differences with the other Gospels and the existence of at least two supplementary endings. It is clear from the considerations of textual criticism that this is the *original* ending, but was it the *intended* ending? There is nothing impossible about ending a sentence (cf. Gen. 18:15; 45:3), or a whole book (See *BAGD* 151b 1.a; van der Horst 1972: 121–124; Danove 1993: 128–129) with *gar*. N. T. Wright (2003: 617–624) argues that it is not the intended ending, as does France (2002: 673, 683) – the latter largely because he finds the subtlety of the literary explanations a little too postmodern for his liking. For cogent literary arguments to the contrary, see Lightfoot 1950e; Boomershine & Bartholomew 1981.

mother of James, and Salome (16:1),[2] came to complete his proper burial.[3] On the Friday just past, these women had gazed upon the crucified Jesus from a distance (15:40). They watched until they saw where his body had been buried (15:47). Now it was Sunday morning, and they arrived at the graveside.

Although the event has been recounted for almost two thousand years, their discovery that morning still shocks and amazes us as we stand at our great distance, contemplating the cross of Christ. They had been worried about who would help them roll away the huge stone that lay across the entrance of the tomb in which the body lay (16:2), but found that it was already rolled back (16:4). No doubt after some hesitation and discussion, the women entered the tomb (16:5).[4] They found a young man, sitting on the right, dressed in white. And then, in one of the greatest understatements of all time, Mark reports: 'and they were alarmed' (NRSV).

The crucified one is risen (16:6)

In particular, this chapter seeks to illuminate the momentous fact revealed to them by this young man in the tomb. 'He said to them, "Do not be alarmed; you are looking for Jesus of Nazareth, who was

[2] Matthew mentions the two Marys (Matt. 28:1), but not Salome. Luke does not initially name any of the women, simply calling them 'the women who had come with him from Galilee' (Luke 23:55, NRSV), but later names the women who reported the empty tomb to the apostles: Mary Magdalene, Joanna, Mary the mother of James, and the other women (Luke 24:10). John mentions only Mary Magdalene, focusing on her story (John 20:1–18).

[3] Although the crucified may not have normally been buried at all, concessions may have been made for the Jews, given that their law forbade leaving bodies hanging up after sunset (Deut. 21:22–23), even the bodies of their enemies (cf. Josh. 8:29; 10:26–27). References in Qumran and Josephus indicate that these sensibilities continued into the first century (see Fitzmyer 1998: 133), and the Romans tended to make concessions to local custom. Joseph of Arimathea may have been the member of the Sanhedrin appointed to ensure the fulfilment of the law. Jewish literature indicates that criminals were not refused burial, but were buried for an initial period in a separate place (see Buchler 1903; Krauss 1934–5). Once this period was over, a secondary burial would take place. This may be confirmed by the fact that the skeleton of Yehoanan, a twenty-five-year-old man crucified in the first century, was discovered in an ossuary, since this indicates a secondary burial – even if we have no evidence of where the first burial took place (see Haas 1973: 49–59; Yadin 1973). For Roman concessions, we should note Philo, In Flaccum 10.83–84, who complains that Flaccus had reversed the earlier Roman practice in Egypt, which allowed the crucified to be taken down and buried by their kinsfolk on the eve of a Roman holiday. Did the Romans make similar concessions in Judea?

[4] France (2002: 678) points out that this 'begins to create a sense of superhuman agency in the narrative'. This is continued by the discovery of the young man in white, and the women's terror.

crucified. He has been raised; he is not here. Look, there is the place they laid him" ' (16:6, NRSV). This announcement has echoed through all lands and across time, with a volume that has not diminished. The one who was crucified has been raised from the dead. The one who has been raised is the one who was crucified.

Everything in Mark's story so far has led up to the moment when Jesus hung on the cross, under a sign that declared him to be the king of the Jews. At that very point he was declared to be the Son of God by a Gentile centurion. The final scene in the Gospel invites us to reflect on the crucifixion in the light of the startling fact that this crucified Son of God has now risen from the dead.

This chapter will attempt to underline the enormous significance of this fact by contrasting Jesus' resurrection with other options available in the ancient world, especially that of *apotheosis*, the belief that a human being could become a god.

The Son of Man is risen!

This final scene in Mark's story draws together several important subplots that have been featured throughout the narrative.

Fulfilment of narrative expectations

Straightforward predictions

Jesus has already predicted in a straightforward manner that the Son of Man would suffer and die, but that after this he would rise again from the dead (8:31; 9:9; 9:31; 10:34; 14:28). This was the resurrection language of Daniel 12:1–2, and so Jesus' predictions would have evoked the expectation of the general resurrection at the end of time.[5] Now, an individual man has risen from the dead.

Apocalyptic predictions

Jesus has also used apocalyptic predictions. He had persistently referred to himself as the Son of Man, that figure who, according to Daniel 7:13–14, would be given the kingdom of God. This kingdom seems to have been getting closer as Mark's story has progressed. Jesus began by saying that the kingdom of God had drawn near (1:15). He spoke of the urgent need to enter the resurrection harvest, because the

---

[5] N. T. Wright (1992: 320–334; 2003: 181, 628), rightly shows that 'resurrection' for the Jews in the first century would have meant the general resurrection at the end of time.

148

kingdom would suddenly interrupt ordinary life (4:26–29) and would encompass the whole earth (4:30–32). Once he began to speak explicitly of his death, he also described the kingdom as being so close that it would come with power even before some of his hearers died (9:1). The only thing left to happen before the great day of resurrection and the coming of the kingdom was the suffering of the Son of Man (9:11–13). And now, the Son of Man has suffered, and he has risen from the dead.

Since in Daniel it was the son of man who would receive this kingdom, it is no surprise that Jesus also looked forward to the imminent coming of the Son of Man. From the beginning of Mark, the expectation of the coming of the Son of Man has been getting more and more intense (8:38 – 9:1; 14:28). Just before the passion narrative began, Jesus stated that the coming would follow the destructive sacrilege and the greatest distress of all time, and, once the Son of Man had come, the kingdom itself would appear (13:29).[6]

The moment has arrived

By interweaving the straightforward predictions of the resurrection and the apocalyptic predictions of the coming of the Son of Man, the narrative forces both sets of predictions to coalesce in the reader's mind. They are speaking of the same event. When we come to Mark 16, this event, predicted so often, has finally arrived.

The significance of this moment

The vindication of the innocent

Although Mark does not make much of it, the resurrection of Christ is a vindication of his innocence. The human courts treated Jesus as a sinner, condemned him to death and handed him over to the wrath of God. His resurrection, however, is a concrete event in human history that announces to the world that the human courts were wrong and that Jesus died as an innocent man.[7] This confirms that he was the obedient Son. His obedience is a crucial factor in the salvation of humanity (cf. 3:31–35; 14:36).

---

[6] The subject of *engys estin* ('is near') should be taken to be the kingdom (cf. 1:15), rather than the Son of Man.
[7] This is a theme in the book of Acts; see 2:23–24, 32, 36–37; 3:13–15; 4:10–12; 5:30–31; 7:52–53; 13:27–28.

The exaltation of the servant

From his baptism through to the cross, Jesus acted as the obedient servant of the Lord. In the final servant song (Isa. 52:13 – 53:12) God promises that the servant will be vindicated because of his willingness to die as the one for the many.

> See, my servant shall prosper;
>> he shall be exalted and lifted up,
>> and shall be very high ...
>
> Out of his anguish *he shall see light*;
> he shall find satisfaction through his knowledge.
>> The righteous one, my servant, shall make many righteous,
>> and he shall bear their iniquities.
> *Therefore I will allot him a portion with the great,*
>> *and he shall divide the spoil with the strong*;
> because he poured out himself to death,
>> and was numbered with the transgressors;
> yet he bore the sin of many,
>> and made intercession for the transgressors.
>> (Isaiah 52:13; 53:11–12, NRSV, italics added)

The resurrection is the vindication of the servant. According to Isaiah 53, this means that his sacrifice on behalf of the many has achieved what it was meant to achieve; that is, the justification of the many! The resurrection of Jesus is a sign that justification has now arrived in the world.[8]

The coming of the Son of Man

As we have seen, following Lightfoot's observations, the passion narrative is built upon the expectation of the coming of the Son of Man. The narrative has quietly but surely presented the moments in which the Son of Man could have been expected, according to the parable of the doorkeeper (13:35). They have all apparently passed by: the last supper in the evening; Gethsemane at midnight; the Jewish trial and Peter's denial at cockcrow; the Roman trial at dawn. Yet, at the end of the crucifixion account, there has been no coming of

---

[8] I suggest that this is also the structure behind Rom. 4:25. The *dia* signifies the 'because' of Isa. 53:12. He was raised because of our justification, that is, because he was willing do die as a ransom for many so that the many could be justified.

the Son of Man, no arrival of the kingdom. This is reinforced by the burial scene, in which Joseph of Arimathea, who places Jesus' corpse in the tomb, is said to be 'waiting expectantly for the kingdom of God' (15:43, NRSV). In a sense, it does not matter what this meant for Joseph himself (see Brown 1998). In terms of its function in the narrative, this verse tells us that the kingdom of God has not yet arrived. The king has been announced, but as yet there is no kingdom come in power. The king was revealed to be a crucified man, a dead man, a buried man. As yet, there is no resurrection, no coming of the Son of Man, no kingdom.

Then, in Mark's closing chapter, we have another dawn. The reference to the time is repeated, to signal to the reader what is going on. A fulfilment is about to occur. The women arrive at the tomb (16:2) 'very early' (*lian prōi*, cf. 13:35), 'after the sun had risen' (*anateilantos tou hēliou*). At this moment, this final apocalyptic scene completes Mark's 'history in the apocalyptic mode',[9] with the declaration, 'He is risen!'

As the foretaste of the exaltation, the resurrection is Mark's way of indicating that the Son of Man has now come to the Ancient of Days.[10] The Son of Man has come and, in fulfilment of Psalm 110:2, is now seated at the right hand of God, installed as Lord (14:62; cf. 12:35–37).

The kingdom come in power

This means that he has also received from the Ancient of Days authority over the kingdom of God, and this will now last for ever. This was the moment to which Jesus had looked forward when he said, 'Truly I tell you, there are some standing here who will not taste death until they see that the kingdom of God has come with power' (9:1, NRSV).

In Jesus' victory over death the kingdom of God comes with power – at least in his case. The world has now seen a resurrection from the dead. The great resurrection day has begun. By this powerful event Jesus himself entered the kingdom of God, and he did so as the

---

[9] A. Y. Collins 1992a, and cf. N. T. Wright's view (1992: 390–396; 2003: 620) that Mark is an apocalypse, pointing to the series of revelatory moments (1:10–11; 8:29; 9:7; 14:61; 15:39). Wright does not understand 'apocalyptic' material in the same way as others; see 1992: ch. 10.

[10] Lightfoot 1950e: 93, drawing upon Dodd (unsourced), notes that the oldest tradition seems to have connected the exaltation more immediately with the resurrection.

glorious Son of Man, who has the position of authority. His coming to his position of authority will have implications for the rest of God's people, for he was the one who died and rose for the many. As Paul will put it, Jesus, the firstfruits from the dead, guarantees the rest of the resurrection harvest (see 1 Cor. 15).

The beginning of the gospel

This is also the beginning of the gospel mission. When they were coming down from the mount of transfiguration, Jesus asked for silence until the Son of Man had risen from the dead (9:9). Now that he had risen, the time for silence is over. In the sequence of events outlined by Jesus' apocalyptic discourse, the great distress would be followed by the coming of the Son of Man, who would then send out his angels to gather the elect from the four corners of the earth (13:27). Now this moment has arrived. The last-days mission to the nations has begun. The young man told the women to go to the disciples and tell them that Jesus would go before them to Galilee (16:7), just as he had promised in the 'mini-apocalyptic discourse' (14:28). This occurrence not only implies the restoration of the disciples after they had deserted Jesus at his hour of need, but also holds promise for the launch of the Gentile mission.[11]

The silence of the women after the young man's command (16:8) is an intriguing feature of this scene, especially since Mark's Gospel closes with these silent, fearful women, who really should have been speaking at this momentous time. The best explanation of Mark's final verse, in my opinion, has been given by Boomershine and Bartholomew (1981). The women's action is plainly wrong. Rather than being silent from fear, they should have been speaking out of faith in this time of mission. But the story portrays these women with great sympathy; so much so that it is impossible for the reader to condemn them. The combination of an action that is clearly wrong and a strong sympathy for the women throws the ending over to the readers,[12] inviting them to repent when they fall into the same trap as the women. Even if fear causes silence, the reader knows that the

[11] See e.g. Senior 1984: 153–158. The proposed journey to Galilee is not for the parousia – as promoted by E. Lohmeyer, R. H. Lightfoot and W. Marxsen (see Marxsen 1969: ch. 2).
[12] It is now fairly usual to speak of the open-endedness that throws Mark's final scene over to the audience for completion. See e.g. Danove 1993: 208–210; Tolbert 1989: 297–299.

story must still be told. The Son of Man has come, it is time to announce the gospel to the ends of the earth, despite our fear.[13] Now this has all happened. A man has risen from the dead. No: more, the Son of God has risen from the dead. The Son of Man has come. The kingdom of God has arrived with power. The last-days mission to the nations has been launched. What an ending to Mark's story! What a moment!

To help us to appreciate the tremendous significance of this event a little more, the next part of the chapter will contrast what actually happened with some other alternatives on offer in the thinking of the ancient world. As they heard Mark's story, the early readers would naturally compare and contrast Jesus' resurrection with these other options that existed in the cultural repertoire of the first century.

The empty tomb: what happened to the body?

Mark tells us that the women came to a tomb in which Jesus' body had previously been laid (15:42–47), but, when they got there, they found the tomb empty.

A lost body?

Some have suggested that the disappearance of the body should be read as a signal either that Jesus had become a hero, or that he had been translated.[14] Although it is possible only to summarize the evidence here, I have argued at greater length elsewhere (Bolt 1996) that Mark's account fits neither of these options.

Hero?

In the ancient world, heroes, valiant people who perform great deeds, were often worshipped at their graveside. Those who had fallen in battle a long way from home often received worship at a specially constructed 'cenotaph' (i.e. an 'empty grave', *kenos taphos*). Does this empty tomb at the end of Mark suggest that he was a hero?[15] No. The hero cult required the body of the hero to be in the grave, for his

---

[13] On this reading of the ending, Mark 1:1 acts as a title to the whole work and indicates that Mark's Gospel is to anchor the gospel mission in the events of Jesus Christ. Cf. Räisänen 1990: 210; and Hickinbotham 1944: 65; they also suggest that 1:1 assumes that the gospel is already known and being proclaimed. It may be of some support to note that all the spurious endings of Mark (the shorter, the longer, and the Freer logion) contain a reference to the beginning of the mission.

[14] Bickermann 1924; Hamilton 1965; A. Y. Collins 1992c; 1995.

[15] As suggested by Bickermann (1924); Hamilton (1965); A. Y. Collins (1992c; 1995).

power was localized around that site. When an 'empty grave' was used, when the hero was known to have died elsewhere, making his body inaccessible, it was erected to do service for the cult as if the body were there.[16] Whereas these 'empty tombs' were known to have been always empty (by definition), Mark's narrative stresses that Jesus' body used to be there, but has now gone; it is an *emptied* tomb.[17] His post-death presence was not localized at the gravesite, as was the case for a hero, for Jesus had promised that he would meet his disciples in Galilee. This is not a story of Jesus' inauguration as a hero.[18]

Translation?

There were also stories about certain great ones who were taken bodily into heaven. Even the Old Testament has two such stories, in the assumptions of Enoch (Gen. 5:24) and Elijah (2 Kgs 2; Palmer 1976: 120),[19] and the Greco-Roman world had its own examples as well. Is the empty tomb a sign of Jesus' translation to heaven,[20] or, to

[16] Thucydides (2.34.3) reports a similar practice: during the *ekphora* for those who had fallen in war, the Athenians 'carried one empty bier for the missing whose bodies could not be found for burial'.

[17] Since the perfective aspect was utilized for the state consequent on an action (McKay 1994: 27, 31; Wallace 1996: 572), we could coin a term and say that it was a *kekenōmenos taphos*, a 'having been emptied and remaining empty tomb'.

[18] It seems odd to argue that 'the focus on the tomb in Mark may have been inspired by the importance of the graves of the heroes in the Graeco-Roman world. Even if the location of the tomb of Jesus was unknown to the author of Mark, and even if there were no cultic observances at the site of the tomb, it would still be important as a *literary* motif in characterising Jesus as hero-like'; A. Y. Collins 1995: 93. If it is a *literary* motif, why is there nothing in Mark's account to suggest a hero cult, and why, in fact, are there features that deny it? In terms of actuality, if the tomb was unknown, and if there was no cult, then there is nothing here either to indicate that Jesus was a hero. It was the cult given at a tomb that made a hero a hero!

[19] Note that Palmer classifies two kinds of assumptions in Jewish Christian literature: first, the taking up of notable figures, especially as the honorific conclusion to a righteous life (Gen. 5:24; Wisdom of Solomon 4:10–11; Sirach 44:16; 48:9; cf. *Gospel of Peter* 5:19; *2 Enoch* 18 [Vaillant] or 67:1–2 [Charles]; cf. interpolation in k [Codex Bobiensis] after Mark 16:3; see Palmer 1976) secondly, 'apocalyptic type', where someone is taken up to heaven temporarily to converse with heavenly figures (*1 Enoch* 39.3ff.; 70–71; *Testament of Levi* 2–5; *3 Baruch*; *Ascension of Isaiah* 7–11); see Mark 9:2–9.

[20] Bultmann (1963: 290) argued that there was no distinction between the resurrection and the ascension in the early days, but the empty tomb does not presuppose an immediate ascension. N. T. Wright (2003: 625–626) offers some critique. Some argue for an ascension directly from the cross (A. Y. Collins 1992c: 147) on the basis of *Gospel of Peter* 5:19 and the addition after Mark 16:3 in Codex Bobiensis. However, this would not be a bodily assumption, but an ascent of the soul (D. A. Smith 2003: 129).

use a synonymous term, of his bodily assumption to heaven?[21] No, for Mark is not narrating a translation story. The stories of people who disappeared, having been translated to another location (be it to some place on or under the earth, or to heaven), did not usually feature tombs – let alone empty ones – because translation avoided death altogether (Bolt 1996: 34).

Once again, these stories do not compare favourably with Mark's account, in which Jesus very definitely dies (in fact, he is crucified), and is buried. His supposed 'translation' occurs far too late, after he has presumably been in the underworld for a period of three days. The young man did not announce Jesus had become a hero, nor that he had been translated; still less an aberrant mixture of the two;[22] but rather that 'he is risen' (*ēgerthē*).[23] What would this mean for Mark's Greco-Roman readers?

Before exploring this further, we should also note another option in the first-century cultural memory.

A left body?

Bodies and shades

The translation stories assumed an older view of the nature of human life. In Homeric tradition, real life was bodily life, and the afterlife could not properly be called 'life' at all (Rohde 1925: 4, 9). Normally, at death, the 'soul' flitted away from the body because its sinews were no longer able to hold the flesh and bones together (*Odyssey* 11.218ff.; cf. *Iliad* 23.97ff.), and went to the afterlife as a shade, not as a body (cf. *Iliad* 1.3–5; *Odyssey* 11; Riley 1995: 29). When the

[21] A. Y. Collins 1995: 88; D. A. Smith 2003: 130, 125. Perkins (1995: 730) argues that if the transfiguration account, with the appearance of Moses and Elijah, provides the key to this episode, then 'Jesus has been translated to heaven just as they were'. (For a brief critique, see N. T. Wright 2003: 625–626.) She also mentions that Mark's readers may have known the story of the emperor who was translated into heaven from the funeral pyre. It is correct to read the transfiguration and resurrection account in terms of translation stories, but there are also differences in both accounts. In the transfiguration, Moses and Elijah appear on earth with Jesus. So too, here, the angel is in the tomb. He plays the role of an apocalyptic interpreter of the event (N. T. Wright 2003: 629). Both of these instances involve, not someone entering heaven, but, in fact, someone from heaven 'coming down' to the earthly realm.
[22] The hero was distinguished from those who have been translated; see Rohde 1925: 121; Bolt 1996: 34–36.
[23] This is not the language of translation, as even Bickermann (1924: 286) admitted. Narratives used a range of language to refer to translations, e.g. the notion of disappearing, or becoming invisible (*aphaniz-*) is frequent; if divinization was involved, the *apotheōs-* or *ektheiōs-* groups can be used; phrases expressing the changed location also occur ('from among men' / 'to among the gods'). Cf. Pease 1942.

privileged few, by contrast, were granted immortality in the myths –
being translated to immortality,[24] or to a special region on the edge
of the world (the Elysian fields,[25] Oceanus,[26] or the Isles of the
Blessed[27]), or even to subterranean regions, separate from Hades[28] –
because they had avoided death altogether, their immortality took
bodily form.[29] Thus 'translations' were also bodily.

Body and soul

Between Homer and Plato this conception changed: the soul was
derived from the upper world, and was set in opposition to the body
(Riley 1995: 29). *Orphism* linked the soul and the air; the soul came
from *to holon*, 'the whole', was borne by the winds, and entered the
body through breathing (Aristotle, *De anima* 410[b]28). At death, the
soul abides in the air, but the body returns to the earth, an idea that
reverberates through literature and inscription.[30] With such beliefs
about the fate of the body at death, how would Greco-Roman readers
have heard the story of the empty tomb?

The apotheosis of virtuous souls

It had long been believed that the virtuous person's death was
somehow different from that of others. Pythagorean philosophy,
propagated by Plato and his followers, spoke of the soul as something
divine. Death was the separation of the soul from the body (e.g. Plato,

[24] Calypso wishes to do so for Odysseus (*Odyssey* 5.135–136; 209–210; 23.335–336).
Odysseus is rescued from the sea by Ino Leucothea, who used to be mortal (*Odyssey*
5.333ff.) – had she been carried away by a god (cf. *Odyssey* 6.280–281)? Ganymede was
similarly carried off (*Iliad* 20.232ff.). Eos bore off the beautiful Orion (*Odyssey* 5.122ff.;
cf. the story of Cleitos, 15.249–250).
[25] Menelaus is informed of the Elysian plain, where Rhadamanthys already dwells
(*Odyssey* 4.560ff.).
[26] To where Penelope wishes to be transported, *Odyssey* 20.61–65; 79ff.
[27] The realm of Hesiod's fourth race, the heroes (*Works and Days* 170ff.).
[28] Rohde (1925: ch. 3) mentions Amphiaraus, Trophonius, Caineus, Althaimenes,
Amphilochus, Laodice and Aristaius. Erechtheus, Hyacinthus and Asclepius are
examples of ancient gods living beneath the earth, whose subterranean dwelling
becomes the 'grave' of their later hero worship.
[29] The post-Homeric poems increased the number of translations: in the *Cypria*
Artemis immortalizes Iphigeneia in the land of the Taurians; the *Aithiopis* has Eos
giving immortality to Memnon, who had been killed by Achilles (by contrast with the
Iliad story, which had Sleep and Death bear off the body of Sarpedon to his own
country for burial), and Thetis carrying the body of Achilles from the funeral pyre and
bringing him to Leuke (contrast *Odyssey* 24.47ff.); in the *Telegoneia*, Odysseus is made
immortal after being slain by Circe, and they dwell over the sea.
[30] E.g. Euripides, *Supplices* 531–536; *IG* I/2: 945.6; *CIL* 6384; Peek, 1960: 353:2ff.
(1st/2nd century AD); Jubilees 23:22; Seneca, *Ad Helviam* 11.7; Philostratus, *Vita
Apollonii* 8.31.

Phaedo 64c), at which time impure souls were subject to reincarnation; that is, they were joined once again to a body. This was undesirable to the Pythagoreans and those influenced by them, who spoke of the body as 'the prison-house of the soul'.[31] The pure soul, by contrast, returned to the realms from which it originally came. It went back to the divine. To this degree, therefore, a good person could hope to become a god, in that his soul, if pure, could return to the gods and never have to face the terrors of bodily life again. It is a small step from this to the idea that someone of great virtue would join the gods in a special sense (cf. Cicero, *De re publica* 2.17; Sirach 45:4–5 [Moses]).[32]

This belief in apotheosis from virtue is also reflected in Jewish writings. In the Septuagint account of Enoch (Gen. 5:22–24, *euērestēsen tōi theōi*, twice, changing MT's *wayithalēk*), which is then transformed by Sirach (44:16) into a paradigm of repentance.[33] When Mattathias addressed his sons before he died (1 Maccabees 2:49ff.), urging them towards zeal for the law, he listed others who had been so zealous (Abraham, Joseph, Phinehas, Joshua, Caleb, David), and then (1 Maccabees 2:58) claimed that 'Elijah, because of his great zeal for the law, was taken up into heaven' (NRSV; *Elias en tōi zēlōsai zēlon nomou anelēmphthē eis ton ouranon*).

Cicero had reported that it was the virtue of Romulus that gave rise to the story of his translation (*De re publica* 1.25; 2.17), and the virtue of the rulers was also a presupposition of their apotheosis.[34] The Stoic philosopher, Seneca, wrote a satire in response to Nero's deification of Claudius in AD 54. This play, as well as the *Panegyricus* of Pliny (AD 100), shows that 'virtue alone entitled the emperor to a place in heaven'.[35] Plutarch considered the connection between virtue and apotheosis to be not only good sense, but, given his view of the soul, *kata physin* ('according to nature'; Plutarch, *Romulus* 28.7–8).

Unlike the older mythological translations, apotheosis involved, not the body, but only the soul. The funeral pyre was said to burn

---

[31] See e.g. the quotations from the Stoics Cicero and Seneca cited below, p. 158.

[32] Cf. Hengel 1976: 25 n. 54, on Hercules' apotheosis.

[33] *Enōch euērestēsen kyriōi kai metetethē hypodeigma metanoias tais geneais* ('Enoch pleased the Lord and was taken up, an example of repentance to all generations'; NRSV).

[34] Pease (1942: 17) suggests that it may have been Augustus' attitude to Hercules and Romulus (Horace, *Odes* 3.3.11–16; *Epistle* 2.1.5–10; Suetonius 2[Augustus].95) which encouraged the notion of an immortality *ex virtute*. The lampooning of Claudius' apotheosis in Seneca, *Apocolocyntosis*, proves the point negatively.

[35] Price 1987: 89. See also Schowalter 1993: 65.

away the body so that the immortal part could ascend to the gods.[36] Heaven was the domain of souls, not bodies – which the virtuous person had spent his lifetime seeking to overcome. To such thinkers, the notion of a risen body would therefore be repulsive.

A risen body?

Repulsive

Seneca wrote that the soul 'regards the body ... since it is a burden which must be borne, not as a thing to love, but as a thing to oversee'; and so, when the soul is about to depart the body, the soul regards the body 'as being of no more concern to itself than is the afterbirth to a child just born' (*Epistle* 92.34). If the body was 'the prison-house of the soul', then life in the body was not really life at all. In Cicero's Dream of Scipio,[37] for example, Scipio says, 'Surely all those who have escaped from the bondage of the body as from a prison are alive; but that so-called "life" of yours is really death' (Cicero, *De re publica* 6.14).

Again, Seneca could say: 'Behold, this clogging burden of a body to which nature has chained me. "I shall die", you say. You mean to say, "I shall cease to run the risk of sickness; I shall cease to run the risk of imprisonment; I shall cease to run the risk of death ... Death either annihilates us or strips us bear. If we are then released, what remains is the better part after the burden has been removed. If we are annihilated, nothing remains; good and bad alike are removed' (*Epistle* 24.18).

Some, such as Plutarch (*De Iside et Osiride* 370C), had heard of certain oriental ideas regarding a more lasting future resurrection. But, given his Platonic views of soul and body, such notions had to be labelled fabulous, for it is simply 'against nature' to insist that the body had a role in the afterlife. In fact, the thought was repulsive to the Platonist. Even the bodily translations of the mythological past were abhorrent to Plutarch (*Romulus* 28.4), 'improbably ascrib[ing] divinity to the mortal features in human nature, as well as to the divine' (6).

---

[36] Apollodorus 2.7.7; Lucian, *Hermotimus* 7; cf. *De morte peregrini* 4, 6, 30, cf. 33; *AG* 16: 185.

[37] It has been claimed that the Dream of Scipio (Cicero, *De re publica* 6) is a pagan example of the apocalypse genre; Attridge 1979: 163. If so, the Dream shares the same generic category as Mark.

We must not, therefore, violate nature by sending the bodies of good men to heaven (*ouden oun dei ta sōmata tōn agathōn synanapempein para physin eis ouranon*),[38] but implicitly believe that their virtues and their souls, in accordance with nature and divine justice, ascend from men to heroes, from heroes to demi-gods, and from demi-gods, after they have been made pure and holy, as in the final rites of initiation and have freed themselves from mortality and sense, to gods, not by civic law, but in very truth and according to right reason, thus achieving the fairest and most blessed consummation. (Plutarch *Romulus* 28.7–8)

Plutarch clearly considers a *bodily* apotheosis to be completely misguided, for 'to send bodies to heaven' is completely 'against nature'.[39] Plutarch's Pythagorean doctrine taught a divinization of the good soul, through the practice of virtue.

When he uses the phrase 'by civic law' (*nomōi poleōs*), he is probably taking a passing shot at a Roman practice that was gaining momentum in his day, namely, that of divinizing rulers by senatorial decision, to which we shall return shortly.

In the second century, Celsus, the famous opponent of Christianity, in one of his vehement attacks against the doctrine of *bodily* resurrection, reminded his audience of an ancient precedent: 'The soul may have everlasting life, but corpses, as Heraclitus said, "ought to be thrown away as worse than dung"' (Origen, *Contra Celsum* 5.14–15).

Crucified?

Even if a bodily apotheosis may have been an option to explain Jesus' disappearance, there would be no possibility that a crucified man might be a candidate for apotheosis. Apotheosis was reserved for the pure of soul, the great ones. A crucified person, however, died under the curse of the gods. The crucified had no hope in the afterlife at all. This can be illustrated by an interchange between a Roman prefect and Justin in the late second century. The prefect calls Justin a 'learned man' and then asks, 'If you shall be scourged and beheaded, are you persuaded that you will ascend to heaven?'.[40] In

---

[38] The Loeb translation adds 'with their souls', no doubt as a rendering of *syn-* in the compound verb.

[39] Celsus sees these as merely the stuff of myths: 'But we must examine the question whether anyone who really died ever rose again with the same body' (Origen, *Contra Celsum* 2.55).

[40] See Stevenson 1957: 30, a translation of *Acta Sancti Justini et sociorum*; original in Gebhardt 1902: 18–21.

other words, a learned man should know that scourging, and beheading – violent deaths – would mean no afterlife hopes at all. This was supremely true for the crucified (see above, p. 137 n. 55). Those violently killed, and especially the crucified, obviously died under the disfavour of the gods. If they had no hope in the afterlife, it would be ridiculous to even speak of the crucified in the same context as apotheosis. Apotheosis was reserved for the virtuous of soul, the great ones of the land. In the first century, this no doubt explains why the apotheosis of the Roman emperors was gradually gathering steam.

The apotheosis of Roman emperors

Mark's Gospel was launched upon the Roman world when the apotheosis of its rulers was still a matter of some debate. This practice began as a sign of great honour, but eventually became simply a matter of custom.

From honour to custom

Romulus

In the background of this practice lay the deification of Romulus, the founder of Rome (Pease 1942: 15). The story of his deification appeared as early as Ennius' *Annals* (65–66, 111–113)[41] in the second century BC. Naturally enough, the events surrounding the moment when Romulus 'vanished from among men' (*ex anthrōpōn ēphanisthē*, Plutarch, *Camillus* 32.5), so that he 'was no more on earth' (Livy 1.15.6), were debated. Some political realists suspected a senatorial conspiracy (Plutarch, *Numa* 2–3), whereas others were convinced he had been 'caught up to the gods' (Plutarch, *Romulus* 27–28), one person even swearing an oath that he had seen him go (28.1).

Caesars

As the imperial power took a new turn with Julius Caesar and then with Augustus, the mythology surrounding Romulus began to be reapplied to Rome's chief man. The prevailing psychology at this time, however, meant that the assumption to heaven was no longer bodily. During the imperial apotheoses, probably from as early as the

[41] Cf. Cicero, *De re publica* 1.25, 2.17.

time of Augustus,[42] the funeral ritual symbolized the heavenly ascent of the soul by releasing an eagle from a cage on top of the pyre.[43] But down below, the body (or an effigy of it) was still burning.

The devaluation of the currency

In time, the apotheosis of the emperor would become so customary that it would lose its significance. But it is important to realize that, at the time of Mark's Gospel, apotheosis was still a valued commodity.

In time, apotheosis of the emperor became something of a formality. This can be illustrated by reference to a papyrus known as the *Feriale Duranum*,[44] a list of religious festivals to be observed by the military from the time of Severus Alexander (AD 224–35). From this document, it seems that in AD 224 some twenty people were worshipped as divine figures, including six women and the early first-century military hero Germanicus (Kreitzer 1996: 72–73). Also in the third century, the biographer Herodian (4.2.1–11) provides an account of the apotheosis ritual current in his time, claiming that 'it is normal Roman practice to deify emperors who die leaving behind children as their successors'.[45] The total statistics seem to be that from Augustus to Constantine, thirty-six of sixty emperors, and twenty-seven of their family members, were apotheosized and given the title *diuus* (Price 1987: 48). It is important to realize, however, that, despite this later devaluation of the currency of apotheosis, in the first century it was still a significant enough issue to cause debate and controversy.[46]

[42] Weinstock (1971: 359, esp. n. 5) refers to a relief in the Vatican Museum, the Paris cameo of the ascension of Germanicus, and 'numerous Greek examples'. Cf. Suetonius 2[Augustus].97.1. L. R. Taylor (1989: 165) also notes that the eagle appeared on an Augustan coin of 27 BC, which she takes as an indication of the emperor's expectation of divinity after his death, since the eagle is 'the most characteristic symbol of apotheosis'.

[43] Dio Cassius 35.4; Herodian 4.2; cf. Lucian, *De morte peregrini* 39.

[44] For a critical edition, see Fink, Hoey & Snyder 1940. See also Benario 1962.

[45] This passage is discussed by Kreitzer (1996: 73–75).

[46] This can be illustrated by the reception given to the apotheosis of Claudius in AD 54 and the debate that lasted at least through to the end of the century. Brandon (1960–1: 134, following Nock 1952: 381–389, 493, 495, 501) claims that 'the deification of the emperor was already a well-known practice' by the days of Titus (AD 79–81), but the fact that its appropriateness was still under discussion is illustrated by an address delivered by Pliny in AD 100 and published in 101 or 103 (Schowalter 1993: 9–10). Pliny (*Panegyricus* 11.1) accepts the deification of the emperors, but cautions Trajan by reference to past excesses: 'Tiberius dedicated Augustus to heaven, only to introduce the crime of high treason; Nero deified Claudius only to make him a laughing stock; Titus deified Vespasian, and Domitian deified Titus, but only so that one would appear to be a son of a god, and the other the brother of a god.'

The early Caesars so honoured

In the early days, not all the Caesars were divinized. Deification had to be ratified by the senate. The ex-soldier Velleius Paterculus, writing in AD 30, just before Jesus' death, listed Julius[47] and Augustus[48] as having received divine honours by his time. When Suetonius took up his pen at the turn of the second century AD, he could add only Claudius, Vespasian and Titus[49] to the list.[50]

Julius

Julius Caesar was the first human to be divinized since Romulus. Although he obviously died a purely human death (Suetonius 1[Julius].83.2), his demise was nevertheless presented like that of Romulus (Appian *Bella civilia* 2.114). Octavian (later Augustus) claimed that a comet had risen to show that Caesar had ascended to the heavens. Basing their decision on this evidence, the senate voted to include him 'among the gods' (Cicero, *Orationes Philippicae* 1.13; 2.110; Schowalter 1993: 62). The comet that appeared at his death provided the basis for the theory that his soul had become a new star (for his apotheosis, see Ovid, *Metamorphoses* 15.745). This heavenly journey became valued as a proof of immortality and as a mythical underpinning of the imperial system (Segal 1980: 1348). Even from the beginning, however, such notions had their critics, as when Propertius (2.15.40–43; cf. 2.5.1f.) contrasted the Roman love of war with his 'war' of love with his mistress. We can imagine him wiping the sweat from his brow in utter exhaustion as he sighs, 'One such night might make any man a god!'

Augustus

During his lifetime, Augustus permitted the provinces to dedicate temples to him, but because he did not want worship independent of Rome (see Suetonius 2[Augustus].53), this was usually alongside Roma, the personification of the ruling city of the empire (Kreitzer

---

[47] See the discussion in Kreitzer 1996: 81–86.

[48] His apotheosis is depicted in the carved sardonyx cameo from AD 9, the *Gemma Augustea* (see Kreitzer 1996: 77–78 and figure 4), and on *The Grand Camée* from AD 17 (see Kreitzer 1996: 78–79 and figure 5).

[49] His apotheosis is depicted in the Arch of Titus; see Kreitzer 1996: 76.

[50] Although receiving many cults in the East, Tiberius did not receive divine honours from the Senate. Caligula, Nero and Domitian were similarly not divinized, despite the fact – or perhaps because of the fact – that each of them had made 'excessive claims to divinity' during their reigns. Kreitzer 1996: 70–71, 90–91.

1996: 86–88). Eventually, the Augustan cult became a structuring force in society (Kreitzer 1996: 96; Price 1984: 248). When Augustus died, the Romulus myth was again pressed into service. Dio Cassius (56.46 1–2), on Augustus, spoke of 'immortalizing him' (*athanatisantes auton*), and of his wife Livia's bestowing a million sesterces upon a certain Numerius Atticus, a senator and expraetor, because he swore that he had seen 'Augustus ascending to heaven after the manner of which tradition tells concerning Proculus and Romulus'.[51]

Claudius?

Augustus' successor, Tiberius, tended to refuse divine honours,[52] although he permitted temples to be dedicated to him.[53] Despite this, Tiberius was never deified after his death.

After Augustus, Claudius was the next to be granted an apotheosis. Avoiding the excesses of his predecessor Caligula,[54] Claudius had actively shunned worship addressed to him during his lifetime. So, for example, in AD 41 he wrote to the Alexandrians dissuading them from their desire to give him divine honours.[55] In AD 54, he was poisoned by his wife Agrippina, Nero's mother, and (strangely enough) Nero took the throne. Perhaps as part of the official denial of his poisoning, which was being spoken of everywhere (Stauffer 1955: 139), Nero had Claudius divinized and issued a series of coins in his honour (Kreitzer 1996: 95). Seneca wrote the funeral oration, Nero delivered it, and Agrippina was made high priestess of the new cult.

---

[51] The pattern was also imitated when, in AD 38, Gaius' sister Drusilla was deified and subsequently named Panthea, and a senator, Livius Geminus, declared on oath that he had seen her ascending to heaven and conversing with the gods (Dio Cassius 59.11.3–4). Jones 1980: 1026.

[52] See Grether 1946: 233 and n. 62; 234–235 and n. 70, 238, 240. It should also be noted, however, that the same deprecation of honours can be found in Claudius, and even in Caligula, and that it probably follows an Augustan precedent; see L. R. Taylor 1929; she also observes that Tiberius' refusals were not successful – cf. next note.

[53] His cult is the closest rival to that of Augustus, who had priests in thirty-four cities. Tacitus (*Annals* 4.55–56) tells of a temple dedicated to him in Smyrna, and archeologists have discovered signs of priests of Tiberius in no fewer than eleven cities. In fact, after Augustus, Tiberius had more temples dedicated to him than any other emperor. Price 1984: 58.

[54] Caligula issued a coin from Amphipolis inscribed KAISAR GERMANICUS THEOS SEBASTOS. Lewis & Bolden 2002: 115. It was rare for the Caesar to be called 'god' on coins during his lifetime. Gaius did not succeed in deifying Tiberius, nor did Gaius' megalomaniac demands for divine honours in his lifetime succeed, but his endeavours certainly kept alive the issue of whether human beings can become gods.

[55] For the Greek text see Charlesworth 1939: 3–5; English translation in Barrett 1987, no. 48, pp. 47–50.

When Claudius was deified, however, it caused great amusement in Rome (Jones 1980: 1028). When Pliny reflected on the event, he could say that 'Nero deified Claudius only to make him a laughing stock' (*Panegyricus* 11.1). Despite having written the funeral oration, Seneca proceeded to write a satirical work ridiculing the apotheosis, called the *Apocolocyntosis of Claudius*, which can be translated as something like 'Claudius is turned into a pumpkin'.[56] In this satire, the gods, climaxing with Augustus himself, express their disgust at Claudius' being placed among them. Clearly, when Mark was being read, apotheosis was an issue still under debate.

Apparently Claudius' deification was met with derision because he did not meet the criteria for the divinization of the emperor. Apotheosis was for the great, the virtuous. The virtuous soul expressed itself through the body in which it resided. Claudius, however, suffered from multiple physical defects that clearly testified to his not being the right calibre of person to join the gods. In Seneca's satire, one of the gods says of him: 'Look at his body, born under the wrath of heaven' (*Apocolocyntosis* 11; cf. 1). The sources speak of his disturbed speech,[57] his weak legs and ungainly gait, his inappropriate laughing fits and slobbering, and his tremor.[58] When he was younger, it had been agreed that he would not sit in the imperial box at the games, so that neither he nor his uncle, Caesar Augustus, might suffer embarrassment.[59]

Modern authors continue to pour scorn upon Claudius, declaring him to be 'an insignificant fool who was ruled by his wife of the moment' (Stauffer 1955: 138). They can probably be forgiven, however, for even his own mother apparently often declared him to be 'a monster: a man whom mother nature had begun to work upon but then flung aside' (Suetonius 5[Claudius].3). These signs have indicated to modern diagnosticians that he may have suffered from congenital cerebral palsy (Moss 1963: 166–167). Whatever the cause, to the ancient world he was definitely not a candidate for becoming a god.

---

[56] For a discussion of Seneca's views on the deification of Claudius, see Altman 1938.
[57] Suetonius 5[Claudius].30; Dio Cassius 60.2. Augustus expressed surprise that he was able to declaim so well, given his problems: 'How in the world anyone who is so unclear in his conversation can speak with clearness and propriety when he declaims is more than I can see' (Suetonius 5[Claudius].4).
[58] Suetonius 5[Claudius].30; 4; Juvenal 6.622–623; Dio Cassius 60.2.
[59] Claudius was often the laughing-stock of others; see Suetonius 5[Claudius].8–9.

Apotheosis and resurrection in Mark's story

It is interesting to reflect on the fact that Mark's Gospel was entering into circulation roughly around the time when the apotheosis of Claudius had occurred and when it was probably being heatedly discussed in Rome. Mark can profitably be read with this debate about apotheosis in mind.

The transfiguration: a missed opportunity?

When the story of Jesus' transfiguration is read from this perspective, it seems like a missed opportunity for a story about a translation, or, as it would be read in Mark's day, about an apotheosis.[60] The transfiguration scene contains some parallels to stories[61] in which a person disappeared or was translated to heaven, or both. In particular, it has several close parallels to Josephus' account of the disappearance of Moses (see Tabor 1989; Begg 1990). Translations could take place upon mountains, and often under changed weather conditions, be it an eclipse or a storm, or, as here, the descent of a cloud.[62] A translation may even involve white garments (v. 3),[63] or a

---

[60] Palmer (1976: 120), who classifies Jewish-Christian assumption stories into two types. Even though Jesus is not technically taken up to heaven, the transfiguration scene has similarities to the 'apocalyptic type', in which a person is temporarily taken to heaven to converse with heavenly figures (cf. *1 Enoch* 39:3ff.; 70–71; *Testament of Levi* 2–5; *3 Baruch*; *Ascension of Isaiah* 7–11).

[61] A. Y. Collins (1992c: 142) claims that 'in the Hellenistic and early Roman periods these traditions of translation and deification were widespread', although, in support, she cites only Josephus and the retelling of the ancient flood story by the Babylonian historian Berossus. The increasing importance of the apotheosis of the Roman rulers, with its backing in the Romulus story, offers further support to her claim.

[62] Mark 9:2; Diodorus Siculus 3.57.8 (Basileia); 4.82.6 (Aristaeus); Josephus, *Antiquities* 4.325–326 (Moses); Cicero, *De re publica* 1.25; 2.17; Dionysius Halicarnassensis 2.56.1–2 (Romulus); Sophocles, *Oedipus Coloneus* 1620 (Oedipus); Livy 1.16; Plutarch, *Romulus* 27.6 (Romulus); Apollodorus 2.7.7 (Hercules).

[63] My basis for suggesting this is a detail in Lucian's mockery of the translation tradition in the *De morte peregreni* (*The Passing of Peregrinus*). When Lucian embellished the story for 'the dullards agog to listen', he added an earthquake, a bellowing of the ground, and a vulture flying out of the flames to heaven with a parting speech (39). The story backfires on him when someone else picks it up, adding the claim that he had seen Peregrinus 'in white raiment a little while ago, and had just now left him walking cheerfully in the Portico of the Seven Voices, wearing a garland of wild olive' (40). The fact that it is a detail added by one who evidently went along with the tradition suggests that it was a part of that tradition, at least by the second century.

voice from heaven (v. 7).[64] Reading this voice from heaven as an expression of divine pleasure in Jesus (v. 7), would be reminiscent of the belief that translations took place because of the virtue of those involved. Of course, a leading and necessary feature of such stories was the person's sudden disappearance,[65] sometimes reinforced by others searching for them. Mark's scene on the mountain concludes with language suggestive of such a search (v. 8): 'looking around (*periblepsamenoi*), they saw no-one'. In a strange twist, however, Mark adds, 'But only Jesus with them'. The person the readers would have expected to disappear is the only one left behind; the heavenly visitors have left without him.

When Mark's transfiguration is read in the light of the translation stories, it appears that here Jesus is presented with an opportunity for apotheosis that he did not take up. Although the voice from heaven, now for the second time, declared Jesus to be the Son of God, he did not 'disappear from among men'. Instead of taking the chance to avoid the death he had predicted (8:31), he came back down the mountain resolved to die, explaining that, before the resurrection can arrive, the Son of Man must suffer (9:9–13). He rejected the opportunity to avoid death through translation or apotheosis and embraced his future suffering for the sake of the divine plan. Thus, in the transfiguration, Jesus continued in his resolve to walk the path of the suffering servant (1:11; 3:31–35; 8:31; 9:11–13; Caird 1955–6: 293).

There would have been no resurrection and no glorious kingdom of God without his prior suffering. From that point onwards, the narrative pressed relentlessly forward to his inevitable death. But now that he has suffered and died, resurrection has occurred: he is risen.

---

[64] Euripides, *Bacchae* 1076–1079 (Dionysus); D. A. Smith 2003: 125. For the language of disappearance, or not seeing cf. Elijah (2 Kgs 2:12, LXX: *kai ouk eiden auton eti*. See also 2 Kgs 2:10); Xisouthros (Berossos, *Babylonia*, fr. 4a: *ouk eti ophthēnai*); Romulus (Plutarch, *Romulus* 27.5: *oute meros ōphthē sōmatos*); and Proteus (Lucian, *De morte peregrini* 39: *ou mēn heōrato ge*). Cf. Mark 9:8: *ouketi oudena eidon*. This language functions synonymously with the *aphan-* disappearance language; see Lohfink 1971: 58. Not seeing suggests the unsuccessful search for a body that is a feature of these accounts (Gen. 5:24, LXX; 2 Kgs 2:16–18; Berossos, *Babylonia* fr. 4a; Plutarch, *Romulus* 27.7; Chariton, *Chaereas and Callirhoe* 3.3; *Testament of Job* 39.8–12; *Protevangelium of James* 24.9). Assumption predictions also figure (2 Kgs 2:3, 5, 10; *1 Enoch* 81:6; *4 Ezra* 14; *2 Baruch* 76:1–5).

[65] Sophocles, *Oedipus Coloneus* 1647–1648 (Oedipus); Cicero, *De re publica* 2.17; Plutarch, *Romulus* 27.6 (Romulus); Diodorus Siculus 2.14.3 (Semiramis); Josephus, *Antiquities* 4.326 (Moses); 2 Kgs 2; Josephus, *Antiquities* 9.27–28 (Elijah). There are many disappearance stories, not all of which are translations to heaven; see Pease 1942.

The resurrection

In direct conflict with beliefs about heroes, translations and apotheoses, Mark's concluding chapter presents an emptied tomb and an announcement that the 'body' that once lay in it 'is risen'. Jesus was not a hero who died and, from the underworld, managed to make his presence still felt in the upper world. Nor was he translated, as one of the privileged few who avoided death altogether. Nor did he receive an apotheosis of soul, as a reward above and beyond the rest of humanity, because of his own great virtue. Jesus' body was once in the tomb, and then it was no longer there, for 'he is risen'. This is clearly a case of resurrection, in which a body returns to life from the grave.

Mark's narrative presented Jesus' death as a divine necessity. He had to die before the resurrection and the kingdom of God could arrive. Refusing to avoid death through apotheosis, Jesus willingly embraced this difficult necessity. When he died, he was recognized as Son of God – a title used for the divine Caesar Augustus. Even then he did not undergo an apotheosis of soul, as the great Caesar had done. Instead, Mark's final chapter shows that he was raised bodily from the dead.

The resurrection of the crucified one

This startling fact does not mean that we can forget the crucifixion. As a part of the young man's momentous announcement, we learn that it is 'Jesus the Nazarene, the crucified one', who is risen and who is no longer there in the tomb. 'Jesus the Nazarene' may reflect what was on the legal charge sheet, reinforcing the fact that he had died as a supposed criminal.[66] It is significant that the Greek uses the

---

[66] This is admittedly speculative. *Nazarēnos* may have no special significance, apart from affirming a continuity from beginning (cf. 1:9) to end; so France 2002: 680. However, this is a rare description of Jesus. Apart from twice in Luke (4:34 [= Mark 1:24]; 24:19 [L]), this description is used only by Mark in the New Testament (1:24; 10:47; 14:67; 16:6). Interestingly, it is always used by someone who is not part of Jesus' group. *Nazōraios* is more common, being used by Matthew and Luke to replace Mark's *Nazarēnos* on a couple of occasions (Matt. 26:71 = Mark 14:67; Luke 18:37 = Mark 10:47). Matthew also uses it once in reference to an enigmatic fulfilment of Scripture, which may be related to Jesus' being the suffering servant (Matt. 2:23). In John, a case could be made for tying this description to the legal charge sheet, since it occurs at the arrest and on the *titulus* (John 18:5, 7; 19:19). This legal entity, 'Jesus Nazoraios', is also referred to in the apostolic preaching in Acts, usually closely related to his crucifixion (Acts 2:22; 3:6; 4:10; 6:14). Paul's use of the term (in Acts) may reflect his former perspective as Saul the persecutor (Acts 26:9), since Jesus identified himself in this way to him on the Damascus road (Acts 22:8). It is also interesting that the followers of Christ became known as 'the sect of the Nazarenes' (Acts 24:5). For a different discussion, see Schaeder 1967.

THE CROSS FROM A DISTANCE

perfective aspect in this description of Jesus, which conveys 'the state or condition of the subject of the verb as a result of an action'.[67] He is *ho estaurōmenos*, 'the one who remains crucified'. The crucified one has risen. The risen one is the crucified one.

What is the significance of the raising from the dead of the crucified one? When the young man closely connected the risen one with the crucified one (v. 6), this would have been seen as a great paradox. For, on the one hand, crucifixion was such a horrendous death that it universally signalled that the crucified person was under a curse. Such a person could not gain rest in the underworld, and, because of his violent death, ran a good risk of becoming a powerful ghost, much sought after to do the magicians' nefarious business (the *biaiothanatoi*). On the other hand, any removal from death was connected with the individual's great virtue. If the apotheosis of Claudius was questioned because his many physical problems showed him to be under the wrath of heaven, how could a crucified man ever be among the likely candidates for an apotheosis? He would, rather, depart to dwell restlessly on the shores of the dark underworld lake.[68] He would never be among the gods.

Crucifixion, resurrection and human hope

Hope that disappoints

In the process of telling the story of Jesus, Mark's Gospel also gives us a slice of life in the first-century world. In the case-studies of the people who are helped by Jesus, recorded in both scene and summary, we gain a picture of first-century life under the shadow of death (see further Bolt 2003).

This picture is not just of the first-century world. It is a slice of life in a world under the shadow of death, showing people struggling against our last and greatest enemy, locked in mortal combat against the grave. The writer to the Hebrews tells us that it is through the fear of death that we are held in slavery all of our lives (Heb. 2:14–15). Our mortality eats away at our existence, as a root cause of the serious problems of life. This was the problem in the ancient world, and, despite our failure to face it squarely in the eye, this is also the problem of our contemporary world. Perhaps life is a little more sophisticated for us, but surely it is still true of our world that, as

---

[67] McKay 1994: 31, cf. 27; Wallace 1996: 572.
[68] Cf. Page 1941: no. 94; see above, pp. 137, 160.

168

Seneca put it, 'most men ebb and flow in wretchedness between the fear of death and the hardships of life' (*Epistle* 4.5). The ancient world had no hope. As Stauffer (1955: 25) summarizes: 'The natural myth of the classical world knew no future, but only perpetual recurrence. The classical myth of fate knew no future, but only the insuperable past. The classical imperial myth knew no future, but only the old wine in new skins.' Indeed, both the Greeks and the Romans had their goddesses of Hope, but they were not considered trustworthy, for they generally let people down (cf. Walsh 1974). Philosophers taught that if people wanted to have an ideal life they should get rid of two things: fear and hope (Bolt 1998c: 65). Hope always disappointed. In this world under the shadow of death, hope soon brings disappointment. Our dreams are not realized. Our goals are not achieved. Our lives keep heading relentlessly towards the grave. Our wishes gradually get smaller, so that the disappointment does not hurt so much. Such life without hope is crippling.

Virtuous souls, heroes, apotheoses and hopelessness

The ideas about virtuous souls, heroes and even apotheoses were of no help to the ordinary person. Heroes gave no promises, and besides, they were already defeated by the grave themselves. For those who were suffering badly in this world, it was no comfort to know that the pure soul might ascend to the gods. Their suffering, especially if from some bodily affliction, already indicated that they were probably, like Claudius, born under the wrath of the gods. In that case, their souls were already impure, and prospects after death were restricted to reincarnation in another revolting body, to endure yet another cycle in this valley of tears.

As for the apotheosis of Caesar, what good was that? Just like the doctrine of the apotheosis of the pure soul, it may speak well of one particular emperor, but what of the rest of humanity? The belief that Julius Caesar, or Augustus, or even Claudius, was great enough to join the gods held out no hope to anyone else, especially to the poor, the powerless, those already broken by this world. All it did was to keep them subjugated under their military and political overlords.[69] Apotheosis was no help at all for those who are perishing. But

[69] The imperial cult also contributed to keeping the provinces poor. It was an expensive effort to maintain the imperial cult, and the elite of the provinces outdid themselves to spend their money, thus bringing the provinces to financial ruin; see Bolt 2003: 251–252.

Mark and his fellow Christians proclaimed the resurrection of the crucified one.

The resurrection of the crucified, and hope

Despite the great differences between the first century and today, we share the same world, because we share the same sentence of death. The good news proclaimed by Mark is that, because Jesus came into *that* world, he has come into *our* world too. The Son of God entered human history at a certain point and time, in order to benefit the world for all time. The Son of God cared for the perishing. He cared enough to do something about our mortal condition – to die on our behalf, even on a cross.

When Augustus was deified, mourning was forbidden. When Jesus died, it was the hour when the bridegroom was taken away (2:20), and a time when mourning was perfectly appropriate. He did not avoid death; he actually died. The normal human repugnance at death, and sorrow before its wicked tyranny, applied in his case too. He lived under the shadow of death, just as we have to do. He went to the grave, just as we shall all have to do.

He died a terrible death: crucified, under the wrath of God. From all ordinary points of view, as a crucified man he left this world in the worst possible way, and he had absolutely no hope in the afterlife. But he died in this way *for us*. His death was an exclusive place-taking death, so that the sting of death might be removed for us. On the third day after his death, the women walked into his emptied tomb and heard the words: 'You are looking for Jesus the Nazarene, who was crucified. He is risen. He is not here.'

According to Daniel 7, when the Son of Man received the kingdom it would flow over to the rest of God's people. If Jesus has now risen and received the promised kingdom, then this holds hope for others. As the one who acted on behalf of the many, his victory is also victory for the many and he will share the kingdom with the many.

But who were these 'many'? Mark's Gospel has already shown us who they are: they are people like the suppliants – those in real need, battered and bruised by the world, afflicted with all kinds of physical, mental and emotional ailments and with all their tragic social consequences. They included the crowds, the children, even the lapsed disciples; people in all manner of the tragic situations so much a part of the first-century world. Apotheosis of the soul held promise only for an elite. Those who were not among the great ones in terms of their achievements or their morality would have little hope. If they had some bodily disability, their chances were perhaps even more remote. Yet 'resurrection' was filled with promise to all those who are among 'the least' of the world – all those in a broken world who could not raise themselves from the dust and whose virtue could not save them. They had a champion who had gone ahead of them and, in so doing, he had provided a ransom that guaranteed their future.

Mark's Gospel spoke of a coming kingdom, which would bring life, not death; salvation, not corruption. For those who continued to live under the shadow of death, Mark presented the assurance that something had been done about human mortality: someone had defeated death – and it was a crucified man. And if a *crucified* man can be raised from the dead, then *anyone* can be raised! Because this crucified man had risen from the dead and ascended to the right hand of the Father,[70] human beings can now be brought to God.[71] Whereas Greeks in the Orphic stream, such as Plutarch, found it abhorrent to speak of a body going to heaven, this is exactly what the resurrection of Christ implied. The early Christians began to proclaim the fact that the risen Christ had taken human flesh to heaven with him,[72] and, that

---

[70] Although it is often claimed that the ascension has been rather neglected in theological enquiry, several recent works have entered the breach. See Donne 1983; Toon 1984; Thomas 1996; Farrow 1999; Atkins 2001. For older works, see Milligan 1898; Davies 1958.

[71] For Cyprian, *Quod idola dii non sint* (c. AD 246), the ascension was so that 'as a consequence he might bring to the Father man whom he loved, whom he put on, whom he shielded from death' (14).

[72] Hippolytus, *Contra Noetum* 21 (?AD 200): 'It is evident therefore that He offered Himself to the Father and before this there was no flesh in heaven'. He repeats this thought in the lost homily *In Helcanam et Annam*: 'He Himself first ascended to heaven and brought man as a gift to God' (*PG* 10.864C). Novatian also affirmed the bringing of flesh to heaven (*De Trinitate* 13, 14). Lactantius discusses ascension in *Divinae institutiones* (c. AD 304). In *Epitome* (after AD 314) he summarizes the first two passages: here the ascension had 'long before' been predicted by Dan. 7:13–14 (*Epitome* 47). According to Leo the Great (*Sermon on Ascension Day, 1 June 444*; Sermon 73.2), the days between the resurrection and the ascension 'provided the opportunity to confirm great mysteries, to reveal great secrets. In these days the fear of dreaded death was removed and the immortality not only of the soul but also of the flesh is assured.' Jesus showed them his wounds: 'He had preserved the wounds of the nails and the lance as signs, to heal the hearts of unbelievers, so that, with a very constant knowledge, not a hesitant faith, they would understand that this nature which had lain in the tomb was to take its place on the throne of God the Father' (3). This had implications for human nature: 'Truly it was a great and indescribable source of rejoicing when, in the sight of the heavenly multitudes, the nature of our human race ascended over the dignity of all heavenly creatures, to pass the angelic orders and to be raised beyond the heights of archangels. In its ascension it did not stop at any other height until this same nature was received at the seat of the eternal Father, to be associated on the throne of the glory of that One to whose nature it was joined in the Son' (4). 'Since the Ascension of Christ is

this, amazingly, guaranteed our own future place in heaven (cf. Col. 3:1–4). The resurrection of the crucified man brings real hope to the world. This is a hope that does not disappoint (cf. Rom. 5:5, in contrast to Eph. 2:12 and 1 Thess. 4:13).

The hope that does not disappoint

The divinities of hope were not trusted in the ancient world, and hope hardly receives a better press in the cynical twenty-first-century West. What can we possibly hope for?[73] Yet Christian hope fills the New Testament. It will not let us down in the end. What we are hoping for *will* be the future. The kingdom of God has been thrown open by Jesus' death as a ransom for many. For those who put their trust in him, the kingdom of God *will* be theirs. The kingdom of God is not just for the virtuous and the bodily whole. It is for believers in Jesus, no matter how lacking in virtue, how broken – physically, emotionally, mentally, spiritually or socially – they may be. It is open to all because entry to the kingdom does not depend on who people are or what they have done. It depends on Jesus, the Son of God, who died as a ransom for many.

If a crucified man can rise, then all of us have hope. And it is a sure hope, because a crucified man has risen from the dead: the Son of God, on our behalf.

The hope that changed the world

This hope once changed the world. Christ gave people back the future. And, having a secure future because of him, lives were transformed. Even in the midst of a suffering world, suffering humans had something that transformed their existence, developed their character, gave them a new zest for life. Because of him, they knew the God of mercy. They had no need to fear the grave any more.

Resurrection hope undercuts the desperate search for security that leads to sin of all kinds. Because Christ has rescued us through the cross, the future is secure already. There is a solid place in which to stand. The future is guaranteed, because of the cross of the crucified God, and this means that the present is transformed in every aspect of life in this world.

---

our elevation, and since, where the glory of the Head has preceded us, there hope for the body is also invited, let us exult ... Today we are established not only as possessors of Paradise, but we have even penetrated the heights of the heavens in Christ ...' (4), recovering what was lost in the fall.

[73] Recall the previous discussion of our present 'world anxiety', p. 112 above; cf. Körtner 1995: ch. 1.

To celebrate his victorious entry into London in the year AD 296, the troops of Caesar Constantius Chlorus glorified him on a gold medallion as the REDDITOR LUCIS AETERNAE, the restorer of eternal light. This was the language of the military god Mithras (Stauffer 1955: 13).[74] A little over a decade later, his son, Constantine the Great, who had been brought up as a believer in Mithras, placed the name of Christ on his imperial standard along with the words SPES PUBLICA, the hope of the world (ibid.). Almost three hundred years after Jesus was crucified by Caesar's representatives as a rebel against Rome, Caesar began to proclaim this crucified man as the hope of the world.

In this book we have seen, in chapter 1, that the cross of Christ has abolished religion, for all that is required is faith in him. In chapter 2, we saw that this world is not in the hands of blind fate or fickle chance. The cross shows God has plans for this world, and they are plans for mercy. In chapter 3, we saw that there is no need for anxiety about our world in turmoil, which the beasts still fill with bloodshed and suffering. The cross was the greatest suffering of all time, and it guarantees that the future lies in the hands of the mighty Son of Man. The fourth chapter showed that, even if the suffering of this world might make us cry out to God from the depths of our being, 'Why have you forsaken me?', the man on the cross has already been in those depths. The Son of God, God himself, endured the wrath of God so that our forsakenness may be overcome once and for all. And, finally, we have seen in this fifth chapter that in our hopeless world a new flag was raised on 3 April 33. We need to look back to that cross constantly.

Although the cross is at a distance from us, it is still in our world. It stands as an ensign, a banner, a signal to the nations for all time, saying: 'Here is the hope of the world.' The Son of Man's mission to the nations continues. Our world is without real hope and will decline further unless the good news of the crucified Christ is widely preached and believed. It is time for a new call to proclaim that the only hope for the world rests in the crucified Son of God. The whole world needs to hear the good news once again. In this cross at a distance, God has come close.

---

[74] The medallion is reproduced as the frontispiece for Stauffer's book and briefly explained on p. 40.

Bibliography

Aichele, G. (1994), 'Fantasy and Myth in the Death of Jesus', *Cross Currents* 44: 85–96.

Alexander, J. A. (1960), *The Gospel According to Mark*, London: Banner of Truth. (Original 1858.)

Altman, M. (1938), 'Ruler Cult in Seneca', *Classical Philology* 33: 198–204.

Andersen, F. I. (1986), 'Yahweh, the Kind and Sensitive God', in P. T. O'Brien & D. G. Peterson (eds.), *God Who is Rich in Mercy: Essays Presented to Dr D. B. Knox*, Homebush West, NSW: ANZEA: 41–88.

Anderson, M., & P. Culbertson (1986), 'The Inadequacy of the Christian Doctrine of Atonement in Light of Levitical Sin Offering', *Anglican Theological Review* 48.4: 303–328.

Atkins, P. (2001), *Ascension Now: The Implications of Christ's Ascension for Today's Church*, Collegeville, MN: Liturgical.

Attridge, H. W. (1979), 'Greek and Latin Apocalypses', *Semeia* 14: 159–186.

Bailey, D. P. (1998), 'Concepts of *Stellvertretung* in the Interpretation of Isaiah 53', in W. H. Bellinger Jr & W. R. Farmer (eds.), *Jesus and the Suffering Servant: Isaiah 53 and Christian Origins*, Harrisburg, PA: Trinity Press International: 223–250.

Barrett, C. K. (1987), *The New Testament Background: Selected Documents*, 2nd edn, London: SPCK.

Barth, K. (1963), *Evangelical Theology: An Introduction*, Edinburgh: T. & T. Clark.

———(1982), *The Theology of Schleiermacher: Lectures at Göttingen Winter Semester 1923/24*, ed. D. Ritschl, trans. G. W. Bromiley, Grand Rapids, MI: Eerdmans. (German: 1978.)

———(1991), *The Göttingen Dogmatics*, ed. H. Reiffen, trans. G. W. Bromiley, Grand Rapids, MI: Eerdmans. (German: 1990.)

Barton, S. (1994), *Discipleship and Family Ties in Mark and Matthew*, Society for New Testament Studies Monograph Series 80; Cambridge: Cambridge University Press.

Bauckham, R. J. (1993), 'Moltmann, Jürgen', in A. E. McGrath (ed.), *The Blackwell Encyclopedia of Modern Christian Thought*, Oxford: Blackwell: 385–388.

Baumgarten, J. M. (1999), 'Messianic Forgiveness of sin in CD 14:19 (4Q266 10 I 12–13)', in D. W. Parry & E. Ulrich (eds.), *The Provo International Conference on the Dead Sea Scrolls: Technological Innovations, New Texts, and Reformulated Issues*, Leiden: Brill: 537–544.

Baur, P. C. (1953), 'Drei Unedierte Festpredigten', *Tradition* 9: 101–126.

Beasley-Murray, G. R. (1986), *Jesus and the Kingdom of God*, Grand Rapids, MI: Eerdmans; Carlisle: Paternoster.

——(1993), *Jesus and the Last Days: The Interpretation of the Olivet Discourse*, Peabody, MA: Hendrickson.

Begg, C. (1990), 'Josephus's Portrayal of the Disappearances of Enoch, Elijah, and Moses: Some Observations', *Journal of Biblical Literature* 109: 691–693.

Bellinger, W. H., Jr & W. R. Farmer (eds.) (1998), *Jesus and the Suffering Servant: Isaiah 53 and Christian Origins*, Harrisburg, PA: Trinity Press International.

Benario, H. W. (1962), 'The Date of the *Feriale Duranum*', *Historia* 11: 192–196.

Best, E. (1990), *Temptation and Passion: The Markan Soteriology*, Society for New Testament Studies Monograph Series 2, 2nd edn, Cambridge: Cambridge University Press.

Bickermann, E. (1924), 'Das leere Grab', *ZNW* 23: 281–291.

Black, C. C. (1996), 'Christ Crucified in Paul and in Mark: Reflections on an Intracanonical Conversation', in E. H. Lovering Jr & J. L. Suney (eds.), *Theology and Ethics in Paul and his Interpreters: Essays in Honor of Victor Paul Furnish*, Nashville, TN: Abingdon: 184–206.

Bligh, P. H. (1968–9), 'A Note on Huios Theou in Mark 15.39', *Expository Times* 80: 51–53.

Bóid, R. (2003), 'A Samaritan Broadside from the Mid Second Century AD', *Australian Biblical Review* 51: 26–36.

Bolle, K. W. (1987), 'Fate', in M. Eliade (ed.), *The Encyclopedia of Religion* 5, New York: Macmillan: 290–298.

Bolt, P. G. (1991a), 'Narrative Integrity of Mark 13.24–27', unpublished MTh thesis, Kensington: Australian College of Theology.

——(1991b), 'The Spirit in the Synoptic Gospels: The Equipment of the Servant', in B. G. Webb (ed.), *Spirit of the Living God*, Part 1, Explorations 5, Sydney: ANZEA: 45–75.

——— (1993), 'The Gospel for Today's Church', in B. G. Webb (ed.), *Exploring the Missionary Church*, Explorations 7, Sydney: ANZEA: 27–59.

——— (1995), 'Mark 13: An Apocalyptic Precursor to the Passion Narrative', *Reformed Theological Review* 54.1: 10–32.

——— (1996), 'Mk 16:1–8: The Empty Tomb of a Hero?', *Tyndale Bulletin* 47.1: 27–37.

——— (1998a), 'Following Jesus and Fishing for People: Evangelistic Mission in the Third Millennium', in R. J. Gibson (ed.), *Ripe for Harvest: Christian Mission in the New Testament and in our World*, Explorations 12, Carlisle: Paternoster; Adelaide: Openbook: 1–35.

——— (1998b), ' "With a View to the Forgiveness of Sins": Jesus and Forgiveness in Mark's Gospel', *Reformed Theological Review* 57.2: 53–69.

——— (1998c), 'Life, Death, and the Afterlife in the Greco-Roman World', in R. N. Longenecker (ed.), *Life in the Face of Death: The Resurrection Message of the New Testament*, McMaster New Testament Studies 3, Grand Rapids, MI: Eerdmans: 51–79.

——— (2000), 'The Philosopher in the Hands of an Angry God', in P. G. Bolt & M. D. Thompson (eds.), *The Gospel to the Nations: Essays Presented to Peter Thomas O'Brien on his Sixty-Fifth Birthday*, Leicester: Inter-Varsity Press: 327–343.

——— (2001), 'Feeling the Cross: Mark's Message of Atonement', *Reformed Theological Review* 60.1: 1–17.

——— (2003), *Jesus' Defeat of Death: Persuading Mark's Early Readers*, Society for New Testament Studies Monograph Series 125, Cambridge: Cambridge University Press.

Boomershine, T. E. (1974), *Mark the Storyteller: A Rhetorical-Critical Investigation of Mark's Passion and Resurrection Narrative*, Ann Arbor, MI: UMI.

——— (1987), 'Peter's Denial as Polemic or Confession: The Implications of Media Criticism for Biblical Hermeneutics', *Semeia* 39: 47–68.

Boomershine, T. E., & G. L. Bartholomew (1981), 'The Narrative Technique of Mark 16.8', *Journal of Biblical Literature* 100.2: 213–223.

Booth, W. C. (1974), *The Rhetoric of Irony*, Chicago, IL: University of Chicago Press.

Bornkamm, G. (1960), *Jesus of Nazareth*, trans. I. and F. McLuskey, London: Hodder & Stoughton.

Boyd, G. A., & P. R. Eddy (2002), *Across The Spectrum: Understanding Issues In Evangelical Theology*, Grand Rapids, MI: Baker Academic.

Brandon, S. G. F. (1960–1), 'The Date of the Markan Gospel', *New Testament Studies* 7: 126–141.

Bremmer, J. (2002), *The Rise and Fall of the Afterlife: The 1995 Read-Tuckwell Lectures at the University of Bristol*, London: Routledge.

Brooten, B. J. (1994), 'Is Belief the Centre of Religion?', in L. Bormann, K. del Tredici & A. Standhartinger (eds.), *Religious Propaganda and Missionary Competition in the New Testament World: Essays Honoring Dieter Georgi, Novum Testamentum Supplement 74*, Leiden: Brill: 471–479.

Brower, K. E. (1997), ' "Let the Reader Understand": Temple and Eschatology in Mark', in K. E. Brower and M. W. Elliott (eds.), *'The Reader Must Understand': Eschatology in Bible and Theology*, Leicester: Inter-Varsity Press: 119–143.

Brown, R. E. (1986), *A Crucified Christ in Holy Week: Essays on the Four Gospel Passion Narratives*, Collegeville, MN: Liturgical.

——(1998), 'The Burial of Jesus (Mark 15.42–47)', *CBQ* 50: 233–245.

Brownlee, W. H. (1956–7), 'Messianic Motifs of Qumran and the New Testament', Part 1, *New Testament Studies* 3: 12–30.

——(1957), 'Messianic Motifs of Qumran and the New Testament', Part 2, *New Testament Studies* 3: 195–210.

Buchler, A. (1903), 'L'Enterrement des criminels', *Revue des études juives* 46: 76–88.

Bultmann, R. (1963), *The History of the Synoptic Tradition*, trans. J. Marsh, Peabody, MA: Hendrickson. (German 5th edn.)

Caird, G. B. (1955–6), 'The Transfiguration', *Expository Times* 67: 291–294.

——(1997), *The Language and Imagery of the Bible*, Grand Rapids, MI: Eerdmans. (Original: 1980.)

Calvin, J. (1979), *Commentaries on the Book of the Prophet Daniel*, trans. T. Myers, Grand Rapids, MI: Baker. (Original: 1561; translation: 1852.)

——(1979), *Commentary on a Harmony of the Evangelists, Matthew, Mark, and Luke*, trans. W. Pringle, Grand Rapids, MI: Baker. (Original: 1545; translation: 1845.)

Camery-Hoggatt, J. (1992), *Irony in Mark's Gospel: Text and Subtext*, Society for New Testament Studies Monograph Series 72, Cambridge: Cambridge University Press.

Campbell, J. McL. (1996), *The Nature of the Atonement and its Relation to Remission of Sins and Eternal Life*, Edinburgh: Handsel; Grand Rapids, MI: Eerdmans. (1856.)

Carson, R. A. G. (1980), *Principal Coins of the Romans* 1, London: British Museum.

Casey, M. (1998), *Aramaic Sources of Mark's Gospel*, Society for New Testament Studies Monograph Series 102, Cambridge: Cambridge University Press.

Cavallin, H. C. (1980), 'Tod und Auferstehung der Weisheitslehrer: Ein Beitrag zur Zeichnung des frame of reference Jesu', *Studien zum Neuen Testament und seiner Umwelt*: 107–121.

Charlesworth, M. P. (ed.) (1939), *Documents Illustrating the Reigns of Claudius and Nero*, Cambridge: Cambridge University Press.

Chilver, G. E. F. (1970), 'Caesar, Julius', *Oxford Classical Dictionary*, 2nd edn, Oxford: Oxford University Press: 189–190.

Chronis, H. L. (1982), 'The Torn Veil: Cultus and Christology in Mark 15.37–38', *Journal of Biblical Literature* 101: 97–114.

Collins, A. Y. (1992a), 'Is Mark a Life of Jesus? The Question of Genre', in idem, *The Beginning of the Gospel: Probings of Mark in Context*, Minneapolis, MN: Fortress: 1–38.

————(1992b), 'Suffering and Healing in the Gospel of Mark', in idem, *The Beginning of the Gospel: Probings of Mark in Context*, Minneapolis, MN: Fortress: 39–72.

————(1992c), 'The Empty Tomb and Resurrection according to Mark', in idem, *The Beginning of the Gospel: Probings of Mark in Context*, Minneapolis, MN: Fortress: 119–148.

————(1993), 'The Genre of the Passion Narrative', *Studia Theologia* 47: 3–28.

————(1994), 'From Noble Death to Crucified Messiah', *New Testament Studies* 40: 481–503.

————(1995), 'Apotheosis and Resurrection', in P. Borgen & S. Giversen (eds.), *The New Testament and Hellenistic Judaism*, Aarhus: Aarhus University Press: 88–100.

————(1997), 'The Signification of Mark 10:45 among Gentile Christians', *Harvard Theological Review* 90.4: 371–382.

————(1999), 'Mark and his Readers: The Son of God among Jews', *Harvard Theological Review* 92.4: 393–408.

Collins, J. J. (1977), *The Apocalyptic Vision of Daniel*, Harvard Semitic Monograph 16, Missoula, MO: Scholars.

Cousar, C. B. (1970), 'Eschatology and Mark's "Theologia Crucis"', *Interpretation* 24: 321–335.

Cranfield, C. E. B. (1977), *The Gospel according to St Mark*, 5th edn, Cambridge Greek Testament Commentary, Cambridge: Cambridge University Press.

Cremer, F. G. (1965), *Die Fastenansage Jesu: Mark 2,20 und parallelen, in der Sicht der patrischen und scholastischen Exegese*, Bonner biblische Beiträge 23, Bonn: Peter Hanstein.

Cullmann, O. (1956), 'The Return of Christ', in idem, *The Early Church*, ed. A. J. B. Higgins, London: SCM: 141–164.

——(1967), *The Christology of the New Testament* 2nd edn, London: SCM. (German: 1957.)

Culpepper, R. A. (1978), 'The Passion and Resurrection in Mark', *Review and Expositor* 75: 583–600.

Danove, P. L. (1993), *The End of Mark's Story: A Methodological Study*, Biblical Interpretation Series 3, Leiden: Brill.

Daube, D. (2000a), 'He that Cometh', in *New Testament Judaism: Collected Works of David Daube* 2, ed. C. Carmichael, Berkeley, CA: Robbins Collection: 429–440.

——(2000b), 'The Significance of the *Afikoman*', in *New Testament Judaism: Collected Works of David Daube* 2, ed. C. Carmichael, Berkeley, CA: Robbins Collection: 425–428.

Davies, J. G. (1958), *He Ascended into Heaven*, London: Lutterworth.

Deissmann, A. (1995), *Light from the Ancient East: The New Testament Illustrated by Recently Discovered Texts of the Graeco-Roman World*, trans. R. M. Strachan, 4th edn, Peabody, MA: Hendrickson (= 4th edn, 1927; German: 4th edn 1922; original 1910).

Decleva-Caizzi, F. (ed.) (1966), *Antisthenes Fragmenta*, Milan: Instituto Editoriale Cisalpino.

Dewey, J. (1980), *Markan Public Debate*, Society of Biblical Literature Dissertation Series 48, Chico, CA: Scholars.

——(1995), 'The Literary Structure of the Controversy Stories', in W. Telford (ed.), *The Interpretation of Mark*, 2nd edn, Edinburgh: T. & T. Clark: 141–152.

Dihle, A. (1982), *The Theory of Will in Classical Antiquity*, Berkeley, CA: University of California Press.

Divjak, J. (1981), *S. Aureli Augustini opera 2.6: Epistolae ex duobus codicibus nuper in lucem prolatae*, Vienna: Corpus scriptorum ecclesiasticorum latinorum 88.

Dodd, C. H. (1961), *The Parables of the Kingdom* rev. edn, London: Collins.

Donahue, J. R., & D. J. Harrington (2002), *The Gospel of Mark*, Sacra Pagina 2, Collegeville, MN: Liturgical.

Donne, B. K. (1983), *Christ Ascended: A Study of the Significance of the Ascension of Jesus Christ in the New Testament*, Exeter: Paternoster.

Doyle, A. D. (1941), 'Pilate's Career and the Date of the Crucifixion', *Journal of Theological Studies* 42: 190–193.

Doyle, B. (2000), *The Apocalypse of Isaiah Metaphorically Speaking: A Study of the Use, Function and Significance of Metaphors in Isaiah 24 – 27*, Leuven: Leuven University Press.

Dumbrell, W. J. (1975), 'Daniel 7 and the Function of Old Testament Apocalyptic', *Reformed Theological Review* 34.1: 16–23.

————(1994), *The Search for Order: Biblical Eschatology in Focus*, Grand Rapids, MI: Baker.

Dyer, K. D. (1999), ' "But Concerning *that* Day . . . " ' (Mark 13.31): "Prophetic" and "Apocalyptic" Eschatology in Mark 13', *Society of Biblical Literature 1999 Seminar Papers*, Atlanta, GA: Scholars: 104–122.

Edwards, J. R. (2002), *The Gospel According to Mark*, Pillar New Testament Commentaries, Grand Rapids, MI: Eerdmans; Leicester: Apollos.

Elliott, J. K. (1972), 'When Jesus was Apart from God: An Examination of Hebrews 2.9', *Expository Times* 83: 339–341.

Evans, C. A. (2001), *Mark 8.27 – 16.20*, Word Biblical Commentary 34B, Nashville, TN: Nelson.

Farley, B. W. (1988), *The Providence of God*, Grand Rapids, MI: Baker.

Farrow, D. (1999), *Ascension and Ecclesia: On the Significance of the Doctrine of the Ascension for Ecclesiology and Christian Cosmology*, Grand Rapids, MI: Eerdmans.

Feuillet, A. (1964), 'Le sens du mot Parousie dans l'Evangile de Matthieu. Comparaison entre Matth. xxiv et Jac. v. 1–11', in W. D. Davies & D. Daube (eds.), *The Background of the New Testament and its Eschatology: In Honour of C. H. Dodd*, Cambridge: Cambridge University Press: 261–280.

Fink, R. O., A. S. Hoey & W. S. Snyder (1940), 'The *Feriale Duranum*', *Yale Classical Studies* 7: 1–222.

Fitzmyer, J. A. (1998), 'Crucifixion in Ancient Palestine, Qumran Literature, and the New Testament', in *To Advance the Gospel: New Testament Studies*, 2nd edn, Grand Rapids, MI: Eerdmans: 125–146. (Original New York: Crossroad, 1981.)

Fledderman, H. (1982), 'A Warning About the Scribes (Mark 12.37b–40)', *Catholic Bible Quarterly* 43.1: 52–67.

Fowler, W. W. (1914), *Roman Ideas of Deity in the Last Century Before the Christian Era*, London: Macmillan.

France, R. T. (1968), 'The Servant of the Lord in the Teaching of Jesus', *Tyndale Bulletin* 19: 26–52.

——— (1982), *Jesus and the Old Testament: His Application of Old Testament Passages to Himself and his Mission*, Grand Rapids, MI: Baker. (Original: Tyndale, 1971.)

——— (1990), *Divine Government: God's Kingship in the Gospel of Mark*, London: SPCK; Sydney: ANZEA.

——— (2002), *The Gospel of Mark*, New International Greek Testament Commentary, Grand Rapids, MI: Eerdmans; Carlisle: Paternoster.

Gaston, L. (1970), *No Stone on Another: Studies in the Significance of the Fall of Jerusalem in the Synoptic Gospels*, Novum Testamentum Supplement 23, Leiden: Brill.

Gebhardt, O. von (ed.) (1902), *Acta Martyrum Selecta*, Berlin: Duncker.

Geddert, T. J. (1989), *Watchwords: Mark 13 in Markan Eschatology*, Journal for the Study of the New Testament Supplement 26, Sheffield: JSOT.

Gill, C. (1985), 'Ancient Psychotherapy', *Journal of the History of Ideas* 46.3: 307–325.

Glasson, T. F. (1945), *The Second Advent: The Origin of the New Testament Doctrine*, London: Epworth.

Goldsworthy, G. (2000), *Preaching the Whole Bible as Christian Scripture: The Application of Biblical Theology to Expository Preaching*, Leicester: Inter-Varsity Press.

Grassi, J. A. (2000), *The Five Wounds of Jesus and Personal Transformation*, New York: Alba House.

Grayston, K. (1990), *Dying, We Live: A New Enquiry into the Death of Christ in the New Testament*, London: Darton, Longman & Todd.

Green, G. L. (2002), *The Letters to the Thessalonians*, Pillar New Testament Commentaries, Grand Rapids, MI: Eerdmans.

Green, J. B., & Baker, M. D. (2000), *Recovering the Scandal of the Cross: Atonement in New Testament and Contemporary Contexts*, Downers Grove, IL: InterVarsity Press.

Grether, G. (1946), 'Livia and the Imperial Cult', *American Journal of Philology* 67: 222–252.

Gundry, R. H. (1993), *Mark: A Commentary on his Apology for the Cross*, Grand Rapids, MI: Eerdmans.

Guthrie, H. H., Jr (1962), 'Fast, Fasting', *Interpreter's Dictionary of the Bible* 2, Nashville, TN: Abingdon: 241–244.

Haas, N. (1973), 'Anthropological Observations on the Skeletal Remains from Giv'at ha-Mivtar', *Israel Exploration Journal* 23: 38–59.

Hagner, D. A. (1998), 'Gospel, Kingdom, and Resurrection in the Synoptic Gospels', in R. N. Longenecker (ed.), *Life in the Face of Death: The Resurrection Message of the New Testament*, McMaster New Testament Studies 3, Grand Rapids, MI: Eerdmans: 99–121.

Hamilton, N. Q. (1965), 'Resurrection Tradition and the Composition of Mark', *Journal of Biblical Literature* 84: 415–421.

Harris, B. F. (1986), 'The Idea of Mercy and its Graeco-Roman Context', in P. T. O'Brien & D. G. Peterson (eds.), *God Who is Rich in Mercy: Essays Presented to Dr D. B. Knox*, Homebush West, NSW: Lancer: 89–105.

Hatina, T. R. (1996), 'The Focus of Mark 13.24–27: The Parousia, or the Destruction of the Temple?', *Bulletin for Biblical Research* 6: 43–66.

Head, P. M. (1995), 'The Self-Offering and Death of Christ as a Sacrifice in the Gospels and the Acts of the Apostles', in R. T. Beckwith & M. J. Selman (eds.), *Sacrifice in the Bible*, Carlisle: Paternoster; Grand Rapids, MI: Baker: 111–129.

Hengel, M. (1976), *The Son of God: The Origin of Christology and the History of Jewish-Hellenistic Religion*, London: SCM. (Reproduced in Hengel 1997.)

———(1977), *Crucifixion in the Ancient World and the Folly of the Message of the Cross*, London: SCM. (Reproduced in Hengel 1997.)

———(1989), *The Zealots: Investigations into the Jewish Freedom Movement in the Period from Herod I until 70 AD*, trans. D. Smith, Edinburgh: T. & T. Clark. (German: 1959.)

———(1997), *The Cross of the Son of God*, London: Xpress Reprints.

Hickinbotham, J. P. (1944), 'The Atonement in St Mark's Gospel', *Churchman* 58: 51–58.

Hoehner, H. W. (1977), *Chronological Aspects of the Life of Christ*, Grand Rapids, MI: Academie.

Hofius, O. (1996), 'Das vierte Gottesknechtslied in den Briefen des

Neuen Testaments', in B. Janowski & P. Stuhlmacher (eds.), *Der leidende Gottesknecht. Jesaja 53 und eine Wirkungsgeschichte*, Tübingen: Mohr: 107–127.

Holloway, R. (1984), *The Killing: Meditations on the Death of Christ*, London: Darton, Longman & Todd.

Hooker, M. D. (1959), *Jesus and the Servant: The Influence of the Servant Concept of Deutero-Isaiah in the New Testament*, London: SPCK.

——(1979), 'Is the Son of Man Problem Really Insoluble?', in E. Best & R. McL. Wilson (eds.), *Text and Interpretation: Studies in the New Testament presented to Matthew Black*, Cambridge: Cambridge University Press: 155–168.

——(1991), *Mark*, Black's New Testament Commentaries, London: Black.

Horst, P. W. van der (1972), 'Can a Book End with GAR? A Note on Mark 16.8', *Journal of Theological Studies* 23: 121–124.

Hughes, P. E. (1977), *A Commentary on the Epistle to the Hebrews*, Grand Rapids, MI: Eerdmans.

Huntingdon, S. P. (1996), *The Clash of Civilizations and the Remaking of World Order*, New York: Simon & Schuster.

Iersel, B. M. F. van (1998), *Mark: A Reader-Response Commentary*, *Journal for the Study of the New Testament* Supplement 164, trans. W. H. Bisscheroux, Sheffield: Sheffield Academic Press.

Iser, W. (1972), 'The Reading Process: A Phenomenological Approach', *New Literary History* 3: 272–299.

——(1980), 'Interaction between Text and Reader', in S. R. Suleiman and I. Crosman (eds.), *The Reader in the Text: Essays on Audience and Interpretation*, Princeton, NJ: Princeton University Press: 106–119.

Iwand, H. J. (1962), *Nachgelassene Werke*, 4: *Gesetz und Evangelium*, Munich: Chr. Kaiser.

Jackson, H. M. (1987), 'The Death of Jesus in Mark and the Miracle from the Cross', *New Testament Studies* 33: 16–37.

Jastrow, M. (1950), *Dictionary of Talmud Babli, Yerushalmi, Midrashic Literature and Targumim*, 2 vols., New York: Pardes.

Jeremias, J. (1963), *The Parables of Jesus*, trans. S. H. Hooke, 2nd edn, London: SCM. (German: 3rd edn 1954, 6th edn 1962.)

Jinkins, M., & S. B. Reid (1997), 'God's Forsakenness: The Cry of Dereliction as an Utterance within the Trinity', *Horizons in Biblical Theology* 19.1: 33–57.

———(1998), 'John McLeod Campbell on Christ's Cry of Dereliction: A Case Study in Trinitarian Hermeneutics', *Evangelical Quarterly* 70.2: 135–150.

Jones, D. L. (1980), 'Christianity and the Roman Imperial Cult', in H. Temporini & W. Haase (eds.), *Aufsteig und Niedergang der römischen Welt* 2 23.2, Berlin: de Gruyter: 1023–1054.

Judge, E. A. (1960), 'The Early Christians as a Scholastic Community', Part 1, *Journal of Religious History* 1: 4–15.

———(1961), 'The Early Christians as a Scholastic Community', Part 2, *Journal of Religious History* 1: 125–137.

———(1980a), *The Conversion of Rome: Ancient Sources of Modern Social Tensions*, Sydney: Macquarie Ancient History Association.

———(1980b), 'The Social Identity of the First Christians: A Question of Method in Religious History', *Journal of Religious History* 11: 201–217.

———(1981), 'The Regional *kanon* for Requisitioned Transport', in G. H. R. Horsley (ed.), *New Documents Illustrating Early Christianity, 1: A Review of the Greek Inscriptions and Papyri Published in 1976*, North Ryde, NSW: Macquarie University Ancient History Documentary Research Centre: 36–45.

———(1986), 'The Quest for Mercy in Late Antiquity', in P. T. O'Brien & D. G. Peterson (eds.), *God Who is Rich in Mercy: Essays Presented to Dr D. B. Knox*, Homebush West, NSW: Lancer: 107–121.

———(1989), 'The Beginning of Religious History', *Journal of Religious History* 15.4: 394–412.

Jung, C. (1936), *Modern Man in Search of a Soul*, London: Kegan Paul, Trench, Trubner.

Jungel, E. (1983), *God as the Mystery of the World*, trans. D. L. Guder, Grand Rapids, MI: Eerdmans. (German: 3rd edn 1977.)

Kähler, M. (1964), *The So-Called Historical Jesus and the Historic Biblical Christ*, Philadelphia, PA: Fortress. (German: 1892.)

Kaiser, O., & E. Lohse (1981), *Death and Life*, Nashville, TN: Abingdon.

Kee, H. C. (1977), *Community of the New Age: Studies in Mark's Gospel*, London: SCM.

Kern, P. H. (forthcoming), 'The Cultural Context of Paul's Gospel: The Cross and Suffering in Galatians', in R. J. Gibson (ed.), *History and the Gospel*, Explorations, Adelaide: Openbook.

Kik, J. M. (1948), *Matthew Twenty-Four: An Exposition*, Philadelphia, PA: Presbyterian and Reformed.

Knox, R. A. (1946), *The Epistles and Gospels for Sundays and Holidays*, London.

Körtner, U. H. J. (1995), *The End of the World: A Theological Interpretation*, trans. D. W. Stott, Louisville, KT: Westminster John Knox. (German: 1988.)

Krauss, S. (1934–5), 'La double inhumation chez les juifs', *Revue des études juives* 97–99: 1–34.

Kreitzer, L. J. (1996), *Striking New Images: Roman Imperial Coinage in the New Testament World*, Journal for the Study of the New Testament Supplement 134; Sheffield: Sheffield Academic Press.

Kyle, R. (1998), *Awaiting the Millennium: A History of End-Time Thinking*, Leicester: Inter-Varsity Press.

Lane, W. L. (1974), *The Gospel of Mark*, New International Commentary on the New Testament, Grand Rapids, MI: Eerdmans.

Lee-Pollard, D. (1987), 'Powerlessness as Power: A Key Emphasis in the Gospel of Mark', *Scottish Journal of Theology* 40.2: 173–188.

Lewis, P., & R. Bolden (2002), *The Pocket Guide To Saint Paul: Coins Encountered by the Apostle on his Travels*, Kent Town, South Australia: Wakefield.

Licht, J. (1978), *Storytelling in the Bible*, Jerusalem: Magnes.

Lightfoot, R. H. (1935), 'The Passion Narrative in St Mark', in idem, *History and Interpretation in the Gospels*, London: Hodder & Stoughton: 126–151.

———(1950a), *The Gospel Message of St Mark*, Oxford: Clarendon.

———(1950b), 'The Reception of St Mark's Gospel in the Church and a Survey of its Contents', in Lightfoot 1950a: 1–14.

———(1950c), 'The Connexion of Chapter Thirteen with the Passion Narrative', in Lightfoot 1950a: 48–59.

———(1950d), 'The Cleansing of the Temple in St Mark's Gospel', in Lightfoot 1950a: 60–69.

———(1950e), 'St Mark's Gospel – Complete or Incomplete?', in Lightfoot 1950a: 80–97.

———(1951), 'A Consideration of Three Passages in St Mark's Gospel', in W. Schmauch (ed.), *In Memoriam Ernst Lohmeyer*, Stuttgart: Evangelisches Verlagswerk: 110–115.

Lohfink, G. (1971), *Die Himmelfahrt Jesu: Untersuchungen zu den Himmelfahrts- und Erhöhungstexten bei Lukas*, Studien zum Alten und Neuen Testament 26, München: Kösel.

———(1985), *Jesus and Community: The Social Dimension of Christian Faith*, trans. J. P. Galvin, London: SPCK. (German: 1982.)

Lohmeyer, E. (1959), *Das Evangelium des Markus und Erganzungs-heft*, Kritisch-exegetischer Kommentar über das Neue Testament, 15th edn, Göttingen: Vandenhoeck & Ruprecht.

Lull, D. J. (1985), 'Interpreting Mark's Story of Jesus' Death: Toward a Theology of Suffering', in K. H. Richards (ed.), *Society of Biblical Literature 1985 Seminar Papers*, Atlanta: GA: Scholars: 1–12.

Lust, J. (2001), 'Cult and Sacrifice in Daniel: The Tamid and the Abomination of Desolation', in J. J. Collins & P. W. Flint (eds.), *The Book of Daniel: Composition and Reception* 2, Leiden: Brill: 671–688.

Luther, M. (1966), *Luther's Works* 8: *Lectures on Genesis 45 – 50*, ed. J. Pelikan & W. A. Hansen, St Louis, MO: Concordia.

Lyonnet, S. (1970), *Sin, Redemption, and Sacrifice: A Biblical and Patristic Study*, Anchor Bible 48, Rome: Biblical Institute Press.

McKay, K. L. (1994), *A New Syntax of the Verb in New Testament Greek: An Aspectual Approach*, Studies in Biblical Greek 5, New York: Peter Lang.

Maier, P. L. (1968), 'Sejanus, Pilate, and the Date of the Crucifixion', *Church History* 37.1: 3–13.

Mann, C. S. (1986), *Mark: A New Translation with Introduction and Commentary*, Anchor Bible 27; New York: Doubleday.

Marshall, C. D. (1989), *Faith as a Theme in Mark's Narrative*, Society for New Testament Studies Monograph Series 64, Cambridge: Cambridge University Press.

Marxsen, W. (1969), *Mark the Evangelist*, Nashville, TN: Abingdon. (German: 1956, 1959.)

Mastin, B. A. (1973), 'The Imperial Cult and the Ascription of the Title *theos* to Jesus (John 20.28)', in E. A. Livingstone (ed.), *Studia Evangelica VI: Papers Presented to the Fourth International Congress on New Testament Studies, held at Oxford, 1969*, Berlin: Akademie-Verlag: 352–365.

Matera, F. (1982), *The Kingship of Jesus: Composition and Theology in Mark 15*, Society of Biblical Literature Dissertation Series 66, Chico, CA: Scholars.

Menzies, R. (1954), 'The Cry of Dereliction', *Expository Times* 65: 183–184.

Michaelis, W. (1981), '*kratos, ktl*', *TDNT* 3: 910–912.

Milgrom, J. (2000), *Leviticus 23 – 27*, Anchor Bible 3B, New York: Doubleday.

Miller-McLemore, B. J. (1988), *Death, Sin and the Moral Life: Contemporary Cultural Interpretations of Death*, American Academy of Religion Academy Series 59, Atlanta, GA: Scholars.

Milligan, W. (1898), *The Ascension and Heavenly Priesthood of our Lord*, London: Macmillan.

Moltmann, J. (1974), *The Crucified God*, London: SCM. (German: 1973.)

Moo, D. J. (1996), *The Epistle to the Romans*, New International Commentary on the New Testament, Grand Rapids, MI: Eerdmans.

Morris, L. L. (1964), *The Abolition of Religion: A Study in 'Religionless Christianity'*, London: Inter-Varsity Press.

———(1972), *Apocalyptic*, Leicester: Inter-Varsity Press; Grand Rapids, MI: Eerdmans.

Moss, G. C. (1963), 'The Mentality and Personality of the Julio-Claudian Emperors', *Medical History* 7: 165–175.

Motyer, J. A. (1993), *The Prophecy of Isaiah: An Introduction and Commentary*, Leicester: Inter-Varsity Press.

Nock, A. D. (1952), 'Religious Developments from the Close of the Republic to the Death of Nero', in S. A. Cook, F. E. Adcock & M. P. Charlesworth (eds.), *Cambridge Ancient History* 10, Cambridge: Cambridge University Press: 465–511.

Noy, D. (1971), 'Afikomen', *Encyclopedia Judaica* 2, Jerusalem: Keter: 329–330.

Oates, W. E. (1995), *Luck: A Secular Faith*, Louisville, KT: Westminster John Knox.

Oepke, A. (1964), '*baptō, ktl*', *TDNT* 1: 529–546.

Ovey, M. (2001), 'The Cross, Creation and the Human Predicament', in D. G. Peterson (ed.), *Where Wrath and Mercy Meet: Proclaiming the Atonement Today*, Carlisle: Paternoster: 100–135.

Page, D. L. (ed.) (1941), *Select Papyri* III, Cambridge, MA: Harvard University Press.

Palmer, D. W. (1976), 'The Origin, Form, and Purpose of Mark XVI.4 in Codex Bobbiensis', *Journal of Theological Studies* 27: 113–122.

Pease, A. S. (1942), 'Some Aspects of Invisibility', *Harvard Studies in Classical Philology* 53: 1–36.

Peek, W. (1960), *Griechische Grabgedichte*, Berlin: Academie-Verlag.

Perkins, P. (1995), 'The Gospel of Mark: Introduction, Commentary, and Reflections', *New Interpreter's Bible* 8, Nashville, TN: Abingdon: 507–733.

Perrin, N. (1976), 'High Priest's Question and Jesus' Answer (Mark 14.61–62)', in W. H. Kelber (ed.), *The Passion in Mark*, Philadelphia, PA: Fortress: 80–95.

Petterson, A. (2000), 'Antecedents of the Christian Hope of Resurrection, Part 1: The Old Testament', *Reformed Theological Review* 59.1: 1–15.

Pilch, J. J. (1995), 'Death With Honor: The Mediterranean Style Death of Jesus in Mark', *Biblical Theology Bulletin* 25: 65–70.

Poole, M. (1963), *A Commentary on the Holy Bible* 3, London: Banner of Truth. (Original: *Annotations on the Holy Bible*, 1683–1685.)

Price, S. R. F. (1984), *Rituals and Power: The Roman Imperial Cult in Asia Minor*, Cambridge: Cambridge University Press.

——— (1987), 'From Noble Funerals to Divine Cult: The Consecration of Roman Emperors', in D. Cannadine & S. Price (eds.), *Rituals of Royalty: Power and Ceremonial in Traditional Societies*, Cambridge: Cambridge University Press: 56–105.

Radcliffe, T. (1987), ' "The Coming of the Son of Man": Mark's Gospel and the Subversion of "the Apocalyptic Imagination" ', in B. Davies (ed.), *Language, Meaning and God: Essays in Honour of Herbert McCabe OP*, London: Chapman: 176–189.

Räisänen, H. (1990), *The "Messianic Secret" in Mark's Gospel*, trans. C. B. Tuckett, Edinburgh: T. & T. Clark. (German: 1976.)

Ramsay, W. M. (1907), *The Church in the Roman Empire before AD 170*, 9th edn, London: Hodder & Stoughton.

Rawlinson, A. E. J. (1931), *St Mark*, 3rd edn, London: Methuen.

Read, D. H. C. (1957), 'The Cry of Dereliction', *Expository Times* 68: 260–262.

Reed, J. P., Jr (1992), 'The Human Cry of Dereliction', *Review and Expositor* 89: 331–345.

Rhoads, D. R., J. Dewey & D. Michie (1999), *Mark as Story: An Introduction to the Narrative of a Gospel*, Minneapolis, MN: Fortress.

Richmond, J. (1963), 'Beyond All Reason', in A. Richardson (ed.), *Four Anchors from the Stern*, London: SCM: 36–46.

Riley, G. J. (1995), *Resurrection Reconsidered: Thomas and John in Controversy*, Minneapolis, MN: Fortress.

Robinson, D. W. B. (1958), *The Meaning of Baptism*, Beecroft, NSW: Evangelical Tracts and Publications. (Soon to be published in a volume of his *Collected Works*, P. G. Bolt & M. D. Thompson, eds.)

—— (1970), 'Jonah', *New Bible Commentary*, 3rd edn, Leicester: Inter-Varsity Press: 746–751.

—— (n.d.), ' "Israel" and the "Gentiles" in the Gospel of Mark', unpublished manuscript. (Soon to be published in a volume of his *Collected Works*, P. G. Bolt & M. D. Thompson, eds.)

Robinson, J. A. T. (1957), *Jesus and his Coming: The Emergence of a Doctrine*, London: SCM.

—— (1963), *Honest to God*, London: SCM.

Rohde, E. (1925), *Psyche: The Cult of Souls and Belief in Immortality among the Greeks*, London: Kegan Paul, Trench, Trubner.

Rossé, G. (1987), *The Cry of Jesus on the Cross: A Biblical and Theological Study*, trans. S. W. Arndt, New York: Paulist.

Russell, E. A. (1985), 'The Gospel of Mark: Pastoral Response to a Life or Death Situation? Some Reflections', *Irish Biblical Studies* 7: 206–223.

Russell, J. S. (1999), *The Parousia: The New Testament Doctrine of our Lord's Second Coming*, Grand Rapids, MI: Baker. (Original: 1878; 2nd edn 1887.)

Sapp, D. A. (1998), 'The LXX, 1QIsa, and MT Versions of Isaiah 53 and the Christian Doctrine of Atonement', in W. H. Bellinger Jr & W. R. Farmer (eds.), *Jesus and the Suffering Servant: Isaiah 53 and Christian Origins*, Harrisburg, PA: Trinity Press International: 170–192.

Schaberg, J. (1985), 'Daniel 7.12 and the New Testament Passion-Resurrection Predictions', *New Testament Studies* 31: 208–222.

Schaeder, H. H. (1967), '*Nazarēnos, Nazōraios*', *TDNT* 4: 874–879.

Schleiermacher, F. (1999), *The Christian Faith*, ed. H. R. Mackintosh & J. S. Stewart, Edinburgh: T. & T. Clark. (German: 2nd edn, 1830.)

Schnackenburg, R. (2002), *The Gospel of Matthew*, Grand Rapids, MI: Eerdmans. (German: 1985.)

Schneider, J. (1971), '*suzēteō, ktl*', *TDNT* 7: 747–748.

Schowalter, D. N. (1993), *The Emperor and the Gods*, Harvard Dissertations in Religion 28, Minneapolis, MN: Fortress.

Schreiber, J. (1967), *Theologie des Vertrauens: Eine redaktionsgeschichtliche Untersuchung des Markusevangeliums*, Hamburg: Furche-Verlag.

Seccombe, D. P. (1986), 'Take up your Cross', in P. T. O'Brien & D. G. Peterson (eds.), *God Who is Rich in Mercy: Essays Presented to Dr D. B. Knox*, Homebush West, NSW: Lancer: 139–151.

Seeley, D. (1990), *The Noble Death*, Journal for the Study of the New Testament Supplement 28, Sheffield: JSOT.

Segal, A. F. (1980), 'Heavenly Ascent in Hellenistic Judaism, Early Christianity and their Environment', in H. Temporini & W. Haase (eds.), *Aufsteig und Niedergang der römischen Welt* 2, 23.2, Berlin: de Gruyter: 1333–1394.

Senior, D. (1984), *The Passion of Jesus in the Gospel of Mark*, Wilmington, DE: Michael Glazier.

Shead, A. G. (2002), 'An Old Testament Theology of the Sabbath Year and Jubilee', *Reformed Theological Review* 61.1: 19–33.

Shotter, D. (1992), *Tiberius Caesar*, London: Routledge.

Smith, D. A. (2003), 'Revisiting the Empty Tomb: The Post-Mortem Vindication of Jesus in Mark and Q', *Novum Testamentum* 45.2: 123–137.

Smith, M. (1981), 'The Composition of Mark 11 – 16', *Heythrop Journal* 22.4: 363–377.

Smith, R. H. (1973), 'Darkness at Noon: Mark's Passion Narrative', *Concordia Theological Monthly* 44.5: 325–338.

Smith, S. H. (1989), 'The Role of Jesus' Opponents in the Markan Drama', *New Testament Studies* 35: 161–182.

Spong, J. S. (1983), *Into the Whirlwind: The Future of the Church*, New York: Seabury.

———— (1998), *Why Christianity Must Change or Die: A Bishop Speaks to Believers in Exile*, San Francisco, CA: HarperSanFrancisco.

———— (2001), *A New Christianity for a New World: Why Traditional Faith is Dying and How a New Faith is Being Born*, San Francisco, CA: HarperSanFrancisco.

———— (ed.) (1999), *The Bishop's Voice: Selected Essays, 1979–1999*, New York: Crossroads.

Stark, R. (1992), 'Epidemics, Networks, and the Rise of Christianity', *Semeia* 56: 159–175. Later revised to become ch. 4 of Stark 1997.

———— (1997), *The Rise of Christianity: How the Obscure, Marginal Jesus Movement became the Dominant Religious Force in the Western World in a Few Centuries*, San Francisco, CA: HarperSanFrancisco.

Stassen, G., M. Tooley & A. Williams (1992), 'Justice and Empowerment as Deliverance from Alienation and Abandonment', *Review and Expositor* 89: 347–358.

Stauffer, E. (1955), *Christ and the Caesars: Historical Sketches*, trans. K. & R. G. Smith, London: SCM. (German: 1952.)

Stevenson, J. (ed.) (1957), *A New Eusebius: Documents Illustrating the History of the Church to AD 337*, London: SPCK.

Stock, A. (1982), *Call To Discipleship: A Literary Study of Mark's Gospel*, Good News Studies, Wilmington, DE: Glazier.

Stott, J. R. W. (1986), *The Cross of Christ*, Leicester: Inter-Varsity Press.

Swete, H. B. (1909), *The Gospel According to St Mark*, London: Macmillan.

Tabor, J. D. (1989), ' "Returning to Divinity": Josephus's Portrayal of the Disappearances of Enoch, Elijah, and Moses', *Journal of Biblical Literature* 108: 225–238.

Tasker, R. V. G. (1961), *The Gospel According to St Matthew*, London: Tyndale.

Taylor, L. R. (1929), 'Tiberius' Refusal of Divine Honours', *Transactions of the American Philological Association* 60: 87–101.

———(1989), *The Divinity of the Roman Emperor*, Middletown, CT: Scholars. (Original: 1931.)

Taylor, V. (1956), *The Cross of Christ*, London: Macmillan.

———(1966), *The Gospel According to St Mark*, 2nd edn, Grand Rapids, MI: Baker. (Original: 1952.)

Teselle, E. (1996), 'The Cross as Ransom', *Journal of Early Christian Studies* 4.2: 147–170.

Thomas, D. (1996), *Taken Up to Heaven: The Ascension of Christ*, Darlington: Evangelical Press.

Thompson, M. D. (2004), 'From the Trinity to the Cross', *Reformed Theological Review* 63.1: 16–28.

Tolbert, M. A. (1989), *Sowing the Gospel: Mark's World in Literary-Historical Perspective*, Minneapolis, MN: Fortress.

Tombs, D. (1999), 'Crucifixion, State Terror, and Sexual Abuse', *Union Seminary Quarterly Review* 53.1–2: 89–109.

Toon, P. (1984), *The Ascension of our Lord*, Nashville, TN: Nelson.

Trudinger, L. P. (1974), ' "Eli, Eli, Lama Sabachthani?": A Cry of Dereliction? Or Victory?', *Journal of the Evangelical Theological Society* 17: 235–238.

Vermes, G. (ed.) (1998), *The Complete Dead Sea Scrolls in English*, Harmondsworth: Penguin.

Vielhauer, P. (1965), 'Erwägungen zur Christologie des Markusevangeliums', *Aufsätze zum Neuen Testament*, Theologische Bücherei 31, Munich: Kaiser Verlag: 199–214.

von Harnack, A. (1904), *The Expansion of Christianity in the First Three Centuries*, London: Williams & Norgate. (German: 1902.)

Walsh, P. G. (1974), 'Spes Romana, Spes Christiana', *Prudentia* 6: 33–43.

Wallace, D. B. (1996), *Greek Grammar Beyond the Basics*, Grand Rapids, MI: Zondervan.

Webb, B. G. (2000), *Five Festal Garments: Christian Reflections on the Song of Songs, Ruth, Lamentations, Ecclesiastes and Esther*, New Studies in Biblical Theology 10, Leicester: Apollos.

Wegener, M. I. (1995), *Cruciformed: The Literary Impact of Mark's Story of Jesus and his Disciples*, Lanham, MD: University Press of America.

Weinandy, T. G. (1995), *The Father's Spirit of Sonship: Reconceiving the Trinity*, Edinburgh: T. & T. Clark.

―――― (2000), *Does God Suffer?*, Edinburgh: T. & T. Clark.

Weinstock, S. (1971), *Diuus Julius*, Oxford: Clarendon.

Wengst, K. (1987), *Pax Romana and the Peace of Jesus Christ*, London: SCM.

Wenham, G. J. (1995), 'The Theology of Old Testament Sacrifice', in R. T. Beckwith & M. J. Selman (eds.), *Sacrifice in the Bible*, Carlisle: Paternoster; Grand Rapids, MI: Baker: 75–87.

Weston, P. (2001), 'Proclaiming Christ Crucified Today: Some Reflections on John's Gospel', in D. G. Peterson (ed.), *Where Wrath and Mercy Meet: Proclaiming the Atonement Today*, Carlisle: Paternoster: 136–163.

Wheaton, D. H. (1962), 'Crucifixion', *New Bible Dictionary*, 1st edn, London: Inter-Varsity Fellowship: 281–282.

Williams, J. F. (1994), *Other Followers of Jesus: Minor Characters as Major Figures in Mark's Gospel*, Journal for the Study of the New Testament Supplement 102, Sheffield: JSOT.

Wright, A. G. (1982), 'The Widow's Mite: Praise or Lament? A Matter of Context', *Catholic Bible Quarterly* 44.2: 256–265.

Wright, N. T. (1992), *The New Testament and the People of God*, Minneapolis, MN: Fortress.

―――― (1996), *Jesus and the Victory of God*, London: SPCK.

―――― (1998), 'The Servant and Jesus: The Relevance of the Colloquy for the Current Quest for Jesus', in W. H. Bellinger Jr & W. R. Farmer (eds.), *Jesus and the Suffering Servant: Isaiah 53 and Christian Origins*, Harrisburg, PA: Trinity Press International: 281–297.

―――― (2003), *The Resurrection of the Son of God*, London: SPCK.

Yadin, Y. (1971), 'Pesher Nahum (4QpNahum) Reconsidered', *Israel Exploration Journal* 21.1: 1–12.

―――― (1973), 'Epigraphy and Crucifixion', *Israel Exploration Journal* 23: 18–22.

Yates, J. E. (1963), *The Spirit and the Kingdom*, London: SPCK.

Yusa, M. (1987), 'Chance', in M. Eliade (ed.), *The Encyclopedia of Religion* 3, New York: Macmillan: 192–196.

Ziesler, J. A. (1972–3), 'The Removal of the Bridegroom: A Note on Mark 2.18–22 and Parallels', *New Testament Studies* 19: 190–194.

Zuntz, G. (1953), *The Text of the Epistles*, London, Oxford University Press.

Index of modern authors

194

195

Index of Scripture references

14:38 110, 140
14:40–41 108
14:41 53, 58, 108, 111
14:43 111
14:43–52 103
14:44 61
14:45 111
14:46 61
14:48 111
14:49 61
14:50 71, 102, 108
14:51 61
14:53–65 118
14:53–72 103
14:54 109
14:58 30, 121
14:61 118, 139, 151
14:62 95–97, 111, 151
14:64 36
14:66–72 108–109
14:67 167
14:72 109
15 55
15:1 52, 117–118
15:1–15 116, 121
15:2 37, 118
15:3–4 120
15:9 118
15:10 40, 52, 119
15:12 118
15:14 119
15:15 52
15:16–20 63, 121
15:16–32 116
15:16–41 121
15:17 55
15:18 118
15:20 55, 122
15:20–27 121
15:21 55
15:23 69
15:24 55
15:26 118, 139
15:27–32 63

15:29 121–124
15:29–30 121
15:29–32 109, 121
15:30 137, 144
15:31 122
15:31–32 37, 121
15:32 37, 44, 118, 121–122, 137, 140, 144
15:33 125
15:33–36 121
15:33–39 116
15:34 69, 109, 121, 125, 127–128, 132, 141
15:35–36 121
15:36 69
15:37 127
15:37–38 30
15:38 122, 125, 127
15:39 34, 116, 119, 125, 138–139, 146, 151
15:40 17, 147
15:40 – 16:8 146
15:42–47 153
15:43 117, 151
15:47 147
16:1 147
16:2 147, 151
16:4 147
16:5 147
16:6 62, 147–148, 167–168
16:7 107, 152
16:8 40, 146, 152
16:13 34
16:14 34
16:16 34
16:17 34

Luke
4:34 167
6:39 76
7:31–35 22
7:34 106

10:24 94
13:28–29 106
14:15–24 106
16:26 134
18:9 64
18:12 21
18:31ff. 56
18:32 59
18:37 167
22:23 61
22:30 106
22:69 96
23:11 64
23:27–31 24
23:55 147
24:7 59
24:10 147
24:15 61
24:19 167
24:30–31 104
24:46 59

John
1:10–11 119
1:14 134
2:11 25
2:17 69
2:19 121
3:22–30 43
3:29 43
4:36 25
5:25–29 60
8:44 74
11:24 62
11:48 58, 133
14:28 95
15:25 69
16:7 95
18:5, 7 167
19:15 119
19:17 55
19:19 167
20:1–18 147

Acts
2:13 25

Index of ancient sources

Porphyry
  PL
    25:569 100
Propertius
  2.15.40–43 162
  2.5.1f. 162
Psalms of Solomon
  8.14 67
  8.14–15 67
  17.4, 21, 26–28 107
Qumran
  1QIsa, on Isa. 61:10 43
  1QM 1.11–12 102
  1QpHab 11.10–15 67
  1Qsa[28a] 2.11–22 106
  4Q371–372 58, 133
  4Q541 124
  4QpNah 137
  CD 19.7–13 107
Rabbinic sources
  Bereshit Rabba
  Gen 22.6 55
  Babylonian Talmud, *Baba Batra*
  49 92
  Babylonian Talmud, *Sanhedrin*
  99a, 98b 104
  Babylonian Talmud, *Sukkah*
  516 92
  Mishnah, *Sanhedrin*
  2.5 86
  Mishnah, *Pesahim*
  10 106
  Ta'anit
  12a 21
  Yadaim
  4.3 24
SEG
  1392 87
Sarcophagus of Adelphia 86
Seneca
  ad Helviam
  11.7 156
  Apocolocyntosis of Claudius 157, 164
  1 164
  11 164

De Clementia
  1.5.2 81
  1.7.2 81
  1.9.12 81
  2.3.1 82
  2.5.4 82
  13.1 81
  19.1 81
  Epistles
  4.5 169
  4.6 41
  8.3f. 75
  13 75
  16.4 75
  16.4ff. 75
  18.6f. 75
  24.18 158
  48.3ff. 75
  63.7f. 75
  72.4 75
  74.6ff. 75
  92.34 158
  98 75
  111.2f. 75
  113.27f. 75
  Questiones naturales
  3, pr.7 75
Sophocles
  Oedipus Coloneus
  1620 165
  1647f. 166
Suetonius 162
  Suet. 1 [*Julius*]
  75 80
  83.2 162
  Suet. 2 [*Augustus*]
  51 81
  53 162
  76.2 21
  95 157
  97.1 161
  Suet. 3 [*Tiberius*]
  59.1 143
  Suet. 5 [*Claudius*]
  3 164